To –
C. W. Unger
with the compliments of
George Korson

MINSTRELS OF THE MINE PATCH

N. BERVINCHAK 1935

Minstrels of the Mine Patch

SONGS AND STORIES
OF THE ANTHRACITE INDUSTRY

By
George Korson

Philadelphia
UNIVERSITY OF PENNSYLVANIA PRESS
1 9 3 8

Manufactured in the United States of America

LONDON
HUMPHREY MILFORD
OXFORD UNIVERSITY PRESS

To

ARNAUD C. MARTS

Preface

[illegible]

The preparation of this book has been made possible by the cooperation of hundreds of persons in the anthracite region and elsewhere. Throughout the book are mentioned the principal sources, particularly the fast-disappearing bards and minstrels who have given so freely and generously of their time, memories, and material. To all of them I am deeply grateful.

For courteous help given in connection with my study of secondary sources I wish to thank the newspapers of the region, and the staffs of the public libraries in Carbondale, Scranton, Wilkes-Barre, Hazleton, Mauch Chunk, and Pottsville; the Pennsylvania State Library, particularly the archives division; the Library of Congress, the New York Public Library, the Historical Society of Pennsylvania, and the Wyoming Historical and Geological Society of Wilkes-Barre.

Gratefully I acknowledge my obligations to the following individuals for valuable services performed by them:

Edith Patterson, librarian of the Pottsville Free Public Library, who was [illegible] helpful during the entire period of research and collecting; Claude W. Unger, president of the Historical Society of Schuylkill County, who for the same length of time generously assisted with suggestions, criticisms, leads, and material; Professor Melvin Le Mon of Bucknell University, who graciously transcribed the melodies used in this volume; Margaret [illegible] of Philadelphia, who gave [illegible] editorial assistance; Nicholas [illegible], one of whose etchings forms a frontispiece

Preface

THE present work has been made possible by the coöperation of hundreds of persons in the anthracite region and elsewhere. Throughout the book are mentioned the principal sources, particularly the few surviving bards and minstrels who have given so freely and generously of their time, memories, and material. To all of them I am deeply grateful.

For courteous help given in connection with my study of secondary sources, I wish to thank the newspapers of the region, and the staffs of the public libraries in Carbondale, Scranton, Wilkes-Barre, Hazleton, Mauch Chunk, and Pottsville; the Pennsylvania State Library, particularly the archives division, the Library of Congress, the New York Public Library, the Historical Society of Pennsylvania, and the Wyoming Historical and Geological Society of Wilkes-Barre.

Gratefully I acknowledge my obligations to the following individuals for valuable services performed by them:

Edith Patterson, librarian of the Pottsville Free Public Library, who was my mainstay during the entire period of research and collecting; Claude W. Unger, president of the Historical Society of Schuylkill County, who for the same length of time generously helped with suggestions, criticisms, leads, and material; Professor Melvin Le Mon of Bucknell University who graciously transcribed the melodies used in this volume; Margaret L. Brady of Philadelphia who was generous with editorial assistance; Nicholas Bervinchak, one of whose etchings forms a frontispiece in this work; Henry W. Shoemaker, state archivist, and president of the Pennsylvania Folk Lore Society, for suggestions and encouragement; Nellie O'Neill of Atlantic City for permission to use "Giant" O'Neill's only copyrighted ballad; and others who have been especially helpful in their own ways, including Frances Dorrance, executive director of the Wyoming Historical and Geological Society; Zelda Popkin of New York; Myra Poland, late librarian of the Osterhout Public Library, Wilkes-Barre, and Florence A. Watts of the same library; Ruth K. Roehrig, Pottsville librarian; and Louis Walton Sipley, executive director of the Pennsylvania Arts and Sciences Society.

I deeply appreciate the courtesies extended to me over a period of years in connection with this research by the following officers of the United Mine Workers of America: Lieutenant Governor Thomas Kennedy, international secretary-treasurer; Mart F. Brennan, chairman of the Anthracite Tri-District Executive Board; and Ellis Searles, editor of the *United Mine Workers Journal.*

In the same connection, various coal company executives have given me coöperation which I am glad to acknowledge with thanks.

I wish to express my deep appreciation also to Dr. Homer P. Rainey, executive director of the American Youth Commission, who, when president of Bucknell University, gave me the opportunity to extend the scope of my research in Pennsylvania folklore; to Bucknell's trustees for sponsoring the Pennsylvania Folk Festival; and to Arnaud C. Marts, president of Bucknell, whose sympathy, counsel, and unstinted support have been a source of inspiration to me.

GEORGE KORSON

Lewisburg, Pennsylvania

Contents

CONTENTS

CONTENTS

CONTENTS

Introduction

ONE evening in 1924 while taking a walk in Pottsville, where I was a newspaper reporter, the question popped in my mind, why had I never heard anthracite miners' songs similar to lumbermen's ballads, cowboy songs, and sailors' chanties? Assuming there was a printed collection, I asked Edith Patterson, the librarian, for a copy. She believed that no such collection existed, and a survey which I subsequently made among the other public libraries in the region confirmed her belief. It was then that she asked me, "Why don't you try to collect these songs yourself?"

I did try, and once started on the hunt I could not stop—I've been collecting ever since. Each ballad discovery acted as a spur to search for others. The circumstances of many of these discoveries are described in the text. Here it is sufficient, I think, to say that the research was not easy, but whatever the disappointments they were more than compensated for by many moments of satisfaction.

The first publication of my findings appeared serially in the *United Mine Workers Journal* in 1926, and the following year this material was published in a small volume entitled *Songs and Ballads of the Anthracite Miner*. It received a fairly good press and in time the edition was exhausted. Continued interest brought my publisher orders which, of course, he could no longer fill. Then rare book dealers began to advertise for copies.

Rather than bring out a new edition as suggested, I decided to compile a much larger collection which would include not only the songs and ballads of the old book, but many other anthracite ballads, together with legends, folk tales, and mining superstitions which I had accumulated in the course of a dozen years of leisurely research. This plan I have tried to follow here.

The Celtic flavor found in the present volume may be ascribed to two sets of circumstances. First, anthracite folklore is part of a chain linked to the balladry of the nation's canals, railroads, and lumber camps where, as in the anthracite mines, a large number of workers in the latter half of the nineteenth century were Irish immigrants with folk songs, come-all-ye's, and fiddle tunes in their hearts. This Irish influence made itself felt in the structure of the texts, and determined the choice of airs to which many were sung. For instance, "The Jam on Gerry's Rocks," most popular of all lumbermen's ballads, was set to an Irish tune.

Secondly, in the anthracite industry the Irish flavor was mixed with Welsh. These races, Irish and Welsh, were still bound by the traditions of their mother countries, and when the need arose to create their own amusements they joined in adapting the bardic and minstrel arts of their common Celtic heritage to the bleak mining environment. This rather loose and wholly spontaneous association between them had historic precedence which reached back into the twelfth century. Thus it may be more than a coincidence that the anthracite region's oldest continuous eisteddfod, which was formed in 1888, has always met on St. Patrick's Day.

All classes of mine workers participated in spontaneous communal gatherings which were usually held on the green, part of every mine patch. Under a starry, moonlit sky of a summer evening, against a background of colliery buildings and culm banks, and in an atmosphere infiltrated with coal dust and brimstone smells, the workers and their families sang together, listened to story tellers, played folk games and danced, as recalled in a ballad:

Let me hear those tales of recess
   That only little folks can tell,
Cuddled up upon the green grass
   Close beside the old town well.
The man in the moon had charge of the light plant,
   Our cottage walls were not of bricks;
Young and old enjoyed the night camp
   On the green at Number Six.

A sheet of iron borrowed from the colliery would be laid on the grass as a sounding board for jigs, reels, hornpipes, and breakdowns as the fiddler scraped out his tunes.

The barroom was another popular resort, particularly in the small towns and patches where it was indeed the "poor man's club," a social center where even miners' wives and daughters went. Given his pipe, a mug of beer, and the companionship of his fellow men after a hard day in the pits, the miner was at peace with the world. Some barrooms were conducted by widows set up in business by the men themselves as an act of charity.

Minstrelsy throve within the mines also. During a lull in work, and nearly always at lunch time, workers would gather at the turnout; this was done not only for diversion, but to escape the grinding stillness of the mine when production had stopped. An old door formerly used to control ventilation became an improvised dance floor. In the eery darkness of this setting, lighted only by tiny yellow flames sputtering from their teapot-shaped lamps, the workers exchanged stories, sang ballads, and danced. Everyone contributed to the fun, even the door boys. Musical notes floated through the mine on the wings of the artificial air currents at other times: mule drivers invariably sang on their long rides, as did miners at the face of the coal when not drilling or blasting.

Entertainments were held nightly on the spacious porches of general stores. The best-known porch in the coal fields was on Mackin Brothers' store in the East End section of Wilkes-Barre, where three generations of mine workers enjoyed themselves. As told in a ballad, "Mackin's Porch":

> Winter or the summer time,
> Whether rain or whether shine,
> Every man is there in line
>   Seated on the step.

Even wakes were social occasions. Everyone went to a wake as there was sure to be plenty to eat and drink, and possibly friends from distant patches. The long hours of the night were passed with story telling and the exchange of gossip and reminiscences. Spooky stories were popular, but occasionally there were hilarious games to keep mourners awake.

The period is also remembered for the number of trials of skill in fiddling, dancing, and ballad singing. Jig-dancing contests were particularly popular and seldom failed to draw large audiences. Gold medals and cash prizes were often awarded to regional champions.

Traditional ballad singers sang without pausing between verses, and usually without accompaniment. Indeed, accompaniment annoyed them, "threw them off the track," they complained. On those rare occasions when they were accompanied, a guitar was the instrument used. The fiddle was sometimes played in unison with the singer. The miner audiences showed a preference for a steady rhythm, one which gave them a chance to tap their feet.

Balladry attained an amazing vogue among the anthracite

mine workers. From the end of the Civil War to the first decade of the present century, no patch or town escaped the fever of improvising or composing songs, ballads, ditties, and doggerel on some phase or other of the mining theme. Unlettered mine workers seemed to have gone daft thinking, talking, writing, and singing in measured and rhymed sentences. Here is an example of a miner's ditty:

Hubbabub hullabaloo,
Two hundred cars will do.

Hoist away, every day,
Clean the coal; make it pay.

In Freeland so frisky,
They sell ice cream and whiskey.

So whack for old Woodside,
It's my darling old place.

The stagecoach driver on the St. Clair-Pottsville line started his daily run from St. Clair with the following cry:

Old Andy at the break of day
Taking all the ladies away,
And a hock ye know!

Even the child workers, many of whom had never attended school, wooed the muse. One of the best-known ballads in this collection, "The Driver Boys of Wadesville Shaft," was improvised by William Keating when he was only twelve years old.

The passwords of the Molly Maguires were frequently cast into blank verse, and one of their chief diversions in jail was improvising and singing ballads. This may be gleaned from the following lines of a poem about the prisoners in the Mauch Chunk jail, written by one of them, and printed in a local paper less than a month before the mass executions:

You may hear them every evening singing a merry song,
Composing rhymes is their delight; they do it very well.

Four of the eight Molly Maguire ballads in this collection were made by imprisoned Mollies, two of whom were subsequently executed.

If a miner bore a grudge against his local boss, he might vent his spite by scrawling a rhymed screed on a scrap of paper which he nailed to a tree for all the world to read. A sample, believed to have been penned by a miner living in the West End of Schuylkill County in the seventies, follows:

One morning of late as I chanced for to stray,
To the Falls of Swatara I straight took my way.
But ere I reached them what was my dismay
To meet with Jim Lloyd, the boss, sir.

Cursing and swearing and damning the mines,
Likewise the poor miners to the flames he consigns.
But little he thought one would make a few lines
To bridle his tongue like a horse, sir.

There was scarcely a mine disaster, a strike, or an event of significance that did not inspire some bard. Men and boys, carried away by their ability to play with words, exercised it even within the mines. While there seems to have been no concerted move among mine bosses to repress the muse, some nevertheless came to regard the whole thing as a nuisance, especially when the bardic art was practised on company time. One of the seemingly unsympathetic bosses was Jack McQuail, superintendent of the Kaska William colliery in the Schuylkill Valley. One day he overheard two company laborers improvising poetry somewhere in the darkness of the gangway. After listening to them a moment or two, and identifying their voices, McQuail fired this broadside at the miscreants in rhythmic syllables:

Paddy Carr and Mickey O'Neill,
You'll work no more for Jack McQuail—

And be jabers, that's poetry too!

Isolation of the mine patch, a semi-primitive plane of living, harsh working conditions, illiteracy, the need for amusement, and folk imagination—these factors produced anthracite folklore.

The contents of the songs and ballads bear out this conclusion. These texts exude sweat and blood, echo every colliery sound, capture every colliery smell. They preserve the miners' changing moods, their thoughts and feelings, their fears, heartaches, hopes and deepest longings, and too, their laughter, wit, and humor. Thus intimately bound up with the anthracite industry, the songs and ballads are true Americana. Whatever may be their intrinsic value as literature or folk music, they are interesting and significant, I believe, as great human documents holding the key to the heart and soul of a departed generation of American industrial workers.

In keeping with tradition, the story for a ballad occurred first to the miner balladist. It was not until after he had improvised his text or perhaps had written it down that he sought a suitable tune. The tune was determined largely by the metre in which his ballad was composed. Current music hall hits, Irish fiddle tunes, come-all-ye's, Welsh, English, Irish, and Scottish folk songs were the sources of anthracite melodies. Where a borrowed tune has been identified, I have given it under the title of the particular song or ballad which was sung to it. However, don't expect to find the tune in its original state. The miners were quite free with these tunes, frequently working them over into an adaptation that suited their purpose best. About fifty tunes, obtained from miners nearly all of whom had previously supplied me with the texts, are preserved at Bucknell University on acetate records which Melvin Le Mon and I made in 1935. Professor Le Mon transcribed the melodies used in the present volume. One of an increasing number of trained musicians finding opportunities for constructive work in the American folk field, he is making a study of the folk music of the anthracite miners. We collaborated on *The Miner Sings*, a collection of ten ballads for which he did the musical arrangements, and which J. Fischer & Bro. of New York, published in 1936.

I do not think that we need be so concerned as to whether a ballad originally had been improvised or deliberately composed so long as it has the traditional ring, acquired by oral transmission. In the last century, the anthracite region, with its many unlettered mine workers, provided a fertile field for the growth of oral tradition. Keeping no records, workers were accustomed to entrusting everything to their memory. Even at that, their minds were not cluttered by too many impressions. Hence, once having heard a ballad they retained it, though they might not sing it exactly the same every time. I have often been amazed to hear miners rattle off ballads from memory which they had heard a half century ago. Variations in ballads might be attributed to faulty hearing of traditional singers, but more often to their obstinate individualism. A singer interpreted a ballad in his own way, and insisted that his was the only way, the result being that ballads underwent many changes through the years, with words, lines, and even verses altered or modified. Being essentially fluid, the ballads lent themselves readily to this folk molding. "Me Johnny Mitchell Man," a ballad in the Slavic-American dialect, is an example of the changes wrought by oral circulation, and for the purpose of comparison, two versions of it are given here. Variants of all other ballads have been excluded to avoid monotony.

While undergoing the process of oral transmission, many ballads lost their individuality as the creation of a single author and took on the character of the mining community as a whole. This was what George Lyman Kittredge of Harvard meant by "collective composition" and what Phillips Barry, another outstanding authority, has called "communal recreation," as I understand the meaning of these terms. However, the part played by the mine workers in the molding of a ballad was as accessories after the fact, to paraphrase Mr. Barry. In other words, first the ballad was created by an individual author and then the traditional singers changed it about. Mencken puts his finger on the nub of the situation when he says, "Folk songs are written, like all other songs, by individuals. All the folk have to do with them is to choose the ones that are to survive. Sometimes, true enough, repetition introduces changes in them, but those changes are not important. The basic song belongs to one bard, and to him alone."

Long before I had begun to theorize about anthracite songs and ballads or to draw conclusions from them, I was moved by an instinctive sense of justice toward the humble mine workers who had created them. I have spent as much time tracing the origin of a ballad as in finding the ballad itself. This is one reason why I was able to identify many of them. In their lifetime these forgotten bards received little attention unless they happened to be minstrels, in which case they were loved and honored. They took their bardic art somewhat casually, with no thought of fame or fortune and none of professionalism. The best proof of this attitude of mind lies in the fact that less than half a dozen in the present collection were originally copyrighted. With the exception of that universal favorite, "Down in a Coal Mine" which, by the way, was not indigenous to the anthracite region, all the copyrighted songs were composed after the turn of the century; they are properly identified through the volume.

Circulation was promoted by visitors from one district to another; by workers changing jobs; by itinerant peddlers, but chiefly, by strolling miner minstrels who transmitted not only songs and ballads, but folk tales, legends, anecdotes, and fiddle tunes. Combining the various minstrel arts, they were for the most part heaven-sent entertainers. Childlike in their simplicity, irresponsible, profligate, and lovable, they were the darlings of the mining community. They had no technical knowledge of music and few had had any schooling. Hence, they sang and played by rote. From village to village and from town to town they strolled with a ballad on their lips, a fiddle or guitar under the arm, and often a bottle on the hip. Every cottage was open to them. At parties, balls, and other entertainments, as in barrooms, they were the center of attraction. While their minstrelsy carried no fee with it, they accepted coins tossed into their weatherbeaten hats.

Some of the minstrels confined their peregrinations to their own county, but others took the whole anthracite region as their stage. Con Carbon of Wilkes-Barre enacted the traditional rôle of "court jester" to John Mitchell, union leader, during the famous 1902 strike. In the darkest hours of that struggle, Mitchell would summon him with some such plea as, "Sing for me, Con," or "Spin me a yarn, Con." Here was minstrelsy dedicated to the cause of labor! Shades of MacLiag and his royal patron, Brian Boru, the Brave!

Among other well-known miner minstrels who have passed on were Giant O'Neill, Poet Mulhall, Ed Foley, Jack Johnson and his brother, Patrick Johnson. True bards and minstrels, they deviated from ancient minstrelsy in one important respect: they served not kings and lords and great ladies, but humble American miners.

Superstitions, legends, folk tales and anecdotes—other folk

expressions found in this volume—are also important in throwing additional light on the anthracite miners. The superstitions and legends generally reflect the miner's fear of lurking death in the mines, of the mysterious sounds which assailed his ears, of underground ghosts, and of poverty. The humorous stories are evidence that the miner could laugh in the face of danger and adversity; the tall story and the anecdote were very popular types, but the miners also liked to sit for hours listening to a long story. In the winter of 1880, a nineteen-year-old mine worker named Martin J. Mulhall invented an oral thriller which he called *Adventures of the Flynn Gang*. For four months, Shenandoah's boy workers would gather every evening at the Mulhall home to listen to young Mulhall improvise a fresh episode of his serial, not a word of which was ever written down.

The editorial matter in each chapter whose object is to orient the songs and ballads, legends and stories, is derived chiefly from personal observation and from interviews with hundreds of mine workers, many of them old-timers, and others connected with the anthracite industry; also local historians. Some of it is the result of deliberate effort, but more came to me casually as I listened hour after hour to old men and women recall the days of their youth in the anthracite region. In some cases, reminiscences were the ore which brought forth precious ballads.

It was a pleasure to hear them talk. Their simple, sincere, and natural manner of speech was full of poetic surprises. For example, one elderly woman recalled that owing to the freezing of the canal, the mines in her patch were closed from late fall *until the blue birds began to sing*.

As resident of the region, newspaperman and folklorist, I have known these people intimately for a quarter of a century, and love them. Unspoiled, hospitable, and gracious, they are to me the salt of the earth.

I would have preferred to confine the editorial matter exclusively to information gleaned from these first-hand, unwritten sources. But for the sake of historical accuracy, I have checked and supplemented it with data obtained from local histories, archives, books, magazine and newspaper files and clippings of current newspapers. For the convenience of those desiring to pursue the historical phase of the subject in more detail I have prepared a bibliography of my secondary sources which may be found in the appendix.

The spread of popular education, the newspaper, the automobile, the movies, and the radio—these have combined to standardize life in the anthracite region as elsewhere in the land. Undoubted blessings, they have nevertheless blighted the folk imagination and checked the growth of folklore. By removing the need for self-amusement, they have deprived the miner of his urge toward self-expression. Coal bootlegging, which has stirred the industry as nothing else since the days of the Molly Maguires, would have inspired many ballads if it had occurred in the last century. As it is, I have found but one ballad having an authentic ring which celebrates this violent symptom of an ailing industry. Composed by one who was bred in the tradition of anthracite minstrelsy, it is published for the first time in this volume. Strangely enough, while ballad-making as a pastime has virtually ceased, a revival of popular interest in anthracite ballads has set in. The folk festival movement in the state, I think, has had something to do with this revival.

CHAPTER ONE

The Mine Patch

GONE is the distinctive flavor of anthracite mining life as it existed for a century. It lingered longest in the mine patch, which was a cluster of squalid hemlock shacks built close to a breaker. Until the barriers of isolation were broken down by modern means of communication it remained as much a closed town as any feudal village in the middle ages. Behind their hills, far removed from the world's activities, the miners worked out their humble destinies. They emerged from their seclusion only on special occasions.

The patch was part of a coal company's property and bore the number of the colliery to which it was attached. Generally only the small, independent operators gave names to their patches. The miners personified their particular company as the Coal King whose power was manifest in the colliery boss. From the time they were brought into the world by a company doctor to the day when their bodies were laid in the grave, they lived in the shadow of the Coal King. Their feeling toward this mythical character is epitomized in the following epitaph on an anthracite miner's tombstone:

> Fourty years I worked with pick & drill
> Down in the mines against my will,
> The Coal Kings slave, but now it's passed;
> Thanks be to God I am free at last.

In the early days of the industry, patches were populated by English-speaking miners—Welsh, Irish, English, and Scottish. In the eighties and nineties came the Slavs and other races. Some patches remained homogeneous, but the tides of immigration overran many of them. Differences of tongue, race, nationality, and religion sometimes led to conflicts. There also existed a social barrier between old and new stock. Life was further complicated by an economic stratification which set the contract miner above the day laborer. Despite these differences and conflicts, inhabitants of a mine patch managed to achieve a fair measure of solidarity. The very smallness of the patch threw them together on terms of intimacy. There was a sharing of meager worldly possessions and an expression of sympathy in times of illness and trouble. No home was ever free of the dread of losing its breadwinner in a mine accident. Hence, when death visited a home everyone attended the funeral and patronized the benefit raffle or dance which followed.

Life was stark, bleak, and semi-primitive. The wretched company houses kept out neither rain, heat, nor cold. They had no plumbing. Water was obtained from a well or from outdoor community hydrants which froze in the winter. Lighting was by tallow candles or kerosene lamps, and streets were dark. Too poor to buy the coal they mined, many workers obtained their fuel from culm banks. Schooling was a luxury. Purchases were made at a company store which generally overcharged its customers. The economic and political life of the little community was in absolute control of the coal operator. Hence, when workers struck they were starved into submission or forced into exile.

Under these circumstances, one would expect former inhabitants of a mine patch to retain bitter memories of the old days. Paradoxically, they don't. Old-timers with whom I have talked were haunted by a nostalgia for them. Time has softened their bitterness but has not effaced from their memory the sentimental side of patch life—the communal sings and dances, the neighborliness and friendships.

Modern communication and mechanical entertainment have dissipated the intimate communal life of the last century. The mine patch, long a symbol of that life, is itself fast disappearing as an independent entity. Many patches have been absorbed by towns and cities which had developed to their boundary line. Some are being ruthlessly uprooted as the industry, harassed by competition, bootlegging, and other troubles, marches toward mechanization and centralization. Some, with their collieries permanently abandoned, are being deserted by their tenants except for those few families who have no other place to go. These patches linger as ghost towns, bereft of song and laughter and utterly dejected in appearance. Their houses wither and decay and eventually tumble into the dark pits below.

Though written forty years ago, "Good-bye Number Three" is timely in view of similar conditions today. Philip Coyle had spent his youth in this Wilkes-Barre Township patch. When he returned after a long absence the sight of the old town going to seed moved him to write this ballad.

"October on Mount Laffee's Hills" expresses the sentimental feeling which miners bear their native heaths. It is also interesting as a reflection of their reaction to the world beyond their own mining environment. Mount Laffee Patch lies in a cove bounded on three sides by gently sloping hills which once were covered with trees and crowned with laurel. The only level stretch is the Pottsville pike at the southern end.

The man who composed this ballad is William Keating, miner bard and strolling minstrel, who was born in the patch. From time to time he had deserted the mines to roam over the country on freight trains, but always to come back to his beloved Mount

Laffee. I asked him how he happened to make this ballad and his written answer follows:

How, When, and Where I "found" and "Framed" (in song) "Autumn Leaves on Mt. Laffee's Hills."

The inspiration: I was born in 1886 in the "cradle" of Mt. Laffee—a Beautiful, (mile-long) verdant valley nestled in the "arms" of low, gently-sloping, Tree-and-Laurel covered Hills. When I was eighteen months old, my Mother died. Untill I became 6 or 7 years old, my 8-year old Sister guarded me, kept me from running "wild" with the other ("mad March Hares") and Rabbits. Between 7 and 10 years of age Mt. Laffee's Hills (and Dales) "mothered" me. therefore I love my Native Hills as Wm. Tell loved his.

It has been truly stated, that we illiterate, unlettered coal-diggers have been neglected, left "out-in-the-cold," left woefully lacking in the art-of-self-expression. We miners (most of us) can think clearly, and feel intensely, but when it comes to saying what we feel and think—then we are stuck; tongue-"tied"—in-ar-tic-u-late. Also, we can (usually) see clearly, too except on "days after-pay-days," then our vision is (like our expression) faulty and blurred, too.

Mt. Laffee's Hills "mothered" me. Mt. Laffee's Vales and grassy Dales were "kind" and "tender" to my bare feet. In all my days of roving (in and out of Armies) the most intense hunger I ever felt, was (Home-sickness) "hunger" for my Hills. My love for my Hills is in-born, deep-rooted, intense, true and life-lasting:

I've written many and many a line
About distant Shores, and "favored" climes—
But, my Heart (never goes)—only into the Rhymes
Which I sing to these Native Hills of mine!

Sure I love every Grass blade on Mt. Laffee's Hills;
My (crude) songs "caught" their "tunes" from Her clear,
    rippling Rills;
And tho Fortune may fare me o'er far Land or Sea—
My "wild" Heart stays, for ever in Old Mount Laffee.

There was no truant officers in my bare-foot days. I was sent to School for one (1) year and played "hooky" six months out of that. At 11 (eleven) years of age I went to work as a Curb-boy (signal tender) in (a P. & R. colliery) Wadesville Shaft (located between Saint Clair and Pottsville, Pa.) Worked at Wadesville for a couple or three years. Heard some of the oldtimers say, "Go West, young man Go West." I went West (by freight train). Arrived in Frisco about a year after the Earthquake. In Frisco they told me: "Go South, young man, Go South." I went south, to New Orleans. There they said: Go "East, young man, Go East." So I roved. Some call it hoboing, some call it "Seeing America First." So since I "left" Home—I've been on the "roam," Rambling all over Creation—. 'Bout a jump-and-a-half in the rear of Success, and two "jumps" ahead of Starvation!

But, no matter where the Hobo goes—Home is where the Heart is.

My Heart always was, and is yet, in Mt. Laffee. Somewhere around the years 1908 or 1909, I happened to be in Florida; working, as a laborer on that once famous (sea-going) "Florida East Coast Railroad." It was late Summer (August). My Heart began "calling" me back, back to Mt. Laffee. I immediately "pulled stakes" and headed north; and arrived in the "Patch" just about the time when Autumn had "painted" my Native Hills in a blaze of colored Beauty!

In glancing over the Editorial-column of Zerbey's "Republican" (on the day of my arrival home) I read, this quotation:

"The Melancholy Days are here
The saddest, gloomiest time o' year."

It struck me like a blow! I threw down that offending "quotation," and looked up at my beautifully-colored, dazzling-bright Hills—and they (my Hills) "told" me that, that "quotation" was a "lie!"

So, early next morning, while the Dew was yet on the leaves and grass, I strolled thru the Woods, and gathered a bunch of Leaves of all different colors and off of different trees, Laurels and Vines.

Then a stroll I took,
To a Leafy nook,
By a clear, babbling Brook
(No pencil, paper, pad, nor Book)
I spread those bright Leaves
On the moss-covered ground
And in their Beauty
This song I "found."

"Dear Old Number Six" recalls happy days spent in this Panther Creek Valley patch which was wiped out about a dozen years ago to make room for a large, mechanized breaker.

Another early patch commemorated in a ballad was Bear Ridge in the Schuylkill Valley. Some of the houses, gloomy and black with coal soot, were still standing when I visited it several years ago. One of the original log cabins built for pioneer miners had been remodeled and was being occupied by a Slavic family. Several landmarks recalled the colliery—small heaps of conglomerate rocks where the breaker had stood; rusty bed-plate bolts which had held the engine in position; a scummy pool which was all that remained of the dam; and the mouth of the mine with a wild cherry tree sprouting from culm and clay with which it had been sealed. Bear Ridge slope, sunk over one hundred years ago, was one of the earliest below-water-level mines in the region. Until the post-Civil War depression caused its abandonment, the colliery had done a flourishing business and had supported a lively community. "Bear Ridge Patch" preserves its story.

Valley Furnace, another patch in the Schuylkill Valley, not far from Bear Ridge, was caught in the same depression. In 1871 it received a blow from which it never recovered; the little mine gave out. Normally the miners might have found jobs at the Shoofly, a nearby colliery. But there a bad vein had been struck and men were being laid off. The only alternative to starvation was to gather meager belongings, leave old associations, and trek across the Broad Mountain into the Mahanoy Valley then being opened to mining.

These troubles were preying on the mind of a little old Irishwoman in Valley Furnace. Her heart was breaking because of the debts she owed in the store and because all her good neighbors were deserting the village. Felix O'Hare, who kept night school for breaker boys at nearby Silver Creek Patch, would pass the woman's cottage to and from school. The simple mining folk believed that his meager book learning, acquired by dint of much whale oil burned after working hours, equipped him to solve all of life's riddles. And so the little old woman would stop him as he went by and pour out her troubles to him. He lent a sympathetic ear and tried to comfort her. One evening he was profoundly moved, his sister, Mrs. Katherine Casserly, told me. He spent half the night trying to put into a ballad some of the things she had told him, and thus created "The Shoofly." Never formally published, this plaintive ballad spread by word of mouth and in a short time the whole region was singing it—and weeping. I am told that music hall audiences in the cities also wept over it. Only his immediate family knew that O'Hare had composed the ballad. The little Irishwoman herself was not told that its author was her schoolmaster confidant. When she heard it for the first time and identified herself with the "old lady" in the ballad, she gave a curse upon the man who had thus exploited her —and not long afterward, O'Hare was drowned in Silver Creek!

B. I. Curran of Centralia supplied the text of "The Shoofly," and Daniel Walsh of the same town sang the tune used here.

The breaker has always been a symbol to the miner. When its whistle blows it is a harbinger of good times. When its ponderous machinery is stilled, sorrow fills the patch. The ballads "When the Breaker Starts Up Full Time," and "When the Black Diamond Breaker Was Burned to the Ground" graphically illustrate these two conditions. "Gossip in a Street Car" mirrors the miners' social life at the turn of the century. All three ballads, the work of Con Carbon, originated in Wilkes-Barre. Daniel Brennan of McAdoo was my source for the first of the three, Dennis P. Coyle for the second, and the third I copied from *Con Carbon's Own Songster*.

"A Miner's Home Sweet Home," by Charles E. Baer and George W. Thornton, published and copyrighted in 1902, is a sentimentalized picture of domestic bliss in a mine patch. It was sung by John Byrne of Philadelphia.

The ballad "When Old Mauch Chunk Was Young" which I dug out of a local history, preserves a picture of the hectic days which marked the founding of Mauch Chunk. Written in a satirical vein by a minister in the 1840's, it is the oldest ballad in this collection.

GOOD-BYE NUMBER THREE

How often, oh, how often, do I think of days gone by
  When we as neighbors lived at Number Three!
How often, oh, how often, do the tears bedim my eyes!
  For they were bright and happy days to me.
We'd gather in the evening when our day's work was done,
  On Cannon's old front porch so merrily,
Singing in the moonlight; the old folks joined the fun,
  When we lived side by side at Number Three.

CHORUS

But those days are gone,
They will come no more.
With a tear in my eye,
Oh, how often I sigh
  For those days of yore.
We lived side by side,
Not a care had we,
Those days they are past,
They were too good to last.
  In old Number Three.

In your travels you may mingle with men of wealth and pomp,
  Whose pockets they are lined with precious gold.

Well, I'd not exchange the pleasures of my childhood's romps,
 That I enjoyed with those dear friends of old.
The neighbors were so pleasant, they'd borrow and they'd lend,
 Their hearts were always happy, light and free.
For a stranger they had welcome, their last farthing they would spend
 When we lived side by side at Number Three.

Now those days are gone forever, they will come no more, I fear,
 The homesteads now are withered and decayed,
Destroyed by cave and culm are the pleasure grounds so dear
 Where in my youth with comrades I have played.
Today I passed the old place and sat upon the hill
 Sweet memories of the past came back to me,
My heart filled with emotion, I sat and cried my fill
 When I saw how time had changed poor Number Three.

OCTOBER ON MOUNT LAFFEE'S HILLS

Sure it's the grandest time of year,
When October days are here
 With their fresh morning frost, their evening dew.
Then Nature decks our hills around,
In a dazzling autumn gown,
 Every color, every shade and every hue.

I have been a roving lad,
The same address I seldom had,
 Since the sweetheart of my boyhood broke her vow.
While my heart for her yet grieves,
I praise these lovely autumn leaves,
 For glad memories they are bringing me now.

Many weary miles I went,
Down the road of discontent,
 Since the wanderlust in youth took hold o' me.
World, I've seen you mostly all,
Yet you cannot hush the call,
 Of native hills 'round dear old Mount Laffee.

Just recently my footsteps led
Back, to the place where I was bred;
  Through Mount Laffee's hills I wandered for a day.
Gathered joys worth more than gold,
Tramped again the trails of old,
  And plucked this bunch of autumn leaves along the way.

White oak leaves of Holly's hill,
Morn's diamond dewdrops dot them still.
  Here's a sprig of evergreen off Green Park's pine.
Scarlet leaves off tall gumberry,
Leaves off wild and tame black cherry,
  And one golden leaf off Murray's wild grape vine.

Silver maple, birch and beech,
Sassafras and garden peach,
  Here's a curly, crispy spear of feeder fern.
While brown autumn leaves downward fall,
Mount Laffee's home scenes seem to call,
  To re-view them in their beauty I return.

My roving footsteps lured me round
Bush bowers that bound the cricket ground;
  Homey pathways give my hobo heart a thrill.
Hawthorn hedge my barefeet knew,
Somber laurel bush, they grew
  All round my dad's log cabin on Mick's hill.

Leaves of hickory, dogwood, plum.
Ho! here's one leaf—am I so dumb?
  Of its history there's nothing I can tell.
I don't even know its name,
Nor the tree whence it came,
  I just found it on the path by Lawler's well.

I have rambled many a mile,
Been everywhere worth while,
  Laughed 'neath Broadway's lights, seen 'Frisco's wonder views.

Seen gay Paree and all the rest,
Yet to me the one joy best
Is to get Mount Laffee's hills beneath my shoes.

Yes, Killarney's Lakes are lovely,
Colorado's canyons grand;
Truly Rocky Mountain's majestic magic thrills.
But to pure beauty you're a stranger,
Till you've gazed on autumn's grandeur,
When October gowns my old Mount Laffee's hills.

They can have their snow-capped mountains,
Woolly prairies and blue seas;
Keep their suffocating cities, large and small.
Let me live in old Mount Laffee,
Bury me 'neath her trees,
To the rest of this weary world you're welcome all.

DEAR OLD NUMBER SIX

Take me back once more to childhood,
Let me climb my mother's knee;
Let me roam the fields and wildwood
As I did in boyish glee.
Let me see the kid goats playing,
Let me feed the baby chicks,
And gather the eggs the hens were laying,
At home, in dear old Number Six.

Let me go back a slate picker—
Just to be a boy once more,
Down the lump coal chutes to flicker,
Rumpety bump and tumble o'er.
Let me hear the old songs o'er,
Let me play those boyish tricks,
Let me chew that Clark & Snover,
At home, in dear old Number Six.

Let me roam the little mountain,
  And cross the dear old Wirley Hill,
Let me hear the hound dogs huntin'
  In the gloaming, calm and still;
Let me hear the catbirds singing,
  Let me fish the little cricks,
Let me with the girls go swinging,
  At home, in dear old Number Six.

Let me go pick huckleberries
  Up the rocks on the mountainside;
Us little lads wi' the little fairies
  Who looked to us to be their guides.
Let me hear the pheasant drumming,
  And watch the woodpecker as he pecks,
Let me see the chipmunks running
  At home, in dear old Number Six.

Let me hear those tales of recess
  That only little folks can tell;
Cuddled up upon the green grass
  Close beside the old town well,
The man in the moon had charge of the light plant,
  Our cottage walls were not of bricks;
Young and old enjoyed the night camp,
  On the green, at Number Six.

Let me see the old-time hoedown,
  Back in the days when we were young,
In all the coal fields there was no town
  Like old Number Six for fun.
The dance went on without a wrangle—
  If they should get in a mix,
Shoue would straighten out the tangle,
  At home, in dear old Number Six.

Number Six is near the number
  Where the silence claims the dead,

Wearing on to peaceful slumber—
  The rock banks for her bed.
When she's down and the rock banks scatter
  O'er the beds of her noisy geese,
On a granite slab in gold letters:
  "May the old town rest in peace."

BEAR RIDGE PATCH

I'd like to see that dear spot
  Where that old breaker stood,
In a place called Bear Ridge
  Where I spent my dear boyhood;
The hillside and the valley, too,
  On them I long to gaze—
In dear old Schuylkill County, boys,
  The place where I was raised.

CHORUS

It makes me sad and lonely now
  When I think of years gone by,
That I spent at the old breaker
  When I was but a boy.
My youthful days are past and gone,
  Old age is coming fast,
The only thing that is left to me
  Is a picture of the past.

When I first went to Bear Ridge
  I mean to let you know;
In eighteen hundred and fifty-six—
  Nearly forty years ago.
I had no fear upon me then,
  My heart was young and gay,
And around the hills of Bear Ridge, boys,
  I spent many a happy day.

Years have brought on changes
  To that dear little town;
The slopes were drowned out
  And the breaker was torn down.
The grass is growing fresh and green
  O'er the place where I used to play,
And the people who were living there
  They all have moved away.

I'd like to meet some comrades, boys,
  That were working with me there;
When the place was shut down,
  We scattered everywhere.
I moved to New Philadelphia,
  And others they went West;
Some of them are now dead and gone—
  I hope they are at rest.

I came to Luzerne County
  In eighteen sixty-seven;
In the month of April
  The date it was eleven.
From there to Carbon County,
  Where I was born, you know;
But my heart still clings to Schuylkill, boys,
  Wherever I may go.

I must leave off writing,
  And bid you all good-bye;
When I think of those happy days
  The tears come to my eye.
I had no trouble on me then,
  No hardships, care, or strife,
But since, like many a poor workingman,
  I've had my ups and downs in life.

THE SHOOFLY

Transcribed by Melvin LeMon

As I went a-walk-ing one fine sum-mer's morn-ing, It's
down by the Fur-nace I chanced for to stroll. I es
pied an old la-dy, I'm sure she was eigh-ty, At the
foot of the bank and she's root-in' for coal; And
[𝄋 Chorus]
Cry-ing "Och-one! Sure I'm near-ly dis-tract-ed, For it's
as I drew nigh her she sat on her hun-kers, And to
down in the Shoo-fly they cut a bad vein; Like-
fill her scut-tle she then did be-gin— To her-
wise they've con-demned the old slope at the Fur-nace, And
self she was hum-ming this mourn-ful dit-ty, And
[fine]
all me fine neigh-bors must leave it a-gain.
this is the song the old la-dy did sing:
[𝄋 to Chorus]

"'Twas only last evenin' that I asked McGinley
  To tell me the reason the Furnace gave o'er.
He told me the company had spent eighty thousand
  And finding no prospects they'd spend no more.
He said that the Diamond it was rather bony,
  Besides too much dirt in the seven-foot vein;
And as for the Mammoth, there's no length of gangway,
  Unless they buy land from Abel and Swayne.

"And as for Michael Rooney, I owe him some money;
  Likewise Patrick Kearns, I owe him some more;
And as for old John Eagen, I ne'er see his wagon,
  But I think of the debt that I owe in his store.
I owe butcher and baker, likewise the shoemaker,
  And for plowing me garden I owe Pat McQuail;
Likewise his old mother, for one thing and th'other,
  And to drive away bother, an odd quart of ale.

"But if God spares me children until the next summer,
  Instead of a burden, they will be a gain;
And out of their earnin's I'll save an odd dollar,
  And build a snug house at the 'Foot of the Plane.'
Then rollin' in riches, in silks and in satins,
  I ne'er shall forget the days I was poor,
And likewise the neighbors that stood by me children,
  Kept want and starvation away from me door.

"And if you should happen to cross the Broad Mountain,
  Step in and sit down on me cane-bottomed chairs;
Take off your fixin's, lay them on the bureau,
  While I in the kitchen refreshments prepare;
And while we are seated so snug at the table,
  Enjoying the fruits of a strong cup of tea,
We'll talk of the quiltin's we had at the Furnace—
  Me heart does rejoice an old neighbor to see."

THE MINE PATCH

WHEN THE BREAKER STARTS UP FULL-TIME

Transcribed by Melvin LeMon

Our trou - bles are o'er, Mrs. Mur - phy, For the
Ditch - man next door tells me straight, That the
mines will start full - time on Mon - day That's
phat he tells me 'tan - ny rate. Sure the
boss, he says, told him this morn - ing, As
he was 'bout en - t'ring the mine, That the
coal is quite scarce roun' 'bout New York, So the
Chorus.
ru - mors is work full - time. And it's boo -
hoo if the news be true, Me store bill's the first thing I'll

pay, A stuff par - lor shuit and a lounge I will
buy, And an or - gan for Brid - gie, hur - ray. Me
cal - i - co skirt I will throw in the dirt— In me
silk one won't I cut a shine? Cheer
up, Mrs. Mur - phy, we all will ate
tur - key, When the break - er starts up full - time.

I'll ne'er stick me fist in a washtub,
  The Chinee man he'll have me trade,
I'll ne'er pick a coal off the dirt bank;
  I'll buy everything ready-made.
We'll dress up our children like fairies,
  We'll build up a house big and fine,
And we'll move away from the Hungaries,
  When the breaker starts up full-time.

The Hungaries won't work with me Paddy;
  They say too much no good his place.
They always lose time after pay day,
  It's meself sure that ne'er liked that race.

They won't load their cairs off the livil,
They want runnin' chutes, do ye mind?
But we'll chase thim away to the divil,
When the breaker starts up full-time.

WHEN THE BLACK DIAMOND BREAKER WAS BURNED TO THE GROUND

(AIR: *The Rakes of Kildare*)

Sure the East End's in mourning, the times are so poor,
The wolf he is knocking at everyone's door;
I can't get a job, faith, for money or love,
One byword I'll use, that I'm not in the shove.
Once I was happy, had money to burn
Though history tells me ev'ry dog has his turn.
Mine came with a vengeance and done me up brown
When the Black Diamond breaker was burned to the ground.

CHORUS

Times are hard, as hard as can be,
And meat in the house is a rare thing to see;
To a bare empty table I have to sit down
Since the Black Diamond breaker was burned to the ground.

I was speakin' to Mackin and Old Foote also,
And sez I, "With the building I think ye are slow;
Put carpenters to work and up with it," sez I.
"If you'll wait," sez Old Foote, "from hunger you'll die."
Be the way that he spoke I could tell very plain
That they never will build the Black Diamond again,
And how we're to live, you all can search me
So we'll get a thermometer and starve by degrees.

Sure I owe twenty dollars to Butcher Gildea,
'Twill be a long time to come when the same I can pay,

For grub I owe thirty at Mackin's cash store,
And beyant at McLaughlin's I owe twenty more.
Tigue the shoemaker I owe for my shoes,
O'Day and Jim Mundy I owe for my booze,
Not speakin' a word of what I owe lower down
Since the Black Diamond breaker was burned to the ground.

GOSSIP IN A STREET CAR

I was riding in a street car, through a little mining town,
Before we reached our destination the car had broken down,
And while the men were fixing it, a miner's wife came in;
With a woman, who was in the car, at once began to chin.
The woman who was in the car from the village moved away,
Where the other one had known her, they were neighbors, I dare say.
They told of all their troubles since the day that they'd been wed,
And if your time's not precious, I will tell you all was said.

"Well, dear ould Mrs. Mulligan, an' how is all yer care?"
"For mesel' I'm feelin' lovely, me heart's as loight as air;
I could sing wid joy this moment, sence Paddy's quit the booze,
'Tis now I kin have dresses, an' me baby kin have shoes."
"But how is all the Gallaghers, an' Murphys, how are they?
An' the Boyles, I didn't see thim sence the day I moved away?
An' how is all yer own care, has Mickey still the cough?
An' how is Jamsey walkin' sence the leg was taken off?"

"Well, Mis' Toole, there's no use grumblin', we're not sent here fer fun,
Me man is sick those two wakes wid a fillon on the thumb,
But Mickey's cough is splanded, no better could I wish.
An' James is walkin' lovely sence he got the artifish.
But did ye hear about the Murphys? No? Well, their little baby died,
An' she made a holy show av hersel', the way she bawled an' cried.
She did cut up ridiculous, she sez, 'Bring back me dear,'
An' the child was hardly buried till the can was sent out fer beer.

"It's Hungaries live in your block, an' they are a dirty clan.
There's only jis wan woman, an' about fifty-seven men.
An' how they live or phat they ate, 'tis more than I can say,
But they all work 'round the breaker fer about fifty cents a day.
An' Mullins' have a piano, an' Maggie's practising,
She's feriver at this song called 'The Marriage Bells did Ring.'
'Pon me soul she has us dafened, fer she's at it noon an' night,
But ye'd ought to see Miss Flannigan, she looks a holy sight.

"She got ivery blessed tooth pulled, let me see, it was las' wake,
An' she looks jis loike a monkey, ivery toime she goes to spake.
An' Paddy Burke is buried, an' so is Cougin's wife,
An' little Jamsey Mack will be a cripple all his life.
He was hurted at the fire, did you not hear av it?
Sure Snyder, the Ditchman's double block, was burnt up ivery bit.
All the ingens in the town was out, they'd niver git it quinch
Af it was not fer my Paddy, ould John Burke and Mickey Lynch.

" 'Twas thim phat got the fire out, fer at it they did stick,
Didn't I laugh at number eight hose cart, till I thought that I'd be sick?
They put their hose across the railroad track, oh Lor', but I did laugh;
An' the noight ixpress run over it, an' cut it roight in half.
Then the horse got frightened, wid the hose cart ran away,
They found the horse nixt mornin' more than twinty miles away.
Oh, it was in all the papers, 'twas a joke wid people here,
An' ye say ye did not raid av it? bedad, I think that's queer."

"Arrah, woman, I hear nothin', people's so strange phere I live,
An' to be once more amongst youse, jis one-half me loife I'd give—
Oh, the noights we sat on my ould porch, af not mine 'twas on yours,
An' af children in the town was sick, 'twas there they got the cures,
The stories phat we used to tell, the jokes an' iverything.
An' the darlin', dear ould Irish come-all-ye's we did sing.
We could tell how much the breaker worked, an' ivery day she lost,
An' how much our men had comin' after payin' all the cost.

"But those days are gone feriver, they will never come again,
As the great Salvation Army sez, till we catch the golden train.

But did Mary Casey marry the dude she used to mash—
The flup phat wore the eye glass an' a seven-hair mustache?
Wid his face so white an' wither, an' thirty-pounder cane,
The wan ye'd think that would dissolve af he stood long in the rain."
"Oh yes, I do remember him. Ah, she gave that thing the slip.
She had two beaus since those bucks; the same Mary is a clip.

"She's at ivery ball an' party, her friends she has disgraced,
An' I'm tould, but don't say nothin', that she laces at the waist.
An' my Mary Ann she tould, that she paints and powders, too,
But fer heaven's sake don't mention it, or spake av it, will you?"
" 'Pon me soul I'll niver mention it, but I'm not at all surprised.
The toime she claned the house fer me, she was powdered to the eyes.
An' paint on top av that again—she wuz a holy sight to see."
The conductor put his head in then and cried out, "Wilkes-Barre."

A MINER'S HOME SWEET HOME

It was on a summer's day in the coal fields far away
  That I chanced upon a miner's lonely cot;
And I marveled much to see how contented he could be,
  For it seemed that he was happy with his lot.
Roses bloomed around the door and a baby on the floor
  Lent a sunshine to that lonely mountainside,
And I said, "Though fate's unkind you are happy here, I find,"
  Then he answered as his face lit up with pride:

CHORUS

There's a light ev'ry night just to show the way,
  A kiss for me at the door,
There's a smile all the while greets me ev'ry day
  I'll cherish forevermore.
For the joy of my life is a trusting wife and baby,
  Why should I roam?
In sunshine or rain it is just the same,
  That's a miner's home sweet home.

I would go upon my way but he answered, "Stranger, stay
  Till you hear the story of a happy life;
All the gold that e'er was mined is not equal, you will find,
  To the blessings of a baby and a wife.
When the sun sinks in the West, 'tis the time I love best,
  Then I look upon my cot with heartfelt pride.
Richer homes I know there are but I'm happier by far
  With my lov'd ones by a miner's fireside."

WHEN OLD MAUCH CHUNK WAS YOUNG

(AIR: *John Anderson, My Jo*)

When old Mauch Chunk was young,
  J—— * used to say,
A man that labored hard should have
  Six Billy cups a day.
And so, with an unsparing hand,
  The whiskey flood was flung,
And drunkards they were made by scores
  When old Mauch Chunk was young.

When old Mauch Chunk was young,
  At noon they blew the horn,
And, gathering thick, came gangs of men,
  And so at eve and morn.
With grace and promptitude and skill
  They moistened lip and tongue,
And went to work in rain and mud,
  When old Mauch Chunk was young.

When old Mauch Chunk was young,
  Lehighton was in prime.
And fights and frolics frequently
  Were had in olden time.

* Joshua White.

Like short-tailed bulls in fly-time
  They at each other sprung,
And many a battle there was fought
  When old Mauch Chunk was young.

When old Mauch Chunk was young
  And Captain Abels preached,
The top notch of intemperance
  By many a one was reached;
And dark the cloud of sorrow
  O'er many a dwelling hung,
With deep disgrace and poverty,
  When old Mauch Chunk was young.

When old Mauch Chunk was young
  A treat was no great shakes,
Unless before the company
  Was set a heap of cakes.
And never better cakes were eat,
  Or better song was sung
Than this which we are laughing at,
  When old Mauch Chunk was young.

CHAPTER TWO

Miners in Good Humor

PART 1: BALLADS

In these humorous ballads we see the anthracite miner holding up the mirror to himself and laughing at his own frailties and troubles.

"A Celebrated Workingman" is a satire on the off-hour braggart whose counterpart may be found in nearly every walk of life. Feeling tipsy after a few drinks on a pay night, the vainglorious one boasts loudly of his skill and prowess in the mines. Every barroom had these fellows and they were laughed at because the miners knew them for the washouts they were outside the barroom. When a bartender thought the crowd had suffered enough from their vaporings he would roar across the smoke-filled room some such sally as, "Here, cut it out. Get a safety, or you'll blow the place up."

This ballad by Ed Foley was immensely popular a generation ago. He first sang it at the wedding of Mr. and Mrs. Thomas Johnson at Kulpmont in 1892. So well was it received that Foley was forced to sing it over and over again until his voice became hoarse. The ballad spread quickly by word of mouth to all corners of the region. Foley must have thought it pretty good himself, for he got off a copy to his former parish priest, Father McMahan at Minersville, who sent back a postscript in the form of a verse written in the metre and spirit of the ballad:

I read your verses o'er and o'er and I think they're simply fine,
And with your kind permission I would like to add a line,
The man who wrote those verses might own a town or mine—
If only he steered clear of the barroom.

"A Celebrated Workingman" was one of the very first ballads to come into my possession when I began collecting. On a rainy March Sunday back in 1925 I was taken on a round of old-time ballad singers in Centralia by B. I. Curran, white-haired school teacher. Some of the singers were at work in the mines, others were out of town. But Mr. Curran said he could recollect some himself if he had a little time. Several weeks later I received this ballad and two others. Variants were also supplied by George Sheibenhood of Ashland and Daniel Walsh of Centralia, who made the record transcribed here.

"Down, Down, Down," another barroom ballad, relates the experiences of a miner reporting for work with a hangover. But it is more than the record of a tipsy worker's muddled thoughts. Rather is it a reflection of the anthracite miner's buffetings which gives it added significance.

"The material for 'Down, Down, Down,'" writes William Keating, its author, "was picked up between gangway roof falls, put together on a mine car bumper, penciled with car sprags, punctuated with mule kicks, tuned to the thunder and vibration of underground blasts and muted to the solitude of the mines, while this mule driver rhymester worked between drunks traveling in and out of the Buck Mountain counter gangway on the third level of Oak Hill shaft at Buckley's Gap, Duncott."

"Down, Down, Down," for a long time an exclusively barroom ballad, has become generally popular. Keating himself, with his resonant bass voice is its best interpreter. The manner in which it was sung in the first years of its existence, and how he happened to compose it, are told by Keating as follows:

In the days when I was hittin' the booze the drinks would come up, up, up when I sang "Down, Down, Down." She was too long to sing straight through, so I broke her up into groups of verses corresponding to levels in a mine. When I got through singing one level, the boys alongside the bar would yell, "Time out for drinks." Then the drinks would go round and Billy Keating would have a drink on the house or on whoever was payin' at the time. As the ballad has about forty verses, you can imagine in what condition the singer and the customers were by the time I got to the end. The barroom floor was me stage for thirty years and, be jabers, I done it up brown when I was at it. But I'm off the hard stuff for life. I've got it licked now.

How did I happen to make up "Down, Down, Down"? Well, about twenty years ago I was drivin' a mule in the Oak Hill mine. Me and the mule were the only livin' things in the gangway unless you count the rats. It got kind o' lonesome, me sittin' there on the bumper with the cars rattlin' along the dark gangways and headin's. To break the loneliness and at the same time show Jerry, me mule, that I wasn't such a bad egg after all, I used to make up ditties out o' me head and sing them as we rode along. One of them was "Down, Down, Down."

"Down, Down, Down" circulated a long time by word of mouth before being set down on paper. Keating was unable to write until he was thirty-two years old and even after he had learned to write, putting things down on paper was too irksome for him. It was so much easier to make up a ballad out of his head and just sing it.

The incentive finally to write out "Down, Down, Down," came to him in the fall of 1927 under the following circumstances: He sang the ballad at a picnic of Oak Hill colliery employees at Duncott, Schuylkill County, and when he had finished, a mine boss named McGee, from the western part of the county, offered him five dollars for a copy of the ballad. This embarrassed Keating as there were no copies in existence, and he promised to make one. However, when he realized the momentous task ahead of him, he promptly forgot the promise.

Then, three weeks later, came a memorable after pay-day spree at Duncott in which the balladist and several butties indulged. Keating had bartered a ham for a quart of moonshine, and after the bottle had made the rounds it became empty. Powerful stuff, the moonshine knocked them out. Stretched out on the grass, they lay moaning and groaning and, even in their stupor, trying to find a way to obtain a refill of the bottle. Finally an idea emerged from the party.

"Say Bill," said one of the boys. "Did you ever write that copy of 'Down, Down, Down,' for that mine boss from the West End—remember, at the Oak Hill picnic he told you he'd give you five bucks for it?"

Keating was in no condition to do any writing, but slowly it penetrated his befogged mind that this was an opportunity to earn enough cash with which to purchase more moonshine.

"We'll go over to my place," he replied at length. "My woman'll raise hell with the whole of us, but I'll write that song, even if it takes me until midnight."

Keating describes the next scene as follows: "We went to my house. I borrowed several sheets of writing-paper from my nearest neighbor and, seated around our middle-room table, with the rest of the fellows helping me with the 'spelling' (while my wife RAVED!), I wrote 'Down, Down, Down.' After several hours' (awful!) efforts, we finished a shamefully 'scribbled!' but possibly readable, copy of my song."

The next problem was to find the boss whose address Keating knew only vaguely as somewhere in the West End. The four booze-thirsty musketeers then got into a rickety automobile and rode to the West End looking for a McGee where the woods could not be seen for McGees. "Finally, after miles of back-tracking, after hootin' and tootin' the flivver's horn through nearly every town, village and 'Patch' in the western end of Schuylkill County without finding 'our' McGee," writes Keating, "we gave up, or rather, we took a different 'tack.' "

They stopped in front of a pool room speakeasy which made them feel at home. The sage behind the bar knew plenty of McGees but not the one the boys were hunting. While Keating poured out his story, the bartender kept his Irish blue eyes glued to the scribbled copy of "Down, Down, Down," smiling as he read. Presently he said, "Say, Butty, is this the only copy ye have of this song?" To which Keating replied, "It is, and it's only through the Mercy of God that I had strength enough in me hand to write that one this evenin'."

"Well," said the bartender, "ye needn't hunt any farther for any McGees. I'll give ye five dollars fer this song, and call your butties in. I'll give ye all a drink and thin ye'll sing this song till I learn the 'chune' av it if it takes from now till mornin'."

"The show was on," Keating adds. "We drank, I sang. We drank again, and I sang again—this song without end. Amen!"

"After a Shaft Pay Day" is still another anthracite ballad redolent of the barroom. But it owes its existence to a spiritual cause. As explained by Henry Carey, sixty, he wrote it a generation ago when his church needed money. "The ballad," said Carey, "was printed on broadsides selling at six cents each, a nickel more than the usual price. I made them redeemable at a local saloon for a schooner of beer or a nickel cigar. The extra cent was turned over to the church fund. The lads fell for the ruse and a lot of broadsides were sold."

The opening stanza was the only one which Carey could recall of his ballad when Le Mon and I called at his little home in the Mahanoy Valley in 1935. The term "shaft" used in the ballad refers to the Lehigh Valley Coal Company's Number Five colliery, known as "the shaft" after the method of entry.

Near Number Five Patch is the village of Lost Creek which

takes its name from a stygian, culm-laden creek running through it. The ballad "Lost Creek" paints a vivid picture of the coarser side of mine patch life in the last century.

The ballad recalls an anecdote. The people of the patch were communicants of the Mary Magdalene Parish formed in 1879. The little red church stood on one side of the road and Number Two colliery faced it on the other.

That little church was built entirely by the miners of the parish, and when completed it lacked only a bell for its belfry. This lack gave concern to the parishioners and their rector, Father Walsh, who would say, "What is a church without a bell to summon the faithful to Mass, to ring the Blessed Angelus and toll for the dead?"

One Sunday morning in 1881, Father Walsh asked his parishioners to remain in their pews after Mass. Laying aside his cassock, he invited suggestions as to how to raise money for the bell.

Among the things suggested were a strawberry festival, a raffle for a goat, picnics and fairs. None, however, seemed adequate to the situation which worried Father Walsh.

No expression, however, had yet come from a rheumatic old miner occupying a back pew who seemed to be surveying Number Two colliery from the window. At length, leaning heavily on his cane, he stood up.

"Beggin' your pardon, your Riverence," he said in a shaky voice.

"Yes, Michael John, what have you to offer?" the priest asked gravely.

"Well, don't ye think, fa-ather," replied the old miner, "that it would be a whole lot ch'aper to use Number Two's steam whistle instead of a bell?"

In the same Mahanoy Valley as Number Five Patch and Lost Creek is the Indian Ridge colliery of the Philadelphia & Reading

Coal and Iron Company. The ballad "Over at Indian Ridge" describes miners building a first-aid station within the mine in 1902, and mocks their unfamiliarity with the building trades. The lesson carried by the ballad seems to be "A miner should stick to his drill." Composed by Harry Tempest, one of the colliery workers, "Over at Indian Ridge" has no refrain or chorus, a piano vamp separating the stanzas.

Foley, the fireboss mentioned in the last stanza, was a colorful character around whom many anecdotes are told in the valley. Once several prosperous-looking New Yorkers were taken through the colliery by Foley and when they came back to the surface, one of them turned to him and said, "Mr. Foley, I wouldn't work in the mines for a million dollars." "Faith," replied Foley, as he gripped the stranger's hand, "there's men a-workin' down there phat's gettin' less than that." On another occasion, at the outbreak of the 1902 strike, Foley's superiors had ordered him to take charge of the engine house. Refusing, he said, "I didn't make a fire for Mrs. Foley this mornin', and I'll be damned if I'm going to make one for the Readin' Company."

Like the preceding piece, "The Broken Shovel" is a nonsense ballad. The fight is supposed to have taken place in Beaver Brook Patch about 1890. One miner accused the other of breaking his new shovel and, being Irish, the accused challenged him to a fist fight. The boys squared off like boxers and pummeled each other until a Casper Milquetoast-like character, a crippled peddler nicknamed Pretta-moor, stepped between them and called a halt. Pretta-moor derived his Gaelic nickname from the potatoes he cried and peddled in the patch. The ballad is believed to have been improvised at the time by a young patcher, Dennis Brady. I first heard it in 1925, in Carbondale, where I found a saloon keeper who said he could sing it. When I asked him to do so, he declined. His reason was that he had given the ballad to a fellow townsman who had promised to reward him with a bottle of whiskey and failed to do so. It was my misfortune to come upon him when he was in this mood. However, after frequent inquiries, I finally was directed to Daniel Brennan of McAdoo who graciously sang it for me.

"Mackin's Porch" turns back the curtain on what probably was the best-known after-hour gathering place of anthracite miners—the porch of Mackin Brothers' general store in the East End of Wilkes-Barre. As they chewed their quids or smoked their clay pipes, the mine workers swore oaths, bandied the gossip of mine and neighborhood, indulged in reminiscences of "the good old days," boasted of their skill as miners, and lied about their earnings. Here too they settled arguments in primitive fashion—with bare fists. The older generation of miners recall feelingly the porch and the lively times associated with it. I obtained this ballad from Dennis P. Coyle, a former miner, who still lives in the neighborhood of the famous porch and has a vivid recollection of it. He was also a close friend of the bard who composed it, Con Carbon.

Coyle also gave me Bob Quigley's ballad, "The Start That Casey Got" which sings of a Wilkes-Barre miner who, weary of the hazards of coal mining, sought a nice, and what he thought would be a safe job in a powder mill at Dupont.

"Jenkin Jenkins" aroused my curiosity when I heard its chorus in Wilkes-Barre in 1936. Since it was most popular with Welsh miners I had Welsh friends help me find it, but when this did not bring the full ballad to light, I made an appeal through the Wilkes-Barre newspapers and received variants from M. P. Kelly and Mrs. Lewis L. Foster.

Another ballad about Welshmen, reminiscent of the third and fourth stanzas of "Jenkin Jenkins" but written by an Irishman, Joseph Gallagher of Lansford, is "Three Jolly Welshmen."

In the spirit of the two preceding ballads, "Jake and Jack Are Miners," satirizes the tired and incompetent miner. Ashland miners can still identify these two characters, though the ballad was written by John Hory over forty years ago.

In the eighties Irish immigrants were still coming into the anthracite region, and fellow countrymen staged welcome parties for them. One such affair in Wilkes-Barre is commemorated in "At Paddy Mayock's Ball," composed by Robert J. Quigley of Parsons in 1886. It was printed in the Wilkes-Barre *Sunday Independent* on May 17, 1936, in connection with the Anthracite Regional Folk Festival held in Wilkes-Barre about that time.

Immigrants, Irish or otherwise, were not always received with balls and parties. "A Tramp Through Carbon County" reflects a hazing which one Irish immigrant received with evident good grace.

Joseph Gallagher, its author, who gave it to me, also made up "Dan McCole," which preserves an early custom in the hard coal fields. Wedding parties marched in a body to the church. Gallagher saw his last outdoor wedding procession in 1870 when twelve couples paraded from the bride's home in Number Six Patch to St. Joseph's Church in Summit Hill. People poured out into the muddy road to gaze upon the blushing bride and bridegroom and their attendants. Gallagher was about six years old then. It made a vivid impression on him, and in 1893 he composed this ballad and sang it at the Lansford Opera House.

"The Pretty Maid Milking Her Goat," with its mocking text, seems out of spirit with its tune, one of the loveliest of all Irish folk melodies. I obtained it from Mr. and Mrs. Thomas Johnson of Kulpmont.

A CELEBRATED WORKINGMAN

Transcribed by Melvin LeMon

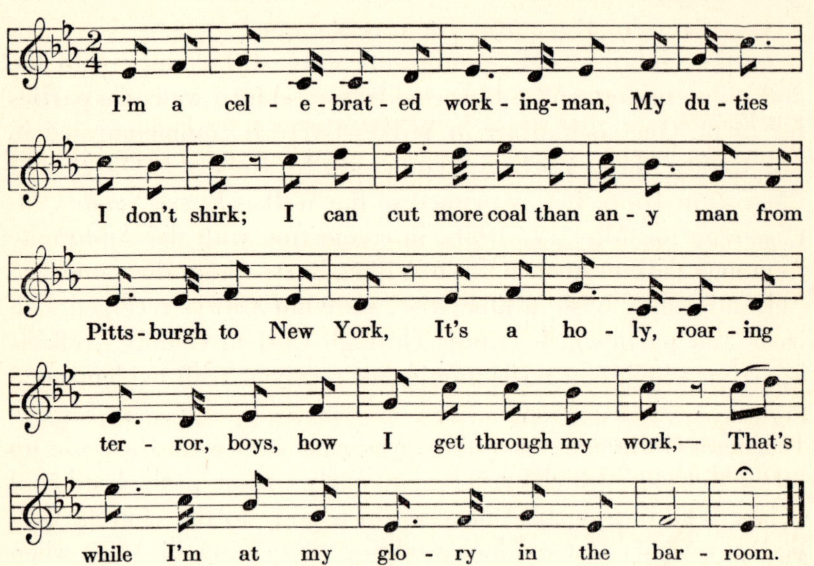
I'm a cel - e - brat - ed work - ing - man, My du - ties
I don't shirk; I can cut more coal than an - y man from
Pitts - burgh to New York, It's a ho - ly, roar - ing
ter - ror, boys, how I get through my work,— That's
while I'm at my glo - ry in the bar - room.

I can stand a double timber, single post, a bar or prop,
I can throw a chain on the bottom or I can throw it on the top,
Give me a pair of double engines and be damned I'll ne'er stop,
Till I land a couple of wagons in the barroom.

I'll go down and work on the platform or go out and run the dump,
I can put pulleys in on the slope or go down and clean the sump,
I can run a 20,000 horse-power steam engine pump—
That's providing that I have it in the barroom.

I'll go down and work the flat vein or go up and work the pitch,
I can work at the Potts or Newside—I don't care the divil which,
I can show the old track layer how to decorate the ditch—
Now haven't I often proved it in the barroom?

Now at driving I'm a daisy; just give me a balky team,
I'll beat anything that e'er went by water, wind, or steam;
There's your balance planes, your endless chains; they're nowhere to be seen,
Now haven't I often proved it in the barroom?

Now at bossing I'm a daisy; I know I'm no disgrace,
For I could raise your wages, boys, twelve cents at the l'ast,
Wasn't the Readin' Company mistaken when they didn't make all haste
And gobble me, before I struck the barroom?

I can show the boss or super how the air should circulate,
I can show the boss fireman how the steam should generate,
And the trouble at the Pottsville shaft I could elucidate,
Now haven't I often proved it in the barroom?

And now my song is o'er and I haven't any other,
For heaven's sake don't fire no more or else we'll surely smother,
The landlord will rather throw us out than go to the bother
Of putting up a ventilator in the barroom.

And now my song is ended and I hope you'll all agree,
That if you want any pointers you'd better send for me,
But I'm not worth a good gol darn till I empty two or three
Of the very biggest schooners in the barroom.

DOWN, DOWN, DOWN

Transcribed by Melvin LeMon

With your kind at - ten - tion, a song I will
trill, All ye who must toil with the pick and the
drill, And sweat for your bread in that hole in Oak
Hill, That goes down, down, down.

When I was a boy says my daddy to me:
"Stay out of Oak Hill, take my warning," says he,
"Or with dust you'll be choked and a pauper you'll be,
Broken down, down, down."

But I went to Oak Hill and I asked for a job,
A mule for to drive or a gangway to rob.
The boss said, "Come out, Bill, and follow the mob
That goes down, down, down."

On the strength of the job and the tune of this rhyme,
I strolled into Tim's an' drank twenty-five shines;
Reported next morning, half dead but on time
To go down, down, down.

Says Pete McAvoy, "Here's Bill Keatin' the scamp."
Just back, Pete supposed, from a million-mile tramp.
Pete showed me the "windie" where I'd get a lamp
To go down, down, down.

The lamp man he squints through the window at me,
"What's your name? What's your age? What's your number?" says he.
"Bill Keatin', I'm thirty, number twenty-three,
Mark that down, down, down."

With a frown of disfavor, my joke it was met,
For an argument plainly, the lamp man was set.
He told me that divil a lamp would I get
To go down, down, down.

Says I, "Mr. Lamp Man, now don't l'ave us fight;
Can't ye see be me eyes I was boozin' all night?
Sure the mines will be dark and I'll have to have light
While I'm down, down, down."

With an old greasy apron, Jim polished his specks,
Declarin' the lamp house rules would be wrecked,
If he'd give out his lantherns 'thout gettin' brass checks
From us Clowns! Clowns! Clowns!

I found the supply clerk, of him I inquired
If he had any checks of the sort Jim desired.
He said: "Here's a check, if you lose it, you're fired,
Mark that down, down, down."

I had the precious lamp check that would pacify Jim,
Flip, into his window, I flung it to him
Sayin', "Now quit your grumbling, an' give me a glim
To go down, down, down."

A contraption Jim gave me, a hose on a box,
'Twas so heavy I thought it was loaded with rocks.
If a car jumped the track, you could use it for blocks
While you're down, down, down.

The box breaks the bones in the small of your back,
Wears the hide off your hips where it hangs be a strap;
Oh! the gawk that transported such lamps to the Gap
May go down, down, down.

When you ask for a lamp you commit an offense,
You'd imagine the lamp man stood all the expense;
While for lamps that won't light we pay sixty-five cents
While we're down, down, down.

We wait at Jim's window while winter winds stab,
While the lamp man unravels a lot of crank gab.
Did ye e'er meet a lamp man that wasn't a crab
In your rounds? Aren't they hounds?

Crabbed lamp lords, ye'll cringe for your cranks whin ye die,
For the way that ye bulldozed me butties and I;
Me and Tracy'll be twanging this ballad on high
While you're down, down, down.

Then into the office I sauntered to Boss Sam.
With a cheery "Good mornin'," says I, "Here I am,
With booze in me bottle and beer in me can
To go down, down, down."

"Well, Billy, me bucko, how are you today?"
"Outside of a headache," says I, "I'm O. K.
I've been samplin' the soda in every café
In the town, town, town."

"Sam, where is my job at?" I wanted to know.
"Was it in the new drift?" Sam shook his head, no.
"When you hit the fifth lift you'll have one more to go,
So get down, down, down."

I asked Sam what tools would I need in the place.
"Very few," said the boss with a grin on his face.
"One seven-size scoop in a coop-stoopy space
Away down, down, down."

With a note from the boss to the shaft I made haste,
Saluted the top-man and in line took me place
Sayin' "Gi' me a cage, for I've no time to waste,
Let me down, down, down."

"All aboard for the bottom!" the top-man did yell,
We stepped on the cage, he ding-donged a bell;
Through that hole in Oak Hill, like a bat out o' hell
We went down, down, down.

In wet or dry weather that shaft always rains,
There's a trembling of timbers and clanking of chains.
Just off of a spree, it flip-flopped me few brains
Going down, down, down.

It happened that something was wrong with the pump;
The water was up—we struck a wet bump.
But the cage kept descending and into the sump
We went down, down, down.

I've been on the outside and inside before,
I fell into oceans and rivers galore,
But that dip in that deep dirty sump made me sore
Away down, down, down.

The fireboss he flagged me, fool questions to ask.
Was I married, or single and where I worked last.
Says I, "Lind me your pincil, me present and past
I'll write down, down, down."

Between the sump bath and headache I felt like a dope,
Going down in the gloom of the underground slope,
On a tricky man-truck and a rotten old rope,
Going down, down, down.

She was blocked from the dish to the knuckle with smoke,
The dust was so thick that I thought I would choke.
Says I to meself I guess here's where I croak
Away down, down, down.

Groped into the gangway they gave me a scoop,
The cut was just fired, muck heaped to the roof.
I stooped an' I scooped till me back looped-the-loop
Stoopin' down, down, down.

That first car we loaded held five tons I swore
And that Buck Mountain coal has the weight of iron ore.
We scooped seven cars but when they brought us one more
I laid down, down, down.

She was heaved on the bottom and cracked on the top
Ne'er a pole, ne'er a slab, ne'er a laggin', nor prop
Pretty soon I expect that Gap Mountain will drop
And come down, down, down

That journey each morning it near breaks me heart;
The steps in the mule-way is ten feet apart;
You must watch your brogans, for if you get a start
You'll roll down, down, down.

The Oak Hill officials are foxy galoots,
With company-store tyrants they're all in cahoots;
With the gangways a river, you're bound to buy boots,
While you're down, down, down.

On pay days I rave; Rube Tracy oft swore,
In fact 'twas enough to make both of us sore,
When our wives drag our wages all out in the store
While we're down, down, down.

But yet I'm in right, for I'm on the ground floor,
In deep in the wet and in deep in the store;
If they sink Oak Hill shaft six or seven lifts more
I'll go down, down, down.

It's a most cruel fate, but continue we must,
Delvin' deep for black diamonds, beneath the earth's crust,
Moil for mush and molasses and eating coal dust
Away down, down, down.

All I drew for a year was a dollar or three,
Those company-store thieves made a pauper of me,
But for ballads like this, I'd have starved for a spree
In the town, town, town.

Toil, you put early-gray on my poor daddy's head,
While he slaved in Oak Hill to provide us with bread;
How I wish I had heeded the warning he plead:
"Don't go down, down, down."

Now my back is toil-bent, my feet work-worn, slow.
Soon the hair on my head will be white as the snow.
Then I fear I'll be shipped to the Pogie below—
Broken-down, a pauperized clown.

AFTER A SHAFT PAY DAY

(AIR: *Just as the Sun Went Down*)

After the roar of a shaft pay night,
 Just at the break of day,
In all directions upon the field
 Our noble heroes lay.
Some were too full for to venture home,
 Some could not find their way;
All this world seemed turned upside down
 After a shaft pay day.

LOST CREEK

(AIR: *The Wearing of the Green*)

Have you ever been to Lost Creek where the women have their rights?
Where the whiskey runs like water and there are lots of brawls and fights?
If you haven't, give attention while I tell you of a day
That I spent among its natives when the miners got their pay.

I was agent for a paper at the time of which I write,
And to canvass went amongst them never dreamin' they were tight.
The first shanty that I entered had a wholesome smell of grog
With a crowd of drunken ruffians and a savage-looking dog

That his owner wouldn't part with for a fifty dollar bill,
He could lick his weight in lions and would either die or kill
The dog that dared to face him, for he never would give up;
And the owner smoothed the ruffles on his darling little pup.

I was standing by unnoticed with me satchel in me hand,
When a greasy-looking loafer came up from behind the stand;
He staggered up against me and said, "Let's see your wares,
Or I'll kick you to the divil, bag and baggage, down the stairs."

I was not intimidated by the drunken bully's speech,
But a little aggravated and felt half inclined to teach
The drunken fool a lesson that he wouldn't soon forget—
And my arms were in position, when a blow of something wet

Closed my eyes and daubed me features with some nasty horrid stuff,
And before I gained my eyesight I was handled pretty rough;
I was kicked and cuffed and pounded as I lay upon the floor
Till I gained my feet and bounded like a rocket through the door.

Through the stumps and stones and bushes like a hunted hare I ran,
While around me fell in showers sticks 'n' stones and old tin cans.
Scores of women drunk as fury charged on me from every side,
Some with clubs and some with bottles, while full many a stone they shied.

Heavens, how I longed for shelter, could I gain some friendly wood!
I could hear them helter-skelter close behind me in the mud.
How I managed to elude them is a mystery to me,
But I beat them all on record till I sighted Number Three!

Then I felt the chase was over, I had won the race at last,
But my heart still thumped my bosom and my breath came thick and fast.
I reached home a sorry agent, changed my clothes and fiercely swore:
If they never get a paper I would visit them no more.

OVER AT INDIAN RIDGE

Now if you'll listen I'll tell you in a bit of a song,
  What's over at Indian Ridge.
I'll tell ye, me boys, and it won't take me long,
  What's over at Indian Ridge.
From the top of the shaft with a rope we're let down—
Yes, many a hundred feet under the ground—
And it's there most any kind of a man can be found,
  Over at Indian Ridge.

They have carpenters and plasterers and stone masons galore,
  Over at Indian Ridge.
They have actors and lawyers and ex-policemen you know,
  Over at Indian Ridge.
The boss came one morning and said to the stone mason:
"You'll try to build me a hospital one story high."
"I'll do," said John, with a wink of the eye,
  Over at Indian Ridge.

Now to build this hospital was all of the rage,
  Over at Indian Ridge.
We had all kinds of mechanics to go down on the cage,
  Over at Indian Ridge.
Jim Dougherty, the steam fitter, said he would do all he could,
While the fireboss, old Foley, was chewing a big tobacco cud,
Old Matthews was building the wall and calling for mud,
  Over at Indian Ridge.

Now I must tell you, me boys, of a great race,
  Over at Indian Ridge.
And if ye listen, I'll tell ye how it took place,
  Over at Indian Ridge.
It was the time of the strike when the Hunks they were out,
Boyd, Mitchell, and Foley were coming the route,
When a clout of a stone knocked old Foley out,
  Over at Indian Ridge.

THE BROKEN SHOVEL

(AIR: *My Brand New Shovel*)

Good Christians all, come lend an ear,
Unto me ditty, and the truth you'll hear;
It's of Barney Gallagher so bold and thrue,
Arrah that broke me shovel,
Arrah that broke me shovel,
That broke me fine new shovel in two.

When the whistle blew and the shovel was broke,
Old Neddy Kearn was the first man spoke,
Saying, "Barney Gallagher, come tell me thrue,
Phat for you broke me shovel,
Phat for you broke me shovel,
Phat for you broke me brand new shovel in two?"

"Oh," said Barney Gallagher in a stuttering way,
"I'll c-c-crack your jaw if I hang this day,
To ins-s-sult a man so b-b-bold and thrue,
About your b-b-bloody shovel,
About your b-b-bloody shovel,
That was broke in two."

Barney and McGlynn, they both pitch in,
Like Corbett and Mitchell they form a ring;
The crowd around began to roar
Phan who the divil entered,
Phan who the divil entered,
But the Pretta-Moor.

"Howlt on," sez the Pretta, "we must have fair play.
"He's a Ross's man and will win the day;
But if you touch him then I'll touch you."
That was all about the shovel,
That was all about the shovel,
That was broke in two.

MACKIN'S PORCH

(AIR: *The Floggin Reel*)

To learn the way of Five Points folk,
If you take and give a joke,
Go on Scott Street for a mope,
  And stop at Mackin's store.
First go to Boyle's and take your wet,
Then go back to Mackin's steps,
Do it quick or you'll be left,
  At eight it won't hold no more.

CHORUS

The Far Downs and Connaught men
Fight, and then make up again;
Dutch and Scotch and English men—
All like chickens in a pen.
The powder smoke does be so thick,
You could not cut it with a pick,
The smell of gas would make you sick,
  In front of Mackin's store.

'Bout half past six or seven o'clock,
Then the men begin to flock,
And tell of cars they were docked;
  Of cars lost and found.
Of dirty coal and lumps of chunks,
Firin' holes and sackin' Hunks,
And the way they have to work and grunt!
  For a livin' underground.

Firing in the face and rib,
Driving headin's, lighting squibs,
Telling big down-country fibs,
  Drilling and tamping holes.

On the bottom raising rock,
Building chutes and standing props,
Waiting at the blacksmith shop,
  And damning laborers' souls.

Working on the flat and pitch,
Laying roads and cleaning ditch,
One day poor and the next day rich,
  Working in bad air.
Lifting cars upon the rail,
Chasing drivers from their pail,
You'd swear it was a sheriff's sale,
  The way they gather there.

This man told tales to the boss,
This man last week two cars lost,
Another man set off the gas,
  Another lost his job.
Yesterday my cars were stopped,
Day before three-quarters docked,
Must load them better at the top
  Be cripes, or I'll be robbed.

Winter or the summer-time,
Whether rain or whether shine,
Every man is there in line,
  Seated on the step.
Some are drawing fine big pays,
Others fifty cents a day,
Not enough to pay their way;
  The half of them's in debt.

SECOND CHORUS

Many and many a man is killed,
Many a quart of blood is spilt,
Some are carried home in quilts,
Burnt that bad their skin does wilt.

The Prospect and Conyngham,
Empire and Nottingham,
At hoisting coal ain't worth a damn
  Compared to Mackin's step.

THE START THAT CASEY GOT

(AIR: *Go 'Way Back and Sit Down*)

Sure Mike Casey got a job in a powder mill
At a dollar and ten a day.
And says he, "By gob, dat's a very good job
And the work is only play";
But he could not read,
So he did not heed,
The sign above the door,
That smokin' on those premises
Is not allowed on any floor;
So the other day with his Henry Clay,
Mike started for the mill,
And if he had left his pipe at home,
He'd have had his ould job still;
But he walked right into the powder mill
Smokin' his Henry Clay,
An explosion occurred
That was plainly heard
One hundred miles away.

FIRST CHORUS

And he went away up far above the town,
But he didn't come down,
(Pause)
No he didn't come down,
For men that travel like Casey did
Are seldom found,
(Pause)
Walkin' around.
If he'd only come down for his family's sake,

Or long enough for to hold a wake,
And go 'way back to the burying ground,
Where he wouldn't be found,
Walkin' around,
He'd be in under the ground,
Sleepin' sound.

SECOND CHORUS

He went away up just a week today,
Far, far away with his Henry Clay;
For men that travel like Casey did,
Will be too far away for to draw their pay,
And the boss says he'll dock him for the time he's been away.
If only half of Mike comes down,
A half a man, a half a day,
And if he lands safe for to tell the tale,
Then he'll win the day,
And they'll raise his pay,
Without delay.

THIRD CHORUS

And he went away up,
And it's safe to bet
That he's goin' yet,
With his cigarette.
For men that get a start like Casey got
Will never forget,
On that you can bet.
He was seen through a telescope passing the moon,
And if he comes down as he went up,
Faith, he'll be due here soon;
And if he strikes hard
Faith, he'll seal his doom,
And then he'll change his tune,
And there'll be a funeral soon,
Some afternoon.

FOURTH CHORUS

Sure he went away up,
And he yelled out loud,
Back to the crowd:
"I have no sh-roud."
Though men that get a push like Casey got
Should feel very proud,
When they're pushin' clouds.
St. Peter said to Casey,
"You're a stranger it appears,
As only one man from Wilkes-Barre
Comes this way every eighty years;
So go 'way down with your Henry Clay,
Where you'll be smokin' away,
Until the Judgment Day;
You'll not be drawin' your pay,
For you'll be in under the clay—
Good day!"

JENKIN JENKINS

My name is Jenkin Jenkins,
I'm a fireboss of renown,
At three each morning
I make my usual round.
I walk through open cross cuts
To get up to the face,
To find how much gas there is
In every miner's place.

CHORUS

My name is Jenkin Jenkins,
I'm a fireboss of renown,
I'm known by all the men and boys,
That work down underground.

I travel over rock and coal
  That fall down in the night.
I grope my way the best I can
  With my small safety light.

At my headquarters at the foot
  When I return from my round,
The miners all depend on me
  For everything safe and sound.
For I am the only person
  That dare go in the mines,
To investigate all dangers
  Before commencing time.

In your place Patsy Patsy,
  I'm sure the roof will drop;
Don't let your laborer load any coal
  Until you stand a prop.
In your place, Evan Evans,
  I find a very bad joint,
You're not arranging your chamber right
  According to the point.

Say, Davis, Smith, and Dougherty—
  Where were you yesterday?
I hear you three have been drinking
  Ever since you got your pay.
You three cannot deny it;
  I see it in your faces.
You three can now take out your tools—
  I've got men in your places.

THREE JOLLY WELSHMEN

They went down to Coaldale to work in the rock,
And when they got there they did nothing but talk.

REFRAIN

John Morgan, John Jenkins, John Jones.

When the boss came around their tools were in stack,
He said, "What have you done?" Says Jones, "Nothing, in fact."
Then he said, "You go home and consider yourselves sacked."

REFRAIN

John Morgan, John Jenkins, John Jones.

They went in the gangway to take out the cut,
And when they got started they got in a rut.

REFRAIN

John Morgan, John Jenkins, John Jones.

Says Morgan to Jones, "You can drill a hole there,
I could always depend that you do what is fair,
As for Jenkins, he should have pins in his hair."

REFRAIN

John Morgan, John Jenkins, John Jones.

They went on the night shift to lower the road,
Two cars is a shift for each man to load.

REFRAIN

John Morgan, John Jenkins, John Jones.

When the boss came around they were swapping old tales.
He said, "You three men can go take your pails
And sing, 'Three Jolly Welshmen going back to Wales.' "

REFRAIN

John Morgan, John Jenkins, John Jones.

JAKE AND JACK ARE MINERS

Jake and Jack are miners,
  Their breast is Number Six,
It's naught but rock and sulphur ball—
  I think they're in a fix.

Jake and Jack are miners,
  The men do laugh and shout;
Every time they fire a shot,
  It blows the tamping out.

Jake and Jack are miners,
  Good people do not grin,
Sometimes they blame the powder,
  Or forget to put some in.

Jake and Jack are miners,
  No coal they'll ever give,
The place where they are working in,
  Will do them while they live.

Jake and Jack are miners,
  Now say they'll go on a tramp,
They do not like the fireboss,
  And curse the safety lamp.

Jake and Jack are miners,
  And do their very best,
But they were born tired,
  So they often want a rest.

AT PADDY MAYOCK'S BALL

Last Thursday night with heart so light just as the clock struck nine,
The neighbors all assembled for to have a jolly time

MINERS IN GOOD HUMOR

In Paddy Mayock's residence on Frog Street, Gravel Hill,
The guests were heartily welcome to eat and drink their fill;
The cause for this rejoicing was paying respects you know
To the greenhorns that just landed from the County Mayo.

CHORUS

There was eatin' and drinkin' and dancin' free for all,
'Twas a grand delight to see the sight at Paddy Mayock's ball.
Oh, my sides were sore with laughter, I thought I'd lose my life
When McCarthy broke the floor through with himself and Ginger's wife.

"Hold on a while," said Ned O'Boyle, "till I get an axe and saw,
On that very spot I'll set a trap for my old mother-in-law.
All this night she's barkin' at me; she'll drive me out of my head;
But for respects to the house I'm in, by croipes I'd kill her dead.
She has me robbed paying life insurance since long ago last Fall;
I'll have to burn the policy or else she won't die at all."

Ned was rarin' and tearin'; he shouted to McGraw
To clear the floor for an hour or two till he'd trap his mother-in-law.
The neighbors tried to pacify him, it was no use at all;
He swore his soul he'd finish her at Paddy Mayock's ball.
At twelve o'clock exactly the guests sat down to eat;
"Now help yourselves," said Paddy, "be gobs don't spare the meat.
For you're welcome, heartily welcome, with your family big or small
To eat and drink till broad daylight, sure I will pay for all.
Arrah, Kerrigan, what ails you, man? Why don't you sit and ate?
There is plenty on the table. Why don't you fill your plate?"
No such eatin' and drinkin' I ever saw before:
They ate McCarthy's old cow, and by croipse they wanted more;
McGee was more than paralyzed, he couldn't stand up at all,
He sat all night in the corner of Paddy Mayock's ball.

When supper was over, Kilban shouted: "Order, men!
Carry out the stove and table, O'Boyle is going to sing,
Just to please the greenhorns, the neighbors one and all,
He will bust his lungs or raise his voice at Paddy Mayock's ball."

When O'Boyle sang eighty verses McGee at him did shout:
"Do you mean to keep the floor all night or what are you about?
I'll swear my life against you, you will kill me out and out,
Sit down there in the corner, don't be wearing out your mouth."

McGee was crazy, he'd amaze ye, he threw off his coat and hat
And swore by his side whiskers he would have no more of that;
"O'Boyle, you dynamite informer, just to please the neighbors all,
I will fight you for the championship of Paddy Mayock's ball."

At five o'clock in the morning McGee and O'Boyle
Stripped off out in the garden, each other for to spoil.
Kilban attended O'Boyle and Kerrigan to McGee;
McCarthy was also chosen to act as referee;
Right and left they pounded, O'Boyle began to shout;
"If you strike me on the nose again by croipse I'll break your mouth;
Why don't you stand forninst me till I smash your Donegal,
Lie down and let me tramp you just to please the neighbors all."

There was thumpin' and bumpin' and fightin' free for all;
'Twas grand delight to see them fight at Paddy Mayock's ball.
McCafferty got paralyzed, O'Boyle he couldn't see,
Kerrigan was tramped a great sight worse than Durkin or McGee;
The Coroner's jury sat on them, their verdict was that all
Committed suicide in self-defense at Paddy Mayock's ball.

A TRAMP THROUGH CARBON COUNTY

(AIR: *Patsy Grant Who Tramped Around the World*)

If you give me your attention, I will give it to you back,
  When I tell you of my travels—well, that's all.
One day I took a notion for to come across the ocean,
  Bid my friends good-bye and left old Donegal.
I arrived at Number Five, to Spring Tunnel made a dive;
  I took in Summit Hill upon me furl,

From that to Number Six, got a reception there with bricks,
 Sure I'm Patsy Grant that tramped around the world.

I went up on the breaker where the boys were picking slate,
 The boss he told me that I stopped the screen;
I was dust up to me collar; be me sowl I thought I'd smother,
 And the boys said it was fallin' from the beam,
I'm sure that Twenty-two had asked me for a chew;
 I towld him that I didn't have a grain,
Then I thought me time had come and I started in to run,
 It was the dust was gettin' loose above again.

I next arrived in Lansford and was walking down the street,
 Says a young lad: "Look at the artificial dude!"
They pulled me by the coat and they struck the highest note,
 And perfumed me with some eggs that was no good.
Then a young lad shouted, "Crabbit, if you guess it you can have it,"
 They said everything about me that was mean,
They argued, they did, and scolded whether I was born or molded,
 Then agreed I was a walkin' slot machine.

I left that part entirely when I tramped it all around,
 From that to sections down the line did hale,
I stopped at old Buck Mountain till I found I wasn't wantin',
 The next I struck was Dock Street in Coaldale.
I stumbled into Fisher's where the boys was drinkin' rum;
 The greatest I have met upon me furl,
Then one spakes out so frisky, "Come, Pat Grant, and have your whiskey,
 It will help you on your trip around the world."

I just received a parcel from a friend in Ireland,
 In a little box a bit of blarney stone,
I got a front tooth pulled and thin I got the blarney stone put in,
 Sure it looks as well as if it was me own.
Now if there's any ladies here that would like to make the boast,
 That they kissed the blarney stone; just raise your hand,
Fall in line, come up this aisle; I'll be waitin' with a smile,
 And I'll give you all the assistance that I can.

CHORUS

With a cigar in me cheek, porous plaster on me feet,
I'm a dandy, I'm a pet among the girls,
While I'm traveling in disguise, sure I live on custard pies;
I'm Patsy Grant that tramped around the world.

DAN McCOLE

You see before you Dan McCole,
A man both strong and hearty,
I'm married now just twenty years
To Bridget Ann McCarthy;
For groomsman I had Pat O'Toole,
For bridesmaid Kate Gildea,
And as we marched off to the church
The people all did say:

CHORUS

Would you look at Dan McCole, gee wiz,
Arrah, boys, don't he look grand?
He's a ladies' pet with eyes black jet,
He's an upright honest man.
My mother called me "Daniel,"
That name's no more on roll,
So when I drop out the boys all shout,
"Would you look at Dan McCole."

When from church we did return,
To pass away our time,
We went into a museum
Admittance fee a dime;
We saw all kinds of pictures,
We watched the monkeys play,
They looked at me and Bridget
As if they'd like to say:

CHORUS

Would you look at Dan McCole, gee wiz,
  Arrah, boys, don't he look grand?
He's a ladies' pet with eyes black jet,
  He's an upright honest man.
My mother called me "Daniel,"
  That name's no more on roll,
So when I drop out the boys all shout,
  "Would you look at Dan McCole."

We then returned to treat our friends
  To a supper and a spree,
We had mutton chops and, troth, we had
  Buckwheat cakes and tea.
We all sat down to ate our fill,
  Some had eggs and others veal,
As I stuck me fork in a little pig
  I thought I heard a squeal.

THE PRETTY MAID MILKING HER GOAT

(AIR: *The Song of the Pretty Girl Milking Her Cow*)

It was a cold winter's morning
  As I went to work for my grub,
I heard a fair maid sing most charming
  As she sat on the heel of a tub;
Her mouth was both large and commodious,
  A small boy might skate down her throat;
Her bullfrog bass voice was melodious,
  As she sat there milking her goat.

I stood and I gazed at this cr'ature,
  I was smashed in two halves by surprise—
Thinks I she's some Goddess of Nature,
  Or the queen of Georgetown in disguise;

I says to her aisy and civil,
  "Do you warble that poem by note?"
I was towld to inquire of the divil
  By the pretty maid milking her goat.

Then I said, "Dearest fairy, have patience,
  Till ye hear what I'm going to propose.
Come, leave all your wealthy relations,
  And travel with me, primrose,
Your everyday dress shall be silken,
  And to show how much on you I dote,
I'll grab howlt of the tail while you're milking,
  And help you to pump the ould goat."

She said, "Don't stand there givin' me taffy
  Or think I'm a foolish galoot,
I know I could ne'er be happy
  With you and your No. 9 boots,
You're nothin' but a common railroader;
  I can tell by the mud on your coat,
And to none but a red-ash coal loader,
  Will my papa give me and the goat."

PART 2: STORIES

Humor, says Charlie Chaplin, is "painful fun," a term peculiarly applicable to the humor of the anthracite industry. It came out of the miners themselves and made them laugh at their own pain and suffering.

Death, the colliery boss, the company, the "pluck me" store, the mine mule, and political authority in the person of the squire, were potential threats to the miner's sense of security. Weighed down by these forces, the miner felt frustrated and insignificant. But when the opportunity arose to get the upper hand over any one of them, he acquired a temporary sense of superiority. In this triumph lay spontaneous humor.

The difficulties encountered by immigrants in adjusting themselves to the mining environment roused laughter in the old-timers. The Welsh and Irish laughed at their own greenhorns, and both races laughed at the Slavs who were borne in on the last wave of immigration.

There were coarse and risqué stories, it is true, but their number was surprisingly small. The tall story was very popular. Following are some examples:

Many years ago I worked in a drift on Big Mountain. When the weather was nice I used to crawl through the air hole and eat my dinner on the surface. I always carried a shotgun with me, seein' as the woods around the mine were full of game. One nice summer day I was a-sittin' under a tree eatin' cherry pie made for me by the little lady back in the shanty. I dropped the cherry pits on the grass there right in front of me.

Well, sir, as I was a-sittin' there, didn't a buck deer suddenly come out of the woods and stop within fifty feet of me! My gun had nothing but birdshot into it so I picked me a handful of the cherry pits and filled my gun with them. I took careful aim of the buck, and ye know, I shot him square in the head. That did not kill him. He stood as if stunned. Then suddenly, he shook his antlers, turned around, and bounded back into the woods. Behold ye! the next summer to the very day the same deer returned and stood before me. How did I know it was the same deer? Out of his head a cherry tree spread in full bloom.

* * *

I worked in the Enterprise mine when it was only a drift many years ago. The vein didn't have much surface on to it and when I throwed a fall, the damn toppin' caved in on me—sand, slate, coal 'n' all. I shook it off all right, but when I cleared me eyes I found meself face to face with a buck which had pretty two-pointed antlers. "I guess we're into it, butty," says I to meself, "and so let's make the best of things." Well, sir, the buck he gave a snort and started to run off. I caught him by the tail and lifted meself on to his back. Then I took hold of his antlers. Bucky ran from one breast to another and then into the gangway, and from the gangway he hopped out of the mine to the surface, and with one leap he bounded up to the top of the mountain. From there he looked down to the cave-in and turned his head as if to ask me if I wanted to get down into the mine again. With one leap he was inside the mine again with me holding on to his antlers. Once again he leaped from breast to breast, into the gangway and up to the top of the mountain and down into the mine again. He repeated this a third time after which wantin' to put an end to the nonsense, I slashed his throat with me big toenail and he bled to death.

* * *

I was comin' home from work one day when I hears somepin go witch-watch-witch. I looks around and don't I see a skeeter as big as a man's arm tryin' to get his bill loose from the bark of an old oak tree! Such hell did he play with that there tree that I saw the roots a-comin' up from the ground. When I seen that the skeeter was capable of such strength, thinks I, I'd better take to me feet, which I did, and don'tcha think I didn't run. To escape the skeeter, I waded through a creek and when I crossed over to the other side of it, me boots and the seat of me pants was chock full of squirmin' fish.

* * *

Two miners made a bet over their beer to see who knew of a deeper shaft.

"I went into a colliery engine house onc't," said one, "and found the h'isting engineer asleep at the lever. Seein' as the engine was at top speed I quick woke him up. The engineer looked at his watch with half an eye open and yawned, 'I got three hours' sleep yet; she won't land on my shift.' "

"Ugh," grunted the other. "That ain't much of a shaft. I went to a mine for a job onc't. It was Wednesday, as I recall. I asked the topman where I could find the boss and he told me the boss had just stepped on the cage at the bottom and if I came back Saturday night I could catch him as he landed."

Other types of humorous stories follow:

DEATH-BED SCENE

Patrick O'Neill became wealthy as a mine contractor, and being a bachelor believed in spending his money during his lifetime. His unconventional manner of living and his neglect of the Church of his fathers over a long period of years brought him a reputation as a libertine. He was quite an old man when he had a stroke. His faithful housekeeper called a doctor. It took the doctor but a minute to tell Patrick that he was in a very bad condition.

"I belave I am," muttered Pat.

"Yes, you are, Pat," said the doctor, "and it will cost you a pretty penny before we of the medical profession have anything to do with you."

"Phat will it cost?" asked Pat, blinking his eyes.

"It will cost at least a thousand dollars," replied the doctor.

"Well, dochtor, don't ye think that's very excessive?"

"Not at all, Pat. You see, never before did we have an opportunity to make a dollar out of you, so it will cost you a thousand dollars before we do anything for you now."

"Very well," says Pat. "I'll give ye the thousand dollars on one condition."

"And what is that?"

"That ye won't let me die without the priest."

"Oh, that will be all right. We can arrange that."

The doctor knew very well that there was no hope for Pat, yet he left him with the feeling that there might be a chance. Several days later, however, he told him the truth. "Well, Pat," says he, "you may call in the priest, for you're not going to get well."

The patient nodded his head in resignation and the priest was sent for.

The priest was an old man himself. When he entered the sick room he took one look at the dying man and said, "Well, you old reprobate, you've sent for me at last. Little you thought of me during the past forty years, running around carousing with nary a thought for the Church of your fathers. And now, Pat, don't you know that after the life you've led it will take a great deal of money for masses, prayers, and offices to be read for you, if your soul's to be saved?"

"Phat will it cost, fa-ather?"

"It will cost at least a thousand dollars."

"Very well, fa-ather, I'll give ye the thousand dollars on one condition."

"And what may that be?"

"Both ye and the dochtor must be here when I'm dying."

"Oh! very well," said the priest. "I suppose that can be arranged."

So the room was cleared and Pat was given the last rites of the Church. Both the priest and the doctor were there. The doctor leaned over the bed to tell Pat that if he had any last request to make, to make it then.

"You have only a few minutes to live," he said.

"You're there yet, fa-ather?" muttered the patient.

"Yes, yes, I'm here," replied the priest.

"Are ye still there, dochtor?" asked Pat.

And the doctor assured him that he was.

"Well, dochtor," said Pat, "ye come around to the other side of the bed."

The priest hereupon leaned over to Pat and in a kindly but firm voice said, "Tut, tut, now, what nonsense is this you're going on with when it's your rosary you should be saying?"

"Well, fa-ather," said Pat as he breathed his last. "As a young man I went to your Church and many's the time I heard ye say from the pulpit that our Savior died between two thieves. I'd like to die the same way."

A STRANGE WAKE

Barney Flaherty was on his way to the slope one morning when he met a red-haired woman. Instead of turning back he went right on and was killed by a fall of rock. His broken body was brought home and preparations were made for the wake. That night the undertaker put the body into a pine box packed tightly with ice which rested on two chairs against the wall of the front room.

Barney's company house had two rooms and a cellar. His corpse lay in the front room and the mourners were entertained in the other. Conversation was carried on in whispers and everything was quiet except for the dripping of the water from the box into a pail.

One of the unexpected mourners was Marty O'Donnell. Falling to his knees before the corpse he offered a prayer for Barney's soul. Hardly had he finished praying when there came a very strange, shrill voice as if from the spirit world. "Marty, you damn hypocrite," said the voice, "it's only a short time ago you scabbed on me—" But Marty had heard enough. Without even stopping to grab his hat from the floor he flew out of the door.

Soon after him came Jerry Donahue, and when he began to pray, the strange voice cried out: "Me sowl won't have rest with you prayin' for me. Sure, you're after squealin' on me to the boss and so it's out of my house for you, Jerry."

And later who should be trooping down the cinder path and into Barney's house but the company storekeeper. He too kneeled as if for prayer, but before he could open his lips the shrill voice of the spirit world screamed: "Another hypocrite. All your life you've skinned me and now you pretend to mourn for me."

He ran out of the house so fast he did not hear half of the things that the spirit said about him.

It was by all odds the strangest, weirdest wake ever held in the county. The mourners would have laughed had they not been so scared at hearing a ghost so plainly. There was no fun at that wake. Everybody was nervous and anxious for the dawn so that they could leave the spooky surroundings.

But when dawn came some of the men investigated to satisfy their curiosity, and this is what they found. A hole had been bored through the floor directly under the pine box into which had been fitted an old water hose stolen from the colliery. This hose extended across the cellar to the outside by means of a tiny window. Two driver boys carried out the hoax. One stationed himself at the hose while the other hid behind a shanty. As a mourner came up the cinder path, the latter would call out his name to the boy at the hose who impersonated Barney Flaherty's ghost.

WHY HE HAD BAD LUCK

I was sitting in a saloon in our patch recently and this is the conversation I overheard:

"So she's not cuttin' so well, eh Tommy?"

"Not so good. No man what'd do what I done could have no luck," the other replied.

"Why, Tommy, what is it you went and done?"

"It's been a secret of me heart for over forty years. But I'll tell you. Remember the hunky what murdered his boardin' missus and another lady over to Bushy Tract?"

"Yes, I was a small lad then."

"If you remember, he socked 'em over the head with a drill, robbed 'em of their money and then set fire to the house. He skipped to Jersey City but they caught him and brought him back to Middleport and gave him in custody to Billy Snyder, the coal and iron cop from up the line.

"Billy wanted a steady and reliable driver to take him and his prisoner to the county jail, and hired me team. Midway down the pike, Billy turns to me and says, says he, 'Let's search this roundheader and see if he has any money on him.'

"So I stopped the team and we began to investigate. When the hunky made a fuss, Bill ups and smacks him on the mouth which made his blood run. We found a hundred and six dollars on him.

" 'I'll split this with you,' says Bill, 'if you promise you won't breathe a word about it to no livin' soul.' Billy he gave me fifty-three dollars and put the other fifty-three in his pocket. 'The county would 'a' taken it off of him anyway,' says Bill, 'and we need the money more'n the county.'

"After we delivered the prisoner at the county jail, Billy went into a restaurant in Pottsville and ordered the biggest steak you ever did see. It weighed eleven pounds. And that night it was meself that went on a jag and when I come to, I was in Minersville and me team was gone which I ain't seen to this day.

"The night they hung the hunky I crawled into bed and pulled the kivers over me head because I was afraid that the hunky's ghost would come back and be lookin' for his money. . . .

"And it's ever since that bad luck has dogged me heels."

TRAPPED BUT LUCKY

Many years ago I was at work robbing pillars in the Holmes vein of the Good Spring colliery. The veins pitched sharp there. There was no scooping, as the coal ran down into the wagon from the chute. Us miners were paid by the number of wagons we loaded. Well, the vein was pretty dirty. When I finished the day's work, the boss said, "Frank, how's the coal in the pillar you're at?"

I told him it was dirty.

"Don't go any higher," he said. "I was on top of the breaker and saw the stuff that was being dumped from the Holmes and it's fit to be dumped on the slush bank. Pull back on that pillar. Get what coal you can."

The next morning I cut the pillar on one side, and when I started cutting it on the other I said to my butty, "Jake, if this side is cut, the pillar will run." But he told me to go ahead, and like a fool I went to work and cut it. I fired a shot and leaped down the manway into the heading. Then I came back, drilled another hole, tamped it nice and tight and just as I was about to fire again, a cloud of dust filled the breast and I knew that the pillar was running.

"Fly, Jake!" I yelled at my butty. He escaped to the heading below and I went right after him. When we got there we found ourselves trapped. Jake lost his head altogether and got down on his knees to pray.

"Let up on that, Jake," says I. "I'm trying to get out of this and if I can so can you."

I worked myself down within ten feet of the battery and called back to him. "Damn it, Jake," says I, "let up on that and follow me. You've only a wife to take care of. I have a wife and kid."

We were penned in for about four hours. It seemed like four years as we sat there with our lamp lights dark, waiting for the rescue gang to dig us out. . . . They hauled away twenty wagonsful of the coal before they reached us. And that experience was a lucky break, for we made more money penned in than when we was working.

A CELEBRATED BAKE-OVEN FIGHT

Who does not remember the bake ovens that were a part of every mine patch? They were stone-arched affairs, usually about fourteen feet long, covered on the outside with lime, their stone floor heated with wood. The ashes were scraped out and the bread pans with their burdens of dough pushed in with a long-handled scoop.

In Johns' patch the ovens were ranged just outside the houses. Since there was one oven for every two families a schedule was kept which enabled each housewife to bake twice a week. The arrangement worked well until some woman went out of her turn.

One bake-oven fight has become a legend. The principals, peace be to their souls, have long since been gathered to their fathers. Their names were—well, let us call them Mrs. Martin Riley and Mrs. Shamus McFadden. Anyway, they were next-door neighbors and shared the same oven. According to the schedule, Mrs. Riley baked on Mondays and Mrs. McFadden on Tuesdays. Until their interests clashed at the bake oven they were on friendly terms, and in this way might have continued indefinitely had not a "Dublin Dan" show picked Tuesday upon which to perform in Pottsville.

Now Mrs. McFadden had come from Ireland but a few years back and was lonesome for the "ould counthry." The "Dublin Dan" shows, popular in those days, invariably staged a parade in the morning, and what with jaunting carts hitched to asses, and gentlemen rigged out in colored breeches and buckled shoes, and bagpipes blowing familiar Irish melodies, they brought a touch of old Ireland to the drab mining country. This is what Mrs. McFadden was most anxious not to miss, and she knew that if she baked on her day she would miss it. That's how she came to do what she did—try to bake on Monday. She got up real early that morning, placed her dough in the oven and returned to her house hoping that the bread might be baked before Mrs. Riley came out. But Mrs. Riley was up early herself, and when she caught sight of her neighbor's dough slowly browning she promptly fished it out and dumped it on the common. Then her geese began eating it. When

Mrs. McFadden, peeping through a hole in her window blind, saw the geese with their bills in her dough, she leaped out of the house, picked up a heavy stick and beat them. Wild and frantic hissing of the geese brought Mrs. Riley out again. She found two or three of her geese dead.

"And phat's the m'anin' of this, Katie McFadden?" she demanded.

"It's punishment I'm after givin' them for 'atin' me foine new dough —that's phat's the m'anin' of it, Mrs. Riley," replied her neighbor.

Whereupon Mrs. Riley snatched Mrs. McFadden's hair and Mrs. McFadden pulled Mrs. Riley's, and the ensuing screams roused the entire patch. Women deserted their housework to pitch into the free-for-all, ranging themselves on whichever side their sympathies or prejudices lay.

That evening Mrs. Riley brought civil action before the village squire for the loss of her geese, and Mrs. McFadden brought a counter-suit asking damages for the dough that the geese had eaten.

The squire, being a candidate for reëlection, was strictly neutral, suggesting that the husbands of the women try to settle the case out of court.

"Squire," spoke up Mart Riley, "that's phat I'm after tryin' for to do —settle this argument out of court. But Shamus here won't do it—he won't fight."

THE GROOD SAVES THE DAY

The Irish miners up our way are united now. But in the old days we were split into two factions, the Kilkennys and the Far Downs, and always battling for the upper hand we were.

Onc't two tickets were put up for election and the ballots were marked Kilkenny and Far Down. When the ballot boxes reached Pottsville, sure, didn't the Court throw them out saying as there was only two parties in this country, Republican and Democratic, and we could have our choice of one or the other. The party labels were changed to carry out the Court order. But nobody was fooled. The voters knew which were the Kilkenny candidates and which the Far Downs.

Those were hot elections we had. Flanagan's barroom over in Silver Creek was the only polling place in Blythe Township, and the voters had to do so much walking to get there that the breaker did not work on election day. The boys whooped it up a bit around the polls, what with one faction or the other trying to steal the election. If we had had a ragman in those days he would have had plenty fine pickings the day after election, what with torn hats, wigs, shirts, neckties, suspenders, and underwear lying around with blood stains on them.

Well, at one of the elections, "Bould Jack" Donahue of Silver Creek was running for tax collector. He took a couple days off in order to cover the entire township, and he canvassed every last home in it—at least he thought he had. And on the night before election he was sitting close to the kitchen stove enjoying a smoke and going over in his mind all the voters that he had solicited just to make sure that he hadn't missed anyone. He almost got a stroke when he discovered that he had somehow passed up "The Grood," an old butty, who lived on Eagle Hill 'way at the other end of the township.

It was a bitter cold and dark night, mind, a night that would have kept a man with less determination from stepping outside of his own door. "Bould Jack" stuck a bottle of rye in his coat pocket and, swinging a lantern, set out for his butty's house.

He got a cool reception from The Grood. They drank out of Jack's bottle, talked about the weather and exchanged township gossip before the candidate got up nerve to solicit his friend's vote.

"Ye know, Grood, I'm in the way of bein' a candidate for tax collector," he said.

"I heerd ye wor."

"I'm countin' on ye for a lift tomorra."

"Well, Jack, I'm after promisin' every son-of-a-gun on both tickets but ye, and I'll be damned if I'm goin' to make any promises to ye."

"Good night."

"Good night."

Jack went home with a heavy heart and with visions of defeat. But he was elected, and it was by the margin of only one vote. He always gave The Grood credit for having saved the day for him.

TEMPERAMENTAL LIZ

Let me tell you of the time Reverend Amandus Diefenderfer tried to break in Liz, the most ornery mule in a mine I worked in. Now there were points to mule-driving that even a eddicated man like the Reverend

Diefenderfer did not know, and that's where he should 'a' stuck to preachin'. Preachers out our way could not always make a living, and they sometimes took a job in the mines to keep the wolf away from the kitchen door. That's how the Reverend Diefenderfer happened to be workin' on this particular day. He was coupled to Bill, the regular driver, who was to teach him the fine points of mule-drivin'. Liz, sly beast that she was, kind of smelled the situation. She turned back to see what the preacher looked like and then let go a kick that struck fire in the top rock. And that was her way of sayin', "Howdy, stranger!" You should 'a' heard her belly laugh after seein' how scared the preacher was. "Ain't she contrary!" he said as he wiped the sweat from his brow.

Bill, who always catered to Lizzie's whims, let her have two or three cuttin' strokes across her back with his leather whip, and they were peppered with a few choice cuss words. Then he shouted "Giddap!" and away they flew, clatterin' down the gangway, turnin' to the right and to the left, pickin' up loaded cars and fetchin' back empties.

Like all other mine mules, Liz knew nothin' about reins, but ran along by the whip and a few orders, but none o' them orders took without cuss words, which went against the preacher's grain.

"My, but you swear so!" he said with a shake of the head; "Can't you use kind words? They always go further than oaths."

"Listen here, Reverend," replied Bill, "I'm drivin' a mule just now and not teachin' Sunday School yet."

To which the preacher said nothing. During that day he picked up more ear-splitting cuss words than he had ever heard before in his whole life. The next day he took charge of Liz himself, but with Bill at his side to check him up.

"Come, come, Elizabeth, giddap!" commanded the preacher as he touched Liz gently with the whip. This must've been too much for the mule. Perkin' up her long ears, she let her hoofs fly, barely missin' the preacher, and this was followed by another one of her belly laughs.

But Reverend Diefenderfer could get no action out of Liz nohow, even when he bore down with the whip just a little harder than his conscience dictated. At last Bill snatched the whip out of his gentle grip and cut Liz somepin awful across her back and let loose some more cuss words. With the preacher on the bumper the work went very slow indeed.

Shortly before dinner-time, Liz was pulling a trip of five empties, and when it got to the turnout, Reverend Diefenderfer commanded, "Gee-wah-haw!" which meant go around. But when he cut the mule harder than his usual stroke, the ornery creature stopped dead in its track and before the men could collect their thoughts, let go a terrific kick against the head-car which almost connected.

"Jump!" yelled Bill. The preacher jumped not a second too soon for Liz had shot over another whopper which would have dispatched him to heaven. "If I wasn't a lover of the Lord," he exploded at the mule, "I'd knock your goddam brains out already!"

This gave Bill a big laugh. "I thought, Reverend," he said, "that kind words went further than oaths."

The dominie clasped his hands, turned up his eyes and prayed, "God forgive me."

KATIE AND PAT

Pat Kane was a clay man, one of a class of itinerant laborers who dug the foundations for boiler houses, coal breakers, and pipeline ditches in the days when the industry was expanding rapidly and collieries were being built all over the region. Unlike other clay men, Pat chose to remain behind when his job at Number Six colliery was ended.

He was put to work driving the mule which pulled an ash cart from the boiler house to the ash dump.

He was tall, lanky, awkward, and not overburdened with intelligence. The mule was named for his wife, Katie. One day he unhitched it and turned it loose in the fields for exercise. Being in one of its playful, mischievous moods, Katie chased him around.

"Look out there, Pat," shouted Gallagher his boss, "she may bite you."

"Sure, it's not Patrick Kane phat's afraid o' the loikes o' that there mule!" he replied.

Gallagher nevertheless repeated the warning. Whereupon Pat assured him that in his day he had driven the wildest horses in all Ireland and he had nothing but contempt for Katie.

"Why," he declared, throwing out his chest, "when I worked over to Hauto there was a little greenhorn mule phat couldn't be harnessed nohow, couldn't be made to come within a mile o' them there shafts of the ca-art, which was a two-wheeled ca-art. A coupla guys tried and failed. Then says I to the boss, says I, 'Begad, it's Patrick Kane as kin put that mule into the ca-art.' Sure, all I done was to take the mule by the bridle and lead it to the shafts. I whispers somepin into its ear, and just like that the mule walks in between the shafts. There was two guys standin' by, and when I gives 'em the high sign, they holds up the shafts and I harness the mule. 'Well, do you think you kin drive the mule?' says the boss. 'Do I think phat?' says Patrick Kane. 'Do the sun shine? Do a cat have little kittens? Sure I kin!' Then I gets on the ca-art and drives the mule. That's all there was to it, boss."

Gallagher chuckled.

"Don't you belave it?" asked Pat resentfully.

"Why, that could happen," replied Gallagher.

"Begad, it did happen."

As he spoke, Katie, her ears standing upright and her teeth showing menacingly, came galloping down the field directly at Pat who, frightened, let out a yell that could be heard all over the valley. He ran as fast as his feet could take him, and reached the engine-house door just in time to save the seat of his pants.

"Begad, boss," said Pat apologetically, as he mopped his brow, "sure she's as sassy as me own Katie."

TOM OF THE GUM BOOT BRIGADE

The Gum Boot Brigade was recruited from itinerant, hard-drinking miners who, when they couldn't get whiskey on tick, bartered gum boots for it.

Tom Garrahan was a distinguished member of this brigade. He was good-natured, sociable, generous, and full of wit. When sober he was a demon miner—but he couldn't stay sober long enough. He worked with me at Silver Creek colliery for a short time in the eighties, and I haven't seen him since, yet he stands out in memory as if I had just passed him on the street.

When he arrived at the colliery he was broke, having guzzled away the equal of three pairs of gum boots at the last place. But he didn't have to starve. His credit at the company store began as soon as his name went on the payroll. Tom would've liked to buy his "drop o' toddy" at the company store, but it wasn't carried. However, for customers like Tom there were Duffy's Malt and Hostetter's Bitters.

Now there were concoctions for you! They not only built up miners' nerves but made them feel between pay days that they were drinking the real stuff.

Tom was sober the first three weeks; at his boarding house he admitted it was the longest dry spell of his career. His resistance, however, broke down in the fourth week. He told the company storekeeper he would simply have to have a pair of gum boots on tick as the water was too deep in his working place. The storekeeper smiled understandingly as he handed the boots over the counter. Without even trying them on Tom tucked them under his arms and made a bee line for the barroom.

On payday Tom got a snake statement in red ink which showed how much he owed the company after working for it a whole month. He wiped out the debt in the second month.

Two weeks later he went to pieces. The desire for drink got the better of him and he couldn't work or sleep. So he decided to quit his job and take a chance on having a balance at the company office.

When he finished his day's work, he came up to Mike Flanagan, the inside boss.

"I want me time, Mr. Flanagan," he said.

"Not leaving us, are you?" the boss asked.

"Yes."

"What's the matter, Garrahan, the life too hard on you?"

"Ugh, it's not that, sir. It's me poor ould mother. . . ."

"Sick, is she?"

"Divil a bit of it. Just lonesome for her one and only b'y."

"Coming back this way sometime again?"

"Guess not. Am thinkin' I'll stay with the ould lady up counthry."

So Tom got his yellow slip, and when he showed it at the company store, he received his balance—two dollars.

He took the train to Pottsville and entered the first saloon he laid eyes on. He had a great time all right. He drank up his money and fell asleep in the saloon.

The next day he was back at Silver Creek with a hangover. Unwashed, unshaved, and his suit all wrinkled, he stood at the entrance to the shaft.

"Who the divil sent for you?" Boss Flanagan shouted when he saw him.

"Who the divil had sent for Columbus?" Tom retorted.

DUTCHY FOGARTY

Dutchy Fogarty has long since been gathered to his fathers. Peace be to his soul. He was a likable old character and one of the best of the old-time fiddlers. His brogue was so broad you could have driven a mine wagon through it, mules and all. But they called him Dutchy because his good old Irish father had married a Dutch girl who was his mother.

Shindigs, raffles, balls, and weddings in McAdoo were not a success without Dutchy Fogarty scraping out the old fiddle tunes. He was unable to read a note of music, yet once started he could go straight through a couple hundred fiddle tunes except for stopping for an occasional schooner of beer. Some fiddlers tune up before they start playing. Dutchy didn't have to. Not a bit of it. His manner of wooing the muse, as it were, was to take his coat off and let his right suspender down. Then the sweetest notes you ever did hear came from that old fiddle of his. His admirers overlooked a lot in him—even the fact that he wore two pairs of pants instead of underwear.

One thing about Dutchy that everybody admitted was his honesty. Yet politics was one of his weaknesses. Warned by friends that as an honest man he had no business in politics, he nevertheless got himself elected high constable. The most responsible duty of the office in those days was to remove dead animals from streets and alleys. He worked on a commission basis—that is, he was paid only for those carcasses that he disposed of, the rates varying with the type of animal. A dead cat, for example, rated fifty cents.

He kept an itemized account of his work and brought it to the borough council for payment once a month. One day he came upon half a cat lying in an alley and in the report of that month was found the item:

"½ cat—$.25."

NO WAY TO TREAT PADDY'S SISTER

Paddy, a driver boy, and his boss met in the gangway of a Schuylkill Valley mine one day.

"Paddy," said the boss, "I was up in New Philadelphia and witnessed the grand walking you Irish had in honor of St. Patrick. One of the oddest things that struck me was Bill Foley's undertaking tally-ho coach in the line of parade with Foley himself wearing a plug hat and holding the reins.

"To be sure," says Pat. "And phat do ye think he was up there af it wasn't to bate up thrade? Sure that fellow visits all the patches round about talkin' to old men and women about his foin hearse and coaches so's they shouldn't forgit to hire him for the funeral when they die. But it's divil a caarpse he'll git up this valley again—that I can tell ye."

The boss looked puzzled.

"Remember when me little sister died?" Paddy began. "Well, I went down to Mr. Foley an' says to him, says I: 'Mr. Foley, phat will ye charge me to bury this sister o' mine?'

" 'Phat size is she?' he towld me.

"And so I towld him her exact size from head to foot.

" 'Fifty dollars on toime or forty-five dollars in cash,' says he.

"I took the cash proposition. Not a hour later he comes up the valley, and onc't he got inside our house bringin' ice tubs and the loikes o' that he had divil a word to say to none of us. Well, we buried this sister o' mine down in St. Stephens' cemetery at Port Carbon, and when the two lads at the head of the coffin let down their end just a bit faster than the lads that held it at the foot, the coffin fell out bewixt the two straps. But it seemed to set all right.

"Then it was an owld woman come to me and says, 'Patrick.'

"I says, 'Ma'am.'

" 'Patrick,' says she. 'Do ye know, I belave your sister's layin' on her side.'

"I was fer goin' immediate to Mr. Foley and gettin' him to open the coffin fer to see af the sister was layin' on her side, and be jabers, I finally did go down to him.

" 'Mr. Foley,' says I, 'ye know, I belave me sister's layin' on her side.'

" 'Go to the divil,' says he.

" 'Cripes,' says I, 'howlt me coat till I lick the son-of-a-bitch.'

"Well, to cut a long story short, Mr. Foley went down to the grave and picked up the coffin and when he opened it, sure wasn't me poor little sister layin' on her side!

"Af that owld woman had towld me mother that we had buried me sister layin' on her side, she'd niver have an aisy day as long as she lived. And it's divil a caarpse he'll ever git up this valley again."

COMPANY HOUSE INHABITANTS

Built of rough hemlock, the company houses were strangely susceptible to bedbug invasion. The belief was that the hemlock wood had a peculiar attraction for them. Once an Irish miner accused his wife of being altogether too tolerant toward the vermin. Resentful, she said, "O! the loikes o' that! Sure oi don't belav th'r's a single one on the primises."

"En bedad!" he quickly answered. "Oi aghrees wid ye, thin, fer the loikes o' thim are all married, en ev lahrge families."

EVEN THE MULE LAUGHED

An old-time Slavic miner, Andrew Mezhanko, had worked in the mines for about forty-five years. One day he came to the momentous decision that he had labored underground long enough, especially since his asthma, contracted in the mine, was bothering him. So he approached Mr. Williams, the outside foreman, for a job in the colliery yard and was told to report the next morning at the colliery office. He was given the job of driving the two-wheeled ash dump cart. The mule was balky and refused to let Andrew put on his hip straps which left the shafts unprotected. When the cart was loaded with ashes the weight forced the shafts to shoot up and carry with them the mule's collar and hames, twisting the mule's head and suspending it in midair.

But let Andrew Mezhanko tell the story in his own way:

"You know I vas vorkin' in de mines forty-five year un I get short breat'—hasthma—un I t'ink mebbe I gonna hask Meester Villiams gimme chob on a houtside. He say shure, Meester Mezhanko, you come in de mornin' on a hoffice. I go on a hoffice—vas shmall shanty, li'le windy two foots long vun foot high. Young clerk seventeen years old, young boy, I'm hask 'im vich kind chob got fer Andrew Mezhanko. He tell me go on a barn. Man vas dere feedin' mules. I hask 'im show me puttin' harness den I know next time self. I vas all time on a coal miner, laborer like dat. He vas kickee son-of-a-gun mule, vite mule, Fanny name. He vunt carry dem straps fer his back nottink. Yoost two shticks on de side, shafts call it, collar un hames, two veels dumb-carp, straps fon de mout'. I'm say giddap fer dat Fanny un go back on a hoffice un haskin' dat boy vat he gon do fer dat mule un two veels dumb-carp. He tell me haul de hashes. He show me vas hashes fer boiler room. Man vas pullin' lever fer de hashes un fall in dumb-carp. After I'm drivin' back again on a hoffice.

"I'm haskin' dat boy vich place puttin' hashes. Dat boy vas laffin. Vas outside boss cummin, Meester Villiams, un I'm tellin' Meester Villiams dat boy vas laffin. Meester Villiams vas look fer dat mule un, son-of-a-gun, he vas laffin. I vas look fer dat mule un son-of-a-gun, I vas laffin. Un mule too, son-of-a-gun, vas laffin."

Popular tradition assigns the rôle of farmer to the Pennsylvania German, but in the West End of Schuylkill County a good many of these people are miners. While they were not pioneers in the anthracite region in the same sense that their forefathers were on the land, nevertheless their early hardships were those associated with pioneering.

Their penetration into the coal townships of this district began in the sixties. They hesitated to cut themselves off from agriculture before they were certain that they would like mine work. Hence, at first they regarded mining chiefly as a source of extra income between seasons. When they came over the mountains they left their families behind. Their farms were located five or more miles from the coal fields which made commuting impracticable. So they brought planks from their village sawmills and hewed saplings for ridgepoles from the woods and built themselves shacks. As a rule a shack was occupied by one man. Here the farmer-miners lived during the week. Saturday nights they trudged home to see their families and attend worship in the little church with the tall spire. They would return to their shacks on Sunday evening with enough provisions to last a week. They did their own cooking.

There are many anecdotes reminiscent of their experiences. Some follow:

Bill Conrad, who worked at the Lincoln colliery, has become a legend. He is said to have been a man of amazing energy and prowess, and to have possessed remarkable powers of endurance. He laughed at danger and regularly took risks which made men of ordinary clay quake in their boots. Yet he lived to be seventy, and to die a natural death. He stood over six feet, had a pair of massive shoulders, and arms and hands so long and powerful that they were the envy of every miner in the township.

One time Bill had a felon on his right forefinger which had begun to fester. Taking a few minutes off from work, he stepped into the colliery smithy and asked the blacksmith for his iron pincers which were used to pull the nails out of mules' shoes.

"Whatcha want with 'em, Bill?" asked the blacksmith.

Bill explained that he was bothered with a felon and reckoned that if he could cut off the last joint of the finger he'd be well rid of it. "Do you want to do the cuttin'?" he asked.

"Not me," said the blacksmith with a shake of the head. "My job's shoein' mules and not cuttin' no fingers off of people yet."

"Let me have them pincers onc't," said Bill.

Whereupon he broke off the end of his finger and nonchalantly returned to work.

* * *

Conrad worked in a flat, three-foot vein. His back must have been made of rubber, else how could he have endured crouching for ten hours a day? To move about he had to hop like a toad or crawl on his hands and knees like a baby. One day he was caught in a squeeze and was buried under a mound of coal and slate. Any other miner might have been crushed to death. Not Bill. He crawled right out and when he got into the heading shook the coal from his back. Bleeding from flesh wounds, he walked to the bottom of the slope and asked the bottom man to take him to the surface.

"I'm cut up a bit," he said. "Mebbe they'll fix me up in the office."

"Sorry, Bill," replied the bottom man. "Can't give you accommodation until after this trip goes up."

"Then you can go to hell, butty," said Bill, as he strode back to work.

* * *

Jack Barr was a day laborer, paid by the miner who employed him. He was no dolt by any means, yet sometimes it suited his purpose to act as one, especially when his fellow workers at the Brookside colliery tried to hoax him.

One day several miners hatched a conspiracy to convince him that he was sick. His own boss started off early in the morning by saying, "Why Jack, you look sick today. What's up?"

"Ach, I never felt better in my life," he replied.

Pretty soon a miner from a nearby breast held his lamp up in front of Barr's face.

"Honest, Jack, you don't look yourself today," he said. "Are you sick?"

"Ach, let me alone. I'm all right."

It was not until a third miner had asked the same question that he sensed the conspiracy, but he didn't betray his suspicions.

"Come to think of it," he said with an air of innocence, "I don't feel so good already."

Not long afterward a fourth conspirator came up to the breast to question the state of his health.

"Really, Jack, you ought to go up to the shack. You're not fit to work," said the man.

This gave the laborer the opening he was waiting for. Turning to his boss, he said, "I guess I better go up already. The air will do me good."

When he reached his shack he laughingly said to himself: "The damn fools think they've played a joke on me. But the joke's on them and the boss. I've got a day's holiday out of it yet."

At another time Barr was injured by a fall of rock. His boss and several others stroked his legs and finding no bones broken winked at one another. Another chance to fool Jack Barr!

"I guess you got a coupla bones broken already," said the boss.

"That's funny," replied Barr, "they hurt a bit where the coal fell on 'em but not like they was broken."

"Well, you better hold your legs stiff-straight out."

They carried him into the gangway, tenderly placed him in a coal car at the bottom of the slope and accompanied him on the upward ride. When they reached the head of the slope they placed him on a plank and carried him to a log wagon upon which was spread a bale of hay for comfort.

"Where are youse takin' me anyhow?" Barr asked.

"Home to the farm," replied one of the men. "A man what's hurt the way you are with a coupla bones broken yet should be tended by your woman."

"But I'm not hurt as bad as that, am I?"

"The hell you ain't. Your legs is broken, man."

Barr nodded as he thought, "You fellows are having a good time at my expense."

His Valley View farm lay several miles away. To a man with broken bones the jolting ride would have been torturous, and Barr suffered only discomfort. This convinced him that his injuries were being exaggerated for the sake of a little fun. When the log wagon finally pulled up in front of his stone farmhouse, the men jumped down all eager to carry him into the house. But he waved them aside and alighted without any assistance whatever.

"Now youse can go to hell," he said. "I'll walk into the house myself —and t'anks for the ride yet."

* * *

John Horner was in a mine car loading coal under a chute that was running an excessive amount of water. When he lifted the chute board, the rush of coal and water buried him. Fortunately for him, men dug him out in jig time. As his head bobbed up out of the coal he announced with an air of triumph in the Pennsylvania German dialect:

"Anyway, I didn't lose my quid."

* * *

A thirteen-year-old boy named John Ney, coming up from his father's farm in Pine Valley, obtained work at the Brookside colliery and was assigned a job wheeling coal from a heading to a chute. The heading was low, narrow, and short, and was like a prison to a boy used to the great open spaces of a farm. He was forced to stoop and bend as he pushed the wheelbarrow of coal for ten long hours. Johnny stuck it out pluckily. When he got home that night, his farmer-father asked him, "What did you work at?"

The youngster shrugged his shoulders.

"Ach, Pop, I didn't work today," he said, "I only pushed a wheelbarrow."

MIRACLES IN A MINE PATCH

Uncle Pete is a fairly good powwower, and admits it. You may guess how chummy we must have been when he cited the following case as an example of his occult powers:

"Jim Leh of Tower City had a wheal in his eye. He went to a doctor and spent his good money with him. But doctoring didn't do him no good. So he thought he'd doctor himself. He went to work and got the marrow of the sassafras tree and made a paste of it. That didn't work. Then he went to work and got store leaves and laid 'em on his eye, and that didn't do no good neither. All this time he was suffering something terrible and was afraid of losing his eye.

"Then someone said to him, 'You ought to take that eye to Uncle Pete.' I was eating my dinner when he came in with his eye all bandaged up. 'Uncle Pete,' he says, 'I'm suffering with my eye. I want you to powwow for it.'

" 'All right,' says I, 'I'll try for it.'

"With that I tears off the handkerchief he had tied around his head, and also the plaster he had on the sore eye. It was so bad, mind, that he couldn't open it. So I put him on the chair and turned his face toward the East. I got the plate I was eatin' out of when he came in, and went to work and made the sign of the cross on the plate three times. Then I held it up even with his eye. 'Look straight at it,' says I. He looked right square at it and then I says:

" 'Dirty plate, I press thee,
Wheal in the eye, do flee.'

"Two hours later I powwowed a second time and I wasn't through more'n a second when Jim says, 'Oh! Uncle Pete, I see already; what's up?'

" 'All right,' says I, 'hold steady, it's takin'. Now go home to rest and come back tomorrow so's I can powwow for the third time.'

"The next day he comes back and says, 'Uncle Pete, this morning when I got up I could see already, and the damn wheal was gone.' "

CHAPTER THREE

Boy Colliers

CHILD labor wrote one of the saddest chapters in the early annals of the anthracite industry. Young boys labored at tasks which stunted their bodies, ground their brains, and warped their souls.

Formerly a miner followed a common pattern in his career. He entered the breaker as a slate picker at eight or nine; went down the mines to tend doors at ten or eleven; and became a mule driver at fourteen or fifteen. From then it was merely a matter of time until he grew to be a laborer, and finally a contract miner.

Education in the hard coal fields during the past century was primitive and sometimes out of reach altogether. Many an old miner will apologize for his illiteracy with an explanation like, "I never had a day's schooling in my life; I was carried into the mines on my father's back."

Employed during the day, most boys could not attend public schools, and this led to the creation of night schools especially for them. The school was a one-room frame building in charge of a master who taught all grades. Parents paid the master and bought the books, and the pupils brought their own lamps for light. They carved their initials and valentines in the rough benches and desks even as boys do in the modern school.

In Scranton the Catholic Church maintained a night school—it was before the parochial school was started—during the winter months, and boys who were able to do so paid from twenty-five to fifty cents a month for tuition. They carried their schoolbooks and catechism in their dinner pails and studied them furtively when the boss was out of sight.

Women teachers were rare, as they were considered too frail to handle the rough, unruly rascals. Nevertheless, in Wilkes-Barre, Mrs. Ellen W. Palmer was their greatest teacher and guide. In the early nineties she conceived the plan of entertaining breaker boys on Saturday evenings. She encountered resistance at first, but eventually won them over. For several years she met with them in vacant storerooms. The movement had grown to such proportions by 1899 that the B. I. A. (Boy's Industrial Association) was chartered, and through the coöperation of the City of Wilkes-Barre and business men, a four-story brick building was erected. This permitted the carrying out of a comprehensive program in their behalf. Classes were held nightly and the boys were taught reading, writing, and arithmetic, and also the various branches of manual training. The tradition of holding a Saturday evening entertainment was continued to the end. All working boys were invited to join the B. I. A., and as a newsboy I enjoyed the privilege and now cherish the memories of those days.

About forty years ago the late Senator William Hines of Wilkes-Barre sponsored the law which brought the night schools of the hard coal fields into the public school system, and this proved a great boon.

In various parts of the region it was the custom in the one-room patch schools to sing the lessons of history, geography, and similar subjects. The master improvised verses containing essential facts and taught his pupils the tunes by which they sang them and committed them to memory. Saturdays were devoted to review and the school resolved itself into a singing school. That it proved an effective memory aid was demonstrated for me and other guests by an eighty-three-year-old St. Clair woman who sang jingle after jingle containing the history and geography lessons which she had learned perhaps three-quarters of a century ago.

I took down the following verse on the Battle of Shiloh as she sang it:

At Pittsburg Landing our troops fought hard,
They killed General Johnston and defeated Beauregard,
The way they slew the Rebels, they knew how it would be
With land force, gun boats, and Union victory.

And she was able to name the county seat of every county in Pennsylvania as she sang the refrain:

Schuylkill County, Schuykill County, Pottsville;
Berks County, Berks County, Reading;
Luzerne County, Luzerne County, Wilkes-Barre.

This custom probably gave the boy colliers the inspiration to cast their own juvenile thoughts and feelings into singing verse. After working hours, and probably after night school, they gathered in a crude shanty on a hillside where in the dim light of their home-made lanterns they improvised ditties and songs. An example of their doggerel follows:

The first comes big Sam with his big leather boots,
He goes down in the breaker and looks down the chutes,
If he sees a cocko he will cry:
"Go down to the shipper and tell a damn lie."

REFRAIN

And it's hard times wherever you go.

Then comes George Shade with a shovel and pick,
He'll go into the drift and sit on a stick,
And if anything ain't right,
He's bound to go out and have a big fight.

REFRAIN

And it's hard times wherever you go.

Other pastimes were games like Rotten Horses, Kick the Wicket, I Spy the Wolf, and Rounders, a crude form of baseball. They also organized circuses, mock Salvation Army meetings and gang fights.

Pay day was red-letter day in a mine patch. The boys turned pay envelopes over to their mothers, but not before they had extracted some of the contents for spending money; this was called the "knockdown." Since the operators did not furnish statements of wages earned, mothers did not know how much their boys withheld for themselves. The boys would get together and agree on a uniform knockdown so that when mothers compared notes there would be no discrepancy. Fathers tolerated the knockdown. "It's an old trick," a father might say with a shrug of the shoulders. "I used to do it myself when I was his age."

And so on pay night the collier lad felt flush. With coins jingling in his pockets, he would strut to the candy shop prepared to blow in his pittance on cigarettes ("coffin nails"), chewing tobacco, craps, and a gamecock fight. At sixteen, he usually said good-bye to the candy shop and the "soft stuff" and began drifting into the saloon to taste of the fellowship of men.

"My Handsome Miner Boy" is that rare anthracite ballad with a love motive. It was composed by John Hory, from whom I obtained it in 1925.

"A White Slave of the Mine," which captures the pathos inherent in the child colliers' lives, was sung in the late Daniel L. Hart's play *Underground* over forty years ago. It was composed by Sam W. Boyd, a Wilkes-Barre newspaperman. Harry Tempest, old-time minstrel, gave it to me.

In the early days a breaker boy worked ten hours a day. Before water was used in processing, the screen room where he picked slate was so thick with coal dust that he could not see beyond his reach. To keep dust out of his mouth he wore a handkerchief and not infrequently took to chewing tobacco to keep from choking. He sat on a narrow plank astride iron-sheathed chutes, crouching over a black stream of clattering coal. His tender little fingers worked fast to pick slate and bony out of the stream and often bled from cuts and bruises. The screen room was stifling in summer and very cold in winter. Every breaker had a stove but because of the building's rambling construction heat did not penetrate the lower reaches, where boys shivered to the marrow and worked with numbed fingers.

At the end of a shift, breaker boys clambered down a rickety wooden stairway, their teeth gleaming through coal-black faces and looking like burnt-cork characters. Their bodies were very tired after the long irksome grind, but a bath in a wooden tub standing in a corner of the kitchen seemed to refresh them. After supper they ran off to night school or to play, free from the intimidating presence of the chute boss and his cutting switch.

They seemed to give fullest play to their animal instincts during lunch hour at the breaker, where they were full of practical jokes. College hazings are mild compared to some of the weird initiations practised on new boys at the breaker.

Strikes and sit-downs of breaker boys occurred frequently. Roused by a grievance, they would swarm out of the breaker as spontaneously as bees leaving a hive. The breaker thereupon suspended operation, throwing the miners, including their own fathers, out of work. The bosses chased after the rebellious boys with whips to drive them back into the breaker. This practice was known as "whipping them in."

On one occasion the operator himself appeared on the scene. He had a reputation as a compromiser, acquired during numerous miners' strikes, and instantly ordered the whipping to stop. Walking into the swarm of striking breaker boys, he took off his hat, bent down his head and called their attention to his baldness.

"Now boys," he said in a somewhat doleful tone, "just look at my head. You see I am an old man as compared to you. I was once a boy. Indeed, when I was about your age I was glad to work for a dollar and a half a week—"

"Sure 'en ye wor a damn fool fer that!" loudly interrupted one of the characteristically Irish boys.

Mothers brought the younger boys to work before seven in the morning and came back for them at the end of the shift. In the winter these trips were made in darkness. They were often tearful events. What of the mother who would come to the breaker to find that her child was not there to be taken home—ever?

At Audenried Patch in the eighties, "a poor Irish widow" had come for her boy, nicknamed Mickey Pick-Slate. But he was not there to greet her. He had fallen into the crusher rolls and was ground up with the coal. The poor woman went out of her mind. Day after day she came back to the breaker to wait for her boy. Her eyes would wander over the coal-smutted faces, and not finding hers among them would shake her head and drag her feet homeward. The ballad "Mickey Pick-Slate" sang of this tragedy, the present version having been given me by Dennis P. Coyle.

The door boy sat at his dungeon-like post in a gangway or heading, where he opened a heavy wooden door for passing mule trips. Compared to picking slate in the breaker or driving a mule, door-tending was not hard labor. But the darkness, stillness, and loneliness combined to oppress a boy's mind, making him serious far beyond his years. It bred in him a sense of responsibility and taught him the lesson of courage. If a roof were "working" in a gangway or heading, the door boy was often the first to hear it and his timely warning saved miners' lives.

The annals of the industry contain the names of many a door-boy hero. One of them, Johnny Clark of Ashley, was publicly hailed "Johnny the Hero" by Mayor Loomis of Wilkes-Barre in 1879. Johnny was employed as a door boy and "patcher" in the Number Ten slope, Sugar Notch, when the roof began to cave in. The mule driver, William "Sult" Kinney, had ordered him to run to safety, but he remained to warn endangered miners, and finally was entombed with Kinney and five other men.

"The Door Boy's Last Good-bye," supplied by William E. Jones, is a copyrighted ballad, composed by Vint. L. Breese and Griffith J. Jones in 1902.

Just as electricity has virtually displaced the boy in the breaker, so has its application to underground transportation eliminated the equally picturesque driver boy and his constant companion in darkness—the mule. A hybrid, the mine mule long held a peculiar niche in the popular imagination, and many legends have grown around it. It bore the brunt of mine haulage for a century or more. Surefooted, less susceptible to sickness than the horse, powerful and tireless, the mule was an indispensable asset underground in the preëlectrical age. The motor which now does its work is called by miners the "electric mule" as a tribute to that hybrid.

The mule had another quality which miners relied upon in emergencies: a remarkable instinct for self-preservation. How that instinct asserted itself is illustrated by this story. An explosion of fire damp rocked the Spencer slope at Black Heath, Schuylkill County, in the fifties. Miners were roasted alive or torn to pieces, while those who escaped the flames and the crashing wreckage dropped in their tracks to escape the dread after-damp. However, none survived. Had the men been able to reach the sump and stick their faces in its turbid water, the oxygen in the water might have sustained them for a while. The only creature to reach the sump, however, was a little black mule. It plunged its snout into the black water and then, as if revived, leaped up the plane to the surface, and its own singed body gave the first alarm of the hell raging below.

Another side to the mule's nature, better known to the outside world, is illustrated by this story. Paddy, a mule driver, was in the colliery yard trying to move his mule, but all his beatings and curses availed him nothing. Into this embarrassing situation stepped Father Whalen, Paddy's parish priest.

"Why, Patrick," said Father Whalen in horror. "What are you doing, abusing the poor little creature that brought our Savior into Jerusalem!"

"Fa-ather," protested Paddy as he wiped the perspiration from his face. "Sure, it wasn't this little son-of-a-bitch or He wouldn't be there yet."

The commonest name for a mine mule was Harry. Among other names were Lizzy or Liz, Fanny, Maud, Mamie, Ginger, Cap, Coalie, Prince, and Fox.

Mules were fed twice a day, morning and evening. But at lunch they would stick their snouts into dinner cans and help themselves to whatever men and boys were eating. They showed a marked taste for hard-boiled eggs, pork chops, bread and jam, and other foods. But they were also satisfied with banana and orange peelings, egg shells, and even bread crusts.

Their own standard food was a balanced ration made up of oats, corn, alfalfa, cake meal, and salt. They liked salt which drivers brought for them from home. They consumed tin dinner cans and parts of miners' clothing without apparently suffering ill effects. Many, addicted to tobacco chewing, refused to budge from their stalls in the morning until bribed with a bite of brown leaf. It was no unusual sight to see a young driver pull a quid of tobacco out of his hip pocket, let his mule have a bite and stick the rest into his own mouth. Mules also liked to grind fine coal between their teeth and swallow it. This was true particularly where the coal had just been shot down, and it was probably the saltpeter in the blasting powder which gave it an appetizing flavor.

When a mischievous mood came over them no more playful pets could be found. Often they would run a race in the gangway with their drivers. Between levels, corresponding to floors in a building, were muleways. A mule raced out of its stall in the morning ready for work and halted immediately in front of the muleway. Then it looked around to see if its young master had caught up with it. If he had, it would bray. The boy grabbed the tail as the animal leaped to the upper level.

The temptation to abuse a mule was by no means small, for it often tried a boy's patience. A driver was expected to produce a certain number of cars during a shift; his job might depend on it. To a mule this meant nothing. If accustomed to pull two cars in a "trip" it would balk at a third being hitched. Though there was no whistle in the mine to blow time, the beast knew instinctively when quitting time had arrived. It would halt, even if the "trip" was in the middle of the way, and no power on earth save dynamite could move it. Nor would it work when tired. In these instances, it earned those adjectives commonly applied to it: balky and stubborn.

A driver anxious to hold his job would do all he could to keep up his quota, and in the face of such exasperating antics he was bound to lose his temper. And when he did, he would twist the mule's long ears, or beat it across the back with a stick, or singe its belly with the flame of his lamp. Of course when caught he was fired. This might be a merciful act on the part of the boss. Even if allowed to remain in the company's employ he would do well to ask to be transferred to another part of the mine. Otherwise he would be in constant danger of injury. The mule was a vindictive beast and with that dogged pertinacity which it inherited from the ass, it often tried to even a score with an abusive driver. Days, weeks, even months, might pass before it got its chance, but when it did, its kick might be fatal. Boys were constantly being kicked in the abdominal region or in the seat of their trousers which sent them crashing against the rib of a gangway. This is not to imply that mules kicked only in revenge, as there were vicious mules just as there were cruel drivers. Sometimes they sank their teeth into a boy's flesh and caused death. Biting, however, was rarer than kicking.

The operators took good care of their mules. In fact, the complaint heard around the mines was that they took better care of them than their workers. This was made the basis for one of the pithiest arguments ever advanced in the region for union organization. It came from the lips of the late Con Foley of Pottsville, an organizer, street-corner Socialist, and Irish wit. While on a round of collieries to organize mine workers many years ago, Foley stopped in front of a colliery where the men worked only three days a week. As he waited just outside the colliery yard, men and mules were being hoisted to the surface at the end of the day's work. The mules were led to the barn in front of which were stacked bales of fodder, while the men struck out for their homes. Foley corralled them a short distance from the colliery. "The mules have more sense than you," was Con's opening shot, and the men laughed. "You work three days a week," he shouted, "and your bosses expect you to feed yourselves seven days. Not so the mules. Look how happy they are at the feed troughs. They work three days just like you, but they get fed seven."

In the larger, well-regulated collieries, every level had its own stable, usually lighted by incandescent lamps; the walls and stalls were whitewashed and the floor either cemented or boarded.

Ventilation and drainage were carefully looked after. The stable was cleansed daily and sprinkled with lime several times a week. The water in the troughs was kept fresh and feed boxes were cleansed regularly. Before it left the stall in the morning, the mule was currycombed and otherwise put into condition for the tiring hours ahead. The harness had been cleansed and made to fit well, especially the collar, to avoid friction which might cause shoulder galls. In more recent years a first-aid cabinet, equipped with medicines, cotton, bandages, and antiseptics, was located in a convenient shanty where it was readily available in case a mule became sick or was injured. Drivers and stable boss knew which first-aid remedies to apply before the colliery veterinarian arrived.

Mules were not permitted to be worked two successive shifts. They were driven singly, and when teamed up it was in tandem. In the latter case the foremost mule carried a small miner's lamp attached to its head or hung on its collar, leading its mates through darkness and rarely making a wrong turn or misstep. No reins were used. The driver sat or stood on the bumper of the front car.

Care had to be exercised in the teaming of mules to avoid serious trouble. The quick could not be teamed with the slow, the dull with the nervous, or the weak with the strong. Thus a driver had to know his mules well to hold his job.

A vivid picture of the life led by driver boys underground is drawn by "The Driver Boys of Wadesville Shaft." It was improvised by William Keating when he was a twelve-year-old door boy in the Wadesville shaft, near Pottsville, in 1898. He had ample time and opportunity to observe the driver boys as they passed through his door. One day rhymes crowded his mind and a suitable tune came with them. As Keating was unable to write, the ballad remained in oral form for many years.

Driver and mule were together for ten hours, and later for eight hours daily. The boy had to be down in the mine before seven, get his mule out of the stable, bring it to the foot of the shaft or slope and hitch it to a trip of empty cars. He hopped on the first car, cracked his long braided leather whip and shouted. When he sang, the ditty probably was "My Sweetheart's the Mule in the Mines," many ribald versions of which echoed through the mines. By a coincidence it was a young fellow in the Schuylkill Valley who sang the present tune, using the words of the first version to shock his grandfather and grandmother. The bowdlerized version was supplied by Thomas E. Heffernan of Wilkes-Barre.

A boy had to learn not only to drive a mule without reins but to govern it with his voice. He had stock cues, but they were not effective unless seasoned with oaths and peppery English.

Driver boys enjoyed a freedom of action denied to breaker boys and door boys, and thus were the most boisterous and defiant of those employed around a colliery. They were always rarin' to do things and chafed under restraint. When his boss was not in sight, a boy sometimes would climb on a mule, lie close to its back and go dashing down the gangway, the flame in his head-lamp a tiny backward streak of blue that gave no light. These bareback rides were forbidden because hazardous, but this meant nothing in their young lives. It was also against the rules to drive a hitched mule faster than a walk. But, he might have asked in his own picturesque way, how could one do justice to such a lively ballad as "Jerusalem Cuckoo," unless one was madly dashing down the gangway?

At the turn of the century, mothers crooned their babies to sleep with "The Driver Boy." It was a doleful story and was sung to a plaintive melody. Many a tear was shed over it. Every mining mother knew that when her son became a driver boy he was lost to her. At fourteen or fifteen he took his place beside the men, sometimes even supporting a family on his meager earnings. This responsibility developed his manliness, which he demonstrated by chewing tobacco, smoking a pipe, drinking liquor, betting on gamecocks and handling a picturesque vocabulary which no conscientious Sunday School teacher approved.

Back in 1925 when I first heard "The Driver Boy" sung by miners' wives in different parts of the region, I sensed its popularity. Until recorded in my previous collection, it had never been published, its circulation being achieved by word of mouth in the traditional manner. I tried for some time to locate the author, and finally found him in John A. Murphy, an elderly Dickson City mine worker. In the same year I asked him to write me about himself and his ballad. His reply, in part, follows:

> The song was inspired and composed through an incident that came under my observation in 1900. A cruel father under the influence of drink was beating his son, a boy about fourteen years of age, when I stepped in and prevented further abuse. Some weeks after, the boy, who was a mule driver in the mines, caught a most severe cold, pneumonia set in and he died. My thoughts drifted back to the night of the beating and being of a poetical turn of mind, it gave me an inspiration to put my little talent to use. The song is written to the tune of "The Little Shoeblack," which I heard in England nearly fifty years ago. . . . I have only a meager education and as you see my grammar is bad, but in the solitude of the mines my thoughts are inspired and drift to what you may term silly effusions. Be that as it may, I get some little pleasure out of it after all. I have been employed as a signal man at the Johnson colliery, Dickson City for a number of years. . . ."

The long association of boy and mule often promoted mutual affection. Most mules responded to kind treatment. For the average boy the mule answered his instinctive craving for a pet and he grew fond of it. Here is how one boy imagined the affection borne him by his mule:

I write these lines down in the slope
Without a glimpse of light or hope
To you, my old friend Johnny O'Brien.

You never gave me a lickin'
And I never gave you a kickin'.

But when you spoke and held the light,
I always drew the wagon right.

These lines recall the tragic story of Martin Crahan, twelve-year-old driver boy who was suffocated with nineteen miners in the West Pittston shaft disaster back in 1871.

The West Pittston mine was small and primitive. Like many in those days, it had but one outlet, and the breaker was built over it. As more men were working than the law permitted, the air was impure. Whether the fan was speeded up beyond its capacity to blow more air into the mine will never be known, but one of its journals became overheated and set fire to the breaker. The engineer quickly signaled to the man in charge of the cage at the bottom of the shaft. As he was about to be hoisted to the top for the last time, this man called Martin Crahan and another boy to go up with him—it was their only chance of saving themselves. The other boy jumped on the cage, but not Martin. He thought of the men still working in distant chambers who were unaware of the fire.

Taking a parting look at the shaft with its flames, crashing timbers, and thick smoke, Martin dashed away to warn the unwary miners deep in the mine.

The burning shaft was their only avenue of escape, which led them to conclude that their hope of survival lay in barricading themselves against deadly gases generated by the fire. Hastily they trimmed large lumps of coal and fitted them together in a solid wall, closing holes and cracks with culm which they scooped up from the tracks in the gangway.

His duty done, Martin retraced his steps to the shaft in the hope of finding the cage still in service, but the hoisting machinery having been destroyed, the cage had already crashed to the bottom. And so he fled back to the miners whom he had risked his own life to warn.

Approaching their barricade, he heard a medley of ghost-like voices coming from behind it. Some of the men were moaning and crying for fresh air; others were singing hymns and still others were praying for deliverance from the horrible death menacing them. His own desperately shrill cry pierced these noises. He begged for admittance, but faltering voices answered that a break in the barricade would let in gases and result in instant death for all of them. Again and again he pleaded with them, beating his little fists against the solid wall of anthracite for emphasis, but all in vain.

Rebuffed by his fellow human beings, he sought the company of his faithful mule, the sharer of his daily labor. Through darkness and smoke, and after much stumbling over débris and bumping into pillars of coal and timbers, he finally groped his way to the mine stable. Finding his mule in its accustomed place, he lay down beside it, but not until after he had feebly written on a board the names of his father and mother and of a little cousin named for him, indicating that his last thoughts were of them.

Rescuers found the brave, self-sacrificing little driver boy, his clothes torn, his face bruised and twisted from the intense agony he must have suffered, lying close to his mule. Like good pals, they had died together.

A short time later, the Pittston *Gazette* printed the following tribute to Martin Crahan under the title, "The Hero of West Pittston Mine," written by W. A. Peters:

Lurid, flashed the awful warning
  Down the depths of Pittston's gloom;
Dirgeful, were the hissing fire-tongues
  Ringing down the miners' doom.

Crackling flames o'erhead, consuming
  Fast, the avenue of hope,
As the noble boy stood yielding,
  With his hand upon the rope.

Yielding to the noblest impulse
  That e'er moved a boyish soul;
Yielding up himself forever
  For those dust-grimed men of coal.

Yielding up, in soul devotion,
  Every thought of self in love;
Yielding that firm law of nature
  While his comrade went above.

Busy thoughts of home were crowding
  O'er him in that inch of time,
But he went to his "father's business"
  Like a hero grand, sublime.

Went, in all his brave devotion,
  Went, through simple love to tell
What we deem the noblest duty,
  Man to man and there he fell.

O ye angels of record in heaven!
  O ye pens of mortality write
Him a place on the roll of martyrs,
  And clothe him in spotless white.

Raise, from the wreck of the body;
  Raise, from the burning mine,
His heroic young spirit to heaven,
  O Christ, for he is thine!

Another poem, entitled "Little Martin Crahan," was written on this touching episode by Zadel Barnes Gustafson. It follows:

A child looks up to the ragged shaft—
  A boy whose meager frame
Shrinks as he hears the roaring draught
  That feeds the eager flame.
He has a single chance; the stakes
  Of life show death at bay
One moment; then his comrade takes
  The hope he casts away.

For while his trembling hand is raised,
  And while his sweet eyes shine,
There dwells above the love of life
  The rush of love divine—
The thought of those unwarned, to whom
  Death steals along the mine.

The while he speeds the darksome way
  Hope paints upon his fears
Soft visions of the light of day;
  Faint songs of birds he hears;
In summer breeze his tangled curls
  Are blown about his ears.

He sees the men; he warns, and now
  His duty bravely done,
Sweet hope may paint the fairest scene
  That spreads beneath the sun.

Back to the burning shaft he flies;
  There bounding pulses fail;
The light forsakes his lifted eyes,
  The glowing cheek is pale.

With wheeling, whirling hungry flame
  The seething shaft is rife;

Where solid chains drip liquid fire,
  What chance for human life?

To die with those he hoped to save,
  Back, back through heat and gloom,
To find a wall, and death and he
  Shut in the larger tomb.

He pleaded to be taken in
  As closer rolled the smoke;
In deathful vapors they could hear
  His piteous accents choke
And they, with shaking voice, refused,
  And then the young heart broke.

Oh love of life! God made it strong,
  And knows how close it pressed,
And death to those who love life least
  Is scarce a welcome guest.

One thought of the poor wife whose head
  Last night lay on his breast—
A quiver runs through lips that mourn
  By children's lips caressed.

These things the sweet, strong thoughts of home,
  Though but a wretched place
To which the sad-eyed miners come
  With Labor's laggard pace—
Remembered in the cavern gloom,
  Illume the haggard face.

Illumed their faces, steeled each heart;
  Oh, God, what mysteries
Of brave and base make sum and part
  Of human histories!
What will not thy creatures do
  To buy an hour of breath?

Well for us all some souls are true
  Above the fear of death!

He wept a little—for they heard
  The sound of sobs, the sighs
That breathed of martyrdom complete
  Unseen of mortal eyes—
And then, no longer swift, his feet
  Passed down the galleries.

He crept and crouched beside his mule,
  Led by its dying moan;
He touched it feebly with a hand
  That shook like palsy's own.
God grant the touch had power to make
  The child feel less alone.

Who knoweth every heart, He knows
  What moved the boyish mind;
What longings grew to passion throes
  For dear ones left behind;
How hardly youth and youth's desires
  Their hold of life resigned.

Death leaned upon him heavily;
  But love, more mighty still,
She lent him slender lease of life
  To work her tender will.

He felt with sightless, sentient hand
  Along the wall and ground,
And there the rude and single page
  For his sweet purpose found.

O'erwritten with the names he loved,
  Clasped to his little side.
Dim eyes the wooden record read
  Hours after he had died.

Thus from all knowledge of his kind,
  In darkness lone and vast
From life to death, from death to life,
  The little hero passed.

And while they listened for the feet
  That would return no more,
Far off they fell in music sweet
  Upon another shore.

* * *

MY HANDSOME MINER BOY

One evening fair as I walked out,
  I heard a maid complain;
By her lamentations
  I knew she was in pain.
She said, "I ne'er will marry him,
  So they need not me annoy:
If e'er I wed with any man
  It's my handsome miner boy.

"He is my joy and heart's delight,
  And evermore will be;
If I cannot be his wife
  I'll live in misery.
For love it has entangled me,
  And that I can't deny,
I'll give my father's fortune
  For my handsome miner boy.

"The first time that I saw him
  Was a cold December day,
He passed me by and cast an eye
  That stole my heart away.
To me he looked so beautiful
  How can I life enjoy,

Forever to be parted from
   My handsome miner boy?

"My parents talk about disgrace,
   And say that he is poor,
To change my resolution
   Or they'll turn me from their door;
But I have money plenty,
   With them I'll not comply,
I'll go and find the lad I love—
   My handsome miner boy."

Then I left my concealment,
   And steered upon my way,
Though unperceived, for her I grieved,
   As homeward I did stray.
She looked so young and innocent
   As she sat down to cry,
I envied him his happiness,
   That handsome miner boy.

A WHITE SLAVE OF THE MINE

I'm a little collier lad,
   Hardworking all the day,
From early morn till late at night
   No time have I to play.
Down in the bowels of the earth
   Where no bright sun rays shine,
You'll find me busy at my work,
   A white slave of the mine.

CHORUS

(*sung twice*)

Our lot in life is full of strife;
   But we make no murmur or sign,

For daily we toil down deep in the soil—
The white slaves of the mine.

When daylight comes I go to work,
When dark I go to bed,
The money that my labor earns,
Keeps us in meat and bread.
Poor father he was killed one day,
Yet mother for him pines,
And that is why you see me here,
A white slave of the mine.

But after all when life is done,
And God has called the roll,
I hope to find He's not forgot
The little collier soul;
Hard work and toil has dwarfed him so,
And ground him down so fine—
That is why you see me here
A white slave of the mine.

MICKEY PICK-SLATE

There came to this country a short time ago,
A poor Irish widow from the County Mayo.
She had but one son, his age it was eight,
And the boss gave him work picking slate.
The first day at the breaker the boys all did stare,
For poor little Mike was the youngest lad there.
They asked him his age; said he, I'm just eight.
So they nicknamed him Mickey Pick-Slate.

FIRST CHORUS

Mickey Pick-Slate, early and late,
That's what they called this poor little waif.
His poor old mother each night she does wait
For her own little Mickey Pick-Slate.

Young Mickey was anxious to learn all he could,
To provide for his mother and keep her in food.
He counted the days and he longed for the time
When he'd start tending doors in the mines.
His mother was longing with joy for the day,
When poor little Mike would be drawing big pay.
The future looked bright though her heart it did ache
For her poor little Mickey Pick-Slate.

One day in the winter with seven below,
While poor little Mike was sifting the coal,
He tripped on a plank that was carelessly placed
And into the rolls he fell to his fate.
His body so mangled it's sad for to say,
The poor little fellow he soon passed away.
His mother demented still lingers and waits
For her poor little Mickey Pick-Slate.

SECOND CHORUS

Mickey Pick-Slate, early and late,
That was this poor little breaker boy's fate;
A poor simple woman at the breaker still waits
To take home her Mickey Pick-Slate.

THE DOOR BOY'S LAST GOOD-BYE

In the mine depths' gloom and silence,
Void of sunlight though 'tis mid-day,
There a fearless little door boy sat alone;
Unseen dangers hover round him
At his post upon the gangway,
While he works, and thinks of mother sick at home;
Without warning there's a cave-in,
Rock and timber downward crashing
Hurl the lad moaning to the rocky floor;
But his pale lips framed this message
As his breath was quick and gasping,
"Good-bye mother, Heav'n protect you evermore."

CHORUS

All his thoughts were of his mother,
All for her his broken pleading
As he lay there, dying, at his shattered door;
Bright-winged angels caught this message
As his life was quickly fleeting,
"Good-bye mother, Heav'n protect you evermore."

In her dreams the mother fancies
She can hear him softly calling,
She can hear him beck'ning from the starry sky;
Soon her lips will close forever,
And the bitter tears cease falling,
She will meet him where they never say good-bye.
Just a door boy in a coal mine,
A brave-hearted manly fellow,
Who lays dying 'neath the wreckage where he fell;
Deathly gases are his mantle,
Splintered roof rock is his pillow,
Just a door boy, but a hero, fare thee well.

THE DRIVER BOYS OF WADESVILLE SHAFT

Transcribed by Melvin LeMon

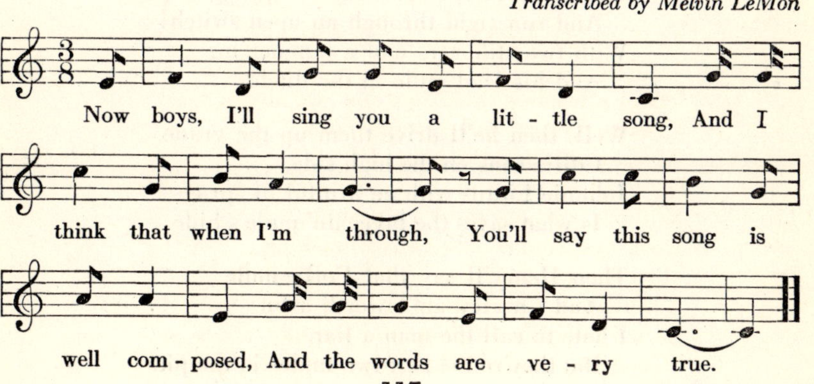
Now boys, I'll sing you a lit - tle song, And I
think that when I'm through, You'll say this song is
well com - posed, And the words are ve - ry true.

It's about a bunch of driver boys,
They worked in Wadesville shaft,
And when I tell you how they toiled
I think 'twill make you laugh.

Well, now to start this little song,
I'll begin with Henry Flynn,
For when it comes to driving mules
He thinks he's the real thing.

He's the first driver from the barn,
With Collie-mule in the lead,
But when he gets back, at quitting time,
He hasn't earned their feed.

He'll leave the Seven-Foot turnout,
With six or seven cars,
They'll run out to the spragging place,
And there he'll be stuck for hours!

He'll drag them then by ones and twos
To the bottom of the shaft;
Then he'll catch his lead mule by the head,
And go for another draft.

Well, then he'll start from the spraggin' place,
And run right through an open switch!
With two stiff cars and a jammer in,
And his lead mule in the ditch.

Well, then he'll drive them up the grade,
Collie runs on the high side,
Johnnie Loftus with an armful of sprags
Is what saves the breechin' mule's hide.

Then Henry'll say that Collie-mule
And Charley ain't worth a bit;
I hate to call the man a liar,
But they're the best two mules in the pit.

It takes us door boys all our time,
To keep Henry Flynn in hemp,
And with weaving lashes for his whip
Our fingernails are bent.

So that's the way he'll run all day,
He'll tally about fourteen cars;
For the longest shift he ever works
Is six or seven hours.

Well, then there's Owney Loftus,
With a team of mules he's slick;
And when he chirrups for the signal light,
Then look out for a big trip.

When Owney's team leaves the Primrose bend,
Their shoes begin to pound,
And until he hits the top of the grade,
He'll never utter a sound.

'Twould do you good to stand upon
The crossroads at the bend;
And watch the curb-boy count Owney's trip—
Twenty cars often mark the end.

He has Fox and Dick and Paddy and Mike;
Lively Lark-mule leads the way,
If all the teams pulled trips like Owney's
Wadesville colliery would surely pay.

Well, here comes Jack McNulty,
Out along the West Skidmore line;
With his feet stretched out on the tail chain,
Old John Garrity nippin' behind.

When Jack's team nears the terminal,
Jack hopes he'll get a through light,
But when he rounds the Skidmore bend,
Then there's no curb-boy in sight!

Then Jack jumps off, sprags up his trip,
At dumb door boys he'll rage and swear;
And if the nipper opens his lip,
Jack hauls him around by the hair!

You see, nearly every trip Jack brings,
He has tunnel-rock cars mixed in,
So, of course, we have to red-light Jack,
So's to white-light Henry Flynn.

Jack drives Punch-mule, Pete, Pet, Prince,
Lazy Mary-mule leads the way.
If Jack would haul more coal, less rock,
Then the breaker could work a full day.

Well, then there's Johnny Baltsis,
He drives the shifting team;
He pulls the cars from the tender shaft,
And keeps the bottom turnout clean.

Johnny Baltsis' the busiest boy about,
The way he slaves is a sin!
Pullin' Jack McNulty's rock cars out,
And side-hitchin' Henry Flynn.

They talk about busy Altoona yards,
But Altoona yards are tame,
You should see John Baltsis shifting cars!
With Jerry-mule and Jane.

Some other time, I'll sing some more,
'Bout the busy driver boys.
At present, I'll page the stable "maids"—
Stable bosses are mostly noise.

Willie Brennan is quiet, seldom gets in a fight,
Bossy Donnagan, he's a darn crank!
They worry me from morn till night,
With their rollin' feed cars and water tank.

They chase me to get the water turned on,
 Then they race me to get it turned off,
But when drivers take their teams for a drink,
 There's never a drop in the water trough!

They haven't the nerve for stable work,
 If a mule shakes his tail they're scared!
And in case of an emergency,
 They never are prepared.

If a hame strap or a tail chain happens to break,
 That team driver's tally will sink,
There's no harness parts in the barn,
 Not even an open link.

Poor mules must stand knee-deep in dung!
 So the company's greatest loss,
Is payin' sixty dollars a month
 To a lazy stable boss.

The firebosses, foremen and driver boss,
 Took a seashore vacation trip;
Willie Brennan carried the bootblack box,
 Jim Donnagan juggled the grips.

The driver boys and the stable boss,
 From my song should learn a lesson,
And now I'll begin with the bottom men,
 For some of them needs a dressin'.

There's easy-going, fat Jack Betzs.
 Jack jokes and loafs all day,
While old "Dutch" Hen is humpty-backed
 Pushin' cars from the cage away.

Matt Reddington, a butty to Betzs,
 And though Matt's a first cousin of mine—
Matt goes to dances and balls every night;
 In the mines he's asleep most of the time.

Mike McNulty gets stuck with an empty trip,
  Jack Betzs bawls all hands out,
Matt Reddington lets a coupling slip
  Onto Dutch Hen's left-foot gout!

"The breaker is waitin'; this won't pay.
  Move those empties," Betzs will shout.
Then Dutch Hen will say in his dutchified way,
  "Be der Lawd Kyist der twack is blocked out!"

In insane asylums madmen rave,
  But where sensible men go daft,
You'd go nutty too with that bughouse crew,
  On the bottom of Wadesville shaft.

Bunker John Kelly and Joe Morley,
  They've the meanest job in the mine;
Double oilcloth suits and high gum boots,
  Yet they're drowned wet all the time.

No moon, no stars, no sun ever gleams
  Through the gloom of the underground;
Here danger, death, and darkness reign,
  Yet humor here is found.

It's quittin' time, I'll close my door,
  Just one request, I pray:
My supper will be a crust, no more,
  Please boost a poor door boy's pay.

MY SWEETHEART'S THE MULE IN THE MINES

(AIR: "*My Sweetheart's the Man in the Moon*")

My sweetheart's the mule in the mines,
I drive her without reins or lines,
On the bumper I sit,
I chew and I spit
All over my sweetheart's behind.

A bowdlerized version follows:

Transcribed by Melvin LeMon

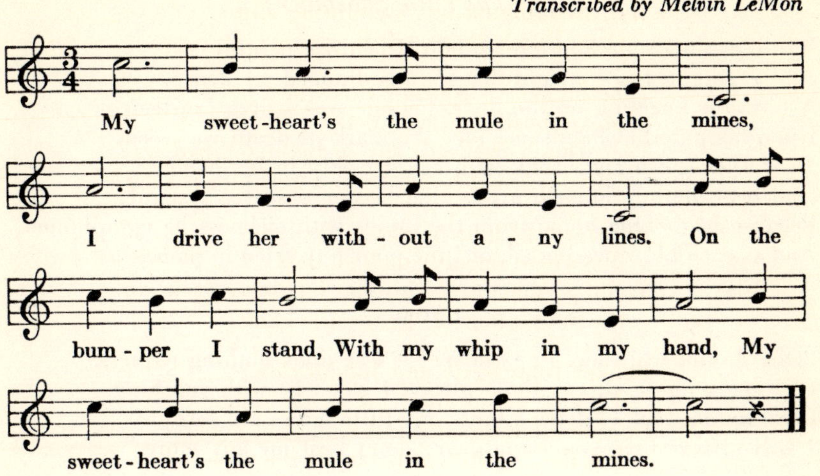
My sweet-heart's the mule in the mines,
I drive her with-out a-ny lines. On the
bum-per I stand, With my whip in my hand, My
sweet-heart's the mule in the mines.

JERUSALEM CUCKOO

I am a donkey driver,
  The best on the line;
There is no donkey on the road
  That can come up to mine.

You may talk about Methuselah
  And other donkeys too;
But no donkey on the road
  Can beat Jerusalem Cuckoo.

Then shout, boys, hurray,
  My troubles they're but few.
No donkey on the road
  Can beat Jerusalem Cuckoo.

THE DRIVER BOY

(AIR: *The Little Shoeblack*)

While passing by a house one night, I heard a painful cry,
And gazing in I saw a sight that soon bedimmed my eye.
A boy was kneeling on the floor, his age was scarce fourteen,
Upon his pale but handsome face the mark of death was seen.
His father, stern and cruel, with a horsewhip in his hand
Had beat the boy in such a way that he could scarcely stand;
Because he'd come home from the mines with sickness he complained,
And as each blow descended, oh! the poor boy cried in pain.

CHORUS

"Oh! do not whip me, Papa dear, for I've done nothing wrong,
Oh! spare me this time, Papa please, I won't be with you long,
For I'm too weak to drive a mule, my little bones are sore;
I will always love you Papa dear; don't beat me any more."

In underground the boy did toil from early morn till night,
His little limbs were growing weak; he could not stand the fight
'Gainst hunger and ill treatment, which no strong man could endure,
So he was forced to leave his work though he begged from door to door.
His mother pleaded, but in vain, to spare her hope and pride.
"Oh! do not kill my darling boy, beat me instead," she cried.
The villain bade her stand aside, her pleadings were in vain,
Again the whip descended and the boy cried out again.

The little fellow then crept off to his cold bed on the floor.
He prayed that God would take him to that bright and golden shore.
"And please forgive my father, for I love him still," said he,
"And he was drunk and ugly or he would not ill-use me."
The parents were soon startled by a wild despairing cry;
They both rushed, frantic, to the room wherein lay their boy,
The father soon repented and these were the words he said:
"Oh! God, I am a murderer!" For his driver boy was dead.

CHAPTER FOUR

Slavs as Miners

SLAVS now move on a plane of equality with their fellow Americans in the anthracite region.

What a far cry from their present position to the almost legendary days of half a century ago! Then they were arriving by the carload and were dumped like cattle on some isolated railroad siding to shift for themselves in a strange, unfriendly land. The natives, suspecting that they concealed horns under their high astrakhan hats and headkerchiefs, regarded them with fear and hatred.

Some of the first immigrants lived in mine breaches like the ancient cave-dwellers because no provision had been made for their accommodation. In one place, it is related, a group lived in such primitive surroundings for three whole months because the men, thwarted by jeers and stones, were unable to reach the colliery to apply for work. They were reduced to the level of animals foraging for food in the woods. When barks and herbs failed to satisfy the hunger of their children they sent their women into the mine patches to beg for food. Unable to speak English, the women made their pathetic pleas by gesticulations.

The transition from these primitive habitations to homes was a slow and painful process. Most of the earliest immigrants were bachelors, or men whose families had remained behind to await passage money. Since no Irish or Welsh family would take them in as boarders they were forced to bunk together in dilapidated barns where unconscionable landlords charged them a dollar a month for a bunk of hay. With the coming of the women a housing shortage set in which the operators partially relieved by building new company houses for the older families, who left their own shacks to the immigrants. Naturally these hovels were the least habitable in the patch. Mere shells, they consisted of rough hemlock boards nailed upright with strips fastened over the cracks and having no foundation, no cellar, and no plaster on the walls. By the turn of the century many old patches were in full possession of the immigrants. The hostility of the older families forced the Slavs to keep together in colonies, though they themselves were hopelessly divided into distinct national groups. Nevertheless many patches were microcosms of Slavic folkways and customs. While they lived in a geographical America they were not part of its life. They occupied a sort of substratum in which their horizons were limited by the church, the saloon, the squire, and the colliery.

Their homes were furnished with a few sticks of furniture, some of which came from a second-hand dealer. The women were too bowed down with work and worry to have the time or incentive to indulge their peasant fancy for pretty things. The wooden washtub was by way of being a symbol of the degradation of womanhood. Every family was crowded with boarders. It was considered part of the housewife's duties to scrub the backs of the men boarders when they returned from the mines in the evening, and children witnessed these daily ablutions.

In his native home the Slav had been accustomed to invest all nature with the poetry of his imagination. But what incentive did he have for such imaginings in the mine patch with its gashed hills; its streams polluted with sulphur water and choked with culm; with dreary culm banks which shut out the sunlight; and the overshadowing breaker? A Slavic miner would dig down through layers of silt and refuse for a patch of fresh earth to plant a few flowers. His love of nature also expressed itself in the bird house he built on the roof of his house or on a flagpole. There he would imprison a song bird and whistle to it in a pathetic effort to induce it to sing, and thus revive memories of a boyhood spent in natural surroundings.

While they have become good miners, at heart many of them remained frustrated farmers. In the last few years, since collieries have closed down throwing them out of work, some have rented or bought old farms in counties adjoining the anthracite region.

The Slav brought his rich heritage of folklore—folk songs, folk games, folk dances, quaint folkways and picturesque customs, superstitions, and strange beliefs. The ridicule of unsympathetic neighbors, however, chilled this folklore in the immigrants.

As popular interest in folklore increases, this suppressed heritage is coming to the surface again through their children and grandchildren. Only when mellow with liquor in the saloons did the old-timers have the courage to sing folk songs. They still sing them under these circumstances and, interestingly enough, English-speaking miners are now learning them.

In the old days the saloon was the only place where the Slavs met their Irish and Welsh fellow workers socially. Sometimes the Slavs asked for liquor "on tick," and being essentially honest received it. The saloon keepers could not pronounce their names, let alone spell them, what with all their consonants jumbled together. They overcame this difficulty by descriptive phrases recorded in their tick books. One Wilkes-Barre tick book contains such identifying touches as the following: "Chicken-Eye Joe; The fellow with big mustache; Pock-marked Andrew; The fellow who talks too much; John Good English; and My Dog Nell." This last allusion was to the customer who always talked about his dog.

The Slav seemed to be the type of peasant to fit perfectly into the coal operators' dream of industrial feudalism. Back home in Southeastern Europe he had subsisted on a simple, coarse diet. He was accustomed to arduous physical labor and long hours in the fields. Moreover he was by nature docile and inured to hardship and oppression. But the operators' plans went astray because they had overestimated the capacity of human endurance, even of European peasants.

What was to become of the Irish, Welsh, and other English-speaking miners who had given the better part of their lives to the industry? Obviously they were to be ousted, and if this proved unfeasible, they were to be intimidated by the threat of more importations from across the seas.

The English-speaking miners took an unfortunate but quite human attitude toward these immigrants. They suspected them for their strange folkways and hated them because they threatened their security, and the Slavs naïvely misunderstood the reason for their neighbors' hostility. They were abused in the press and from the platform, stoned when they dared venture from their patches, jeered at and intimidated in and around the mines, and in every other way were denied the rights and decencies of civilized men.

The most potent of all weapons employed against them was economic. Unable for some time to learn mining technique because of the hatred borne them, they remained unskilled laborers, employed by contract miners, some of whom cheated and persecuted them. One of those early laborers, John Subalko, waited many years for his revenge. He was now a miner and his former employer, Davy Jones, had retired. One evening in a saloon Jones began to boast of the great things he had accomplished in his day and turned to Subalko, his one-time laborer, for corroboration. "Tell 'em, John," he said, "what kind of a miner *I* was."

Subalko gulped his beer down, smiled and then said, "Yea, Davy, you vas great miner all right. You come in morning, look at place un say, 'John, no got coal dese time,' un wid foots pointing you say, 'drilling hole dese place, drilling hole dat place.' Den you sitting down on tool box un laborer drilling hole, shooting coal down un loading car. Next shift, Mister Davy, you coming un looking round place same like boss. You telling laborer —dat's me—wid de foots pointing, too lazy bending over wid de hands—'drilling hole dese place, drilling hole dat place.' Den mebbe you going home. Me no see miner all day. Yea, Davy, you vas bully gut miner—tool box miner, dat be kind o' miner you vas."

"He Wouldn't Load the Lumps" reflects the brutality with which the Slavic immigrants were often manhandled around the mines. "A Hungarian Christening" gives a glimpse into the social relations existing between them and the Irish. In both ballads Wilkes-Barre is the setting, which strengthens the common belief that they were composed by Con Carbon, the period, probably the nineties. I have heard variants sung in different parts of the region.

"A Greenhorn Makes Good" was sung by John Quinn at the 1936 Anthracite Regional Folk Festival in Wilkes-Barre, and he was also my source for the two previously mentioned ballads. "A Greenhorn Makes Good" sings of the Slavs' ambition to rise in the mining scale. Their attempts in this direction were often pathetic, as illustrated by this anecdote. A Slavic laborer approached an official for a contract miner's certificate. "I like fer be miner," he exclaimed. "How fer come dose papers?"

"You can't get papers yet," replied the official. "You don't know enough about mining. How would you mine coal where there was gas?"

"Dat be easy, John. Coal same one place like yudder place, yes?"

"Yes, I know that, but would you fire a shot in a place where you knew there was gas?"

"Sure me fire shot lotsa times every place. Gas no bodder me. Get lotsa coal down—dat be vat you calling good miner man."

"That's what you would call a dead miner man," retorted the official, refusing the application.

Being fatalistic they were indifferent to danger and took chances that seasoned miners avoided. Hence a great many were maimed or killed, and newspapers in the loose journalism of the day would report so many Polanders or Hungarians had been injured or killed when they could not get their names. Yet when the Slavs were given the opportunity to learn mining technique they made good miners.

Before the Workmen's Compensation Act was passed, benefit balls would be held to raise money for widows and orphans of men killed in the mines. While admission was open to all, the appeal was directed particularly toward the victim's own countrymen. Among the Slavs a benefit ball was a joyous occasion when countrymen from scattered districts would spend a few hours together dancing, drinking, and singing folk songs. Liquor was freely consumed and fights sometimes broke out, but only when English-speaking rowdies invaded the stuffy halls did the brawls develop into riots. The rowdies were sometimes runners for unconscionable squires who paid them to stir trouble. This created an excuse for constables to raid the hall and drag "hunkies" off to a hearing where they were charged with disturbing the peace and fined and assessed with the "costs" which, in Pennsylvania's antiquated petty court system, belonged to the squire. Invariably such raids were staged on pay days. A record of one of those old-time ballroom brawls is preserved in "The Hungarian Ball," a Con Carbon ballad. Versions were supplied by Dennis P. Coyle of Wilkes-Barre and Jerry Byrne of Buck Run.

"Polinky" commemorates what once was the Slav's favorite refreshment and worst enemy. Its effect on the drinker was to stir within him a desire to engage in physical combat with everything animate or inanimate—buzz saws and wildcats preferred. Here is a recipe for making polinky: "Take an ordinary washtub or wash boiler, pour into it one keg of beer, one gallon of whiskey and half a pound of red pepper. Stir with a broom handle and drink from a tin cup at indiscretion."

It needs no emphasis to discern that polinky and discretion did not mix well. When Prohibition came, many Slavic mine workers were already adepts at making moonshine.

HE WOULDN'T LOAD THE LUMPS

If you'll lend me your attention for a little while,
Sure I'll sing you a song and it won't take very long,
It's all about the miners, the laborers and the mines
Where the sun does ne'er shine, but where the drivers have good times.
I ne'er can forget the happy days I drove a mule,
Playing tricks on the miners we ne'er learned in school.
And I'll tell you on the quiet, how 'tis we the miners fooled
As we'd go through their box, steal their oil and break their locks.
You may talk of side-shows and of fun,
Go down the mines and listen to an Irishman and a Hun,
And of all the shows you've ever seen, you'll say it takes the bun.
Listen to my tale of woe, for I'm going to let 'er go.

Paddy Glennon had a laborer with a very funny name,
Now the Hun was not to blame for he couldn't change his name,

Paddy liked the laborer, but he couldn't pronounce his name,
So he told the Hun quite plain: "John, you'll have to change your name."
The Hun he sez, "Shot op, you fool, you talkin' like cow,
I'm no change dat name, you no can tell me how.
My daddy fon old country sure is gib it me dat name,
You son-of-a-gun, I'm no can change, I'm leave it just de same."
Paddy then sure he lost his temper quite,
And at the poor Hungarian he swore with all his might,
He sez, "Me buck, you'll change your name, or me you'll have to fight."
Now the fighting is in vain for the Hun won't change his name.

I knew another miner, he was cunning as a fox,
He would sleep all day on the box,
His laborer workin' like an ox.
The other day while passing,
He was talking to the Hun,
Sez he, "John, load plenty lumps
Or they'll dock you at the dump."
"How I'm gonna load de lumps?
No got one coal fon de breast—
Ev'ry time you fire hole,
You make nottink but dust.
You t'ink I'm gonna steal it
Fon miners yudder breast?"
So with that he plunked the Hun
Sure he laid him in a lump
And the miner sacked the Hun
'Cause he wouldn't load the lumps.

On the eighth day of November I was huntin' with a gun,
Just above at Laurel Run, for it was there I seen the fun.
Standing at a pay-car was a miner and a Hun,
And the miner had the mon' but he wouldn't pay the Hun.
Paddy sez, "Now John, you got all you're gonna get."
The Hun he sez, "You son-of-a-gun, I'm get em two shifts yet."
Paddy sez, "You'll get it, but you'll get it in the neck."
And with that he plunked the Hun and he laid him in a lump.
"All right, Paddy, I'm tomorra fixin' squire."

"I don't care," sez Paddy, "if you go and fetch the Mayor."
And with that I seen a Hun go flying through the air.
Listen to me while I speak:
At the Huns' there is a wake,
And his funeral is tomorrow.
He received a nasty thump,
And they'll bury him in sorrow,
'Cause he wouldn't load the lumps.

A HUNGARIAN CHRISTENING

(AIR: *Happy to Meet and Sorry to Part*)

On Chewsday last week as I laid on the sofa
Me backbone was sore, for that day I worked hard,
When in came the woman and sez to me, "Dinny,
There's a Hungarian man wants you in the yard."
Well, I pulled on me boots and went out in the garden,
There stood John Shalonsky; sez he as he smiled,
"I want yerself and the woman on next Sunday morning
To come to the Duck Pond and stand for me child."

CHORUS

Well, I tried to refuse but he'd take no excuse,
For Hungarians are divils whene'er they get riled;
The woman says no, but sez I, "Yes, we'll go
On next Sunday morning and stand for the child."

When Sunday came round, sure I dressed in my latest,
Shirt, necktie and collar and brand new black suit;
And me wife, Mary Ann, in her silk and her ribbons,
Faith, Old Jay Gould's daughter ne'er looked so cute.
Well, we christened the child and it cost five dollars,
When I handed it over, the clergyman smiled,
And sez he, "You're the first Far Down e'er came from Ireland
To stand for a Slavish Hungarian man's child."

SECOND CHORUS

The Hungarians and Slavish ate cornbeef and cabbage
And poured whiskey in them till I thought they'd go wild;
I sat on me sate and 'fraid for to spake—
The day that I stood for the Hungarian child.

When we got to the house, sure I gazed on the dinner.
My woman then she sez "We'll ate none o' their rot."
There were lumps of boloney with fat pork and cabbage
And dried up store cakes with raisins on top.
They asked me to ate, I refused them politely.
Oh, my, when I did, sure I thought they'd go wild,
If I hadn't run, they would kill me complately
The day that I stood for the Hungarian child.

THIRD CHORUS

I made a bolt for the door, at the wife gave a roar,
"Come on, Mary Ann, for begorra they're wild."
There was a car passing by, I jumped on, on the fly,
With a curse on me lip for the Hun and his child.

A GREENHORN MAKES GOOD

Me vorking fer Prospect, me gotta gut job,
Ev'ry day mus' load six car un t'row slate fer gob.
Me no like dat Prospect, me go Number Two
Me asking Manus Vaters, he say no job fer you.

Me go Condy Cannon, asking him fer vork,
Condy no gibing, me asking Paddy Burke.
Paddy gibing job, now me vorking 'gain,
Me no like dat Paddy, him too lazy man.

Me betcha glass beer, Paddy drilling seven hole,
You go look fer his place, no got vun car coal.

Me bully gut laborer, boss telling me right,
Small drivers telling me Paddy Burke out o' sight.

Yest'day, sure, vas pay day, me vas go fer mine pay,
Me vas pass Paddy Burke's house; him live far away;
Un him holler, "Hello, Joe, how much shifts you got?"
Me telling him got seven shift un two car o' rock.

"Come on fer mine shanty, me pay dat fer you."
Him gib me t'backy box; "Joe you like chew?
Me no can pay you today, Joe, no got very much stuff,
You mus' lend me tventy-five cents, I no got 'nough."

"Checkai, Paddy Burke, me no vork you more,
You no can pay laborer, you no can pay store."
Me go asking boss fer breast on a flat
Him telling me go courthouse, get c'tificat'.

Me vas go fer courthouse; Judge gibing me note,
I dunt know whatchicallit, but somet'ing it wrote;
Un it say fon dat paper dat's de bully gut man you.
Showing fer de boss, get em Breast Number Two.

You know Pete, Paddy's brudder? Him laborer fer me.
Him used to vas laborer Pat Coyle, Number Three.
Dat's de bully gut laborer; ev'ry day load full coal
Dat's me cuckoo miner; me drilling plenty hole.

Me out o' sight miner, ev'ry mont's get beeg pay,
Me no greeny, ah me Engleesh vershtay.
But me nevair forgetting first time me vork
Fer dat lazy old son-of-a-gun, Paddy Burke.

THE HUNGARIAN BALL

Ah me last night got plenty fun,
At beeg, beeg ball fer vidow voman;
Costing feefty cents fer ticket,
George Shlavonsky him got kick-ed.

Four Engleesh boys punch his head,
Me ketch dat boys me kick em dead;
Dat mine brudder, George Shlavonsky,
Me helping him.
Me ketch dat boys me gib em kill,
Yes, me vill.
Me t'ink em come fon Brewery Hill, Viskey Hill,
Me dunt care fon v'ere em come,
Dat son-of-a-gun.
Me strong like onion—
Me kill em right away.

FIRST CHORUS

Me have gut time fer dat ball,
Me dance fer ev'ry gal,
Kate Kilbunk un Mary Slotsky,
Me dance fer Rosy Plotsky.
Me dancing Engleesh dance,
George Kabuch busting pants,
Me telling him crazy man,
Him telling me, "All right."

George Monsory too much drunk,
Him vant fight fer Andrew Bunk,
Andrew telling him "Dunt get fonny,
Go un fight dat George Zaloni."
George him say, "No sir, Mike,
Dat son-of-a-gun, him too gut fight."
Den dat man him going outside
Un taking sneak fer home.
George him say, "Me de stuff, dat man bluff,
Me fight you all,
Any man fer dese ball,
Beeg un small,
Me dunt care fer feefty men, hoondret men."
Me go op fer dat fella
Un me telling, "You shot op!"

SECOND CHORUS

Den him gib me fer crack,
Me gib him yudder one back,
Him get mine nose fer his mout'
Me tell him, "Son-of-a-gun, look out!"
Me t'rowing him down on floor,
Dat son-of-a-gun, me kick him sore,
Ev'ry voman starting roar
Un busting Hungarian ball.

POLINKY

Didja ever drink dat moo'shi'
  Lotsa people make?
Better you drink de rop on rats,
  Un eat de bleeny cake.
Ven you take it vun drink,
  Make you lotsa talk,
Op you take it yudder,
  Nevair you can valk.

CHORUS

Undertaker laffin'
  Ven him see you drink.
"Pulley soon a coffin
  Fer dat man," he's t'ink.
Den he's take de measure,
  Vantsa fix you nice;
He no vantsa see you drink again,
  He vantsa see you on de ice.

Make you feel de fonny,
  Yust like circy clown
Ven some people holler,
  "Enoch opside down."

V'ere is it moo'shi', no su'shi',
  No madder vat you sed,
Op you drink dat vooden viskey,
  Soon you goin' in debt.

Doctor come un tol' me,
  "Enoch, you too risky,
You vear dat vite-pine overcoach,
  Op you drink dat vooden viskey."
No more dat fonny biziness,
  I gonna tell you right,
I'm nevair keep de still again,
  I'm yus' meself keep qviet.

CHAPTER FIVE

Superstitions and Legends

THE miner made daily genuflections to the goddess Luck. He followed omens and carried charms and amulets. On the day shift of the mining necromancy were the devil, the "wise woman," or witch, and fairies. Ghosts haunted the mines and appeared in the patch at night.

The most common source of legends was strange sounds heard in the mines. The roar of accustomed noises which dazed a visitor from the surface left the miner undisturbed. But what ground his brain were the mysterious knocking, creaking, groaning and wailing which he heard during a lull in mining. Somewhere a rock or a large lump of coal, loosened from a cranny by some mysterious force, would drop suddenly with a tremendous thud. Far above his head there might be a crackling as the strata settled after a day of blasting. Deadly gases seeped through crevices in the coal, making a sound like the murmur of trickling water. Underground railway tracks would contract at night to the accompaniment of terrifying knocking. Water dripping on the reverse side of a shovel or on a hollow lump of coal in an isolated section of the mine might become so magnified in the awful stillness as to sound like alternate blows of a steel drill, as illustrated in the story "Ghostly Miners." These sounds once petrified miners and led to the spread of legends. The present-day miner recognizes them and is unmoved by them, but he hears noises of his own.

Mysterious knockings are heard in other kinds of mines and

are interpreted by the miners in accordance with varying local tradition. For example, in England the Cornish miners associate them with "knockers," mythical noise-making spirits believed to haunt their workings. In our Western mines, the knockings are believed to be the work of mischievous gnomes known as "tommy-knockers." Workers in the bituminous coal mines of Central and Western Pennsylvania have still different conceptions of their mysterious sounds, according to Colonel Henry W. Shoemaker, president of the Pennsylvania Folk Lore Society. "Some years ago," he states, "old miners employed in the Peale district of the bituminous coal fields in western Center County believed the knocking to come from small, but able-bodied beneficent spirits, dressed in gray, who went about the entries sounding the mine supports with small hammers to test their safety and giving voice to sounds like shrill whistles where a cave-in was imminent. Older miners in the Broad Top district of Huntingdon County ascribed the knocking to the throbbing of the earth, put to great pain by the miners' diggings and borings."

But in the anthracite industry, unknown sounds were always associated with ghosts, especially the ghosts of miners who had been killed while at work. Most of the ghosts were cripples who lacked limbs which had been blasted away. In a certain Schuylkill County mine, the headless ghost of a miner is supposed to have been seen riding through the labyrinthian tunnels on a mule.

Ghosts had various motives for returning to a mine. Revenge, as in the Hudsonryder legend, was one of them. Anxiety to complete a particular piece of work left unfinished by a fatal accident, as in "Ghostly Miners," was another. A third was a desire to help a former butty in his work, as illustrated by the following incident. In the Wyoming Valley was a Welsh miner who could load his mine car in less time than it took two miners working in an adjoining chamber to load theirs. Since his prodigiousness was of recent origin, his feat was attributed to the help that he was receiving from the ghost of a former butty who had been killed a short time before. The two miners regarded the common rumor with skepticism and decided to investigate. Leaving two laborers behind to load their own car, they entered the Welshman's chamber and gossiped with him so long that he could not possibly load any coal. But when they finally left him and came out into the heading again, there, to their utter amazement, was the Welshman's car loaded to the top with coal, waiting for the mules!

It is significant that apparitions were most commonly seen in the mines after a fatal accident. Undoubtedly optical illusions were more likely to be experienced during the mental strain and emotional disturbance that followed an accident. After the Avondale mine disaster in which one hundred and ten lives were lost, many men and boys refused to return to the mine because of a rumor that it was haunted. The legend originated shortly after the accident when a miner tried to strike a lucifer match, then an innovation, on his wet clothes. While he himself was not visible in the blackness of the gangway, the coruscation of the match gave the impression of a disembodied spirit. When another miner saw the coruscating flashes from a distance, he dropped his tools and ran helter-skelter, crying that he had seen ghosts of disaster victims.

Similarly, workers in a certain Schuylkill County colliery believed that the ghost of one of their fellow miners had visited the underground workings. The legend sprang up in the sixties shortly after a miner had been killed, and it passed into anthracite folklore. Several years ago I learned that the legend originated in a hoax played by two mischievous boys. They had smuggled a goat into the slope, tied a lighted candle between its horns and turned it loose in the gangway. Naturally the gangway was dark and the eery bobbing of the candle light through that blackness fairly petrified miners who saw it. Too frightened to investigate, they carried to the patch the news of a ghostly visitation and shocked the patchers into believing their story. The young rascals who had perpetrated the hoax held their tongues as they feared being trounced by their respective fathers, and thus abetted the perpetuation of the legend.

Anthracite miners did not welcome ghosts. They believed that the way to ward them off was to remain away from the workings several days after a fatal accident. Miners would drop their tools instantly on hearing that one of their comrades had been killed. To prevent a sudden shutdown, bosses would try to suppress the news until after the shift, but they rarely succeeded, owing to the efficiency with which the underground grapevine worked. The men would not return to their jobs until after the victim's funeral. This hoary custom clashed with the emergency created by the World War when uninterrupted production was necessary. The miners sacrificed it only when the operators had agreed to compensate them by allowing a full day's wages to pallbearers and donating one hundred and fifty dollars toward funeral expenses; this agreement between the union and the anthracite operators is still in force.

It was believed that mules, horses, dogs, and other domestic animals were able to see specters that were invisible to the human eye; this superstition is part of the Hudsonryder legend. There the mules balked at pulling the shattered body, apparently because they were frightened by Hudsonryder's apparition. A dog howling in the night portended an approaching death in the family, presumably because it had the power to see the apparition of death. The story is told of a dog that barked all night in Lannigan's Patch, Schuylkill County, and kept its master from going to work in the mines the next morning. The miner felt secure enough to see a baseball game in the afternoon, however. On his way home from the game he was killed by a fast freight train. Recently I asked a skeptical old miner whether it was really true that the nightly howling of a dog was a sign of death. "It would be," he said with a twinkle in his eye, "if I could get hold of a good-sized rock to throw at him."

The mining folk had a deep-seated fear of the night. They believed that the night air held all sorts of evil. One old Irish miner told me that his people fought like wildcats during the day, but that when night came they lost their nerve. A legend growing out of this fear centers around a large rock on the outskirts of Silver Creek Patch in the Schuylkill Valley. The Molly Maguires had murdered a peddler at this rock, so the legend goes, and to avenge his death, the peddler's ghost haunted it—at night. There were people living in Silver Creek a half century ago who swore by all that was sacred that they had seen the ghost and even heard it wail. So vivid and terrible was this illusion that even strong men would take to their heels when they passed the rock "after lamplight." One poor soul imagined that the ghost was following him all the way to the nearby town of New Philadelphia, and ran so heedlessly that he plunged into the creek and was drowned.

With the introduction of technological improvements and safety appliances, anthracite mines are becoming less spooky, but it is doubtful that they ever will be entirely free of ghosts. In 1927 an explosion rocked the Woodward colliery, one of the most scientifically equipped in the Wyoming Valley. Many workers were injured and seven were killed. Despite repeated searches, five of the bodies have not been recovered. This has given rise to a legend that the ghosts of the five miners stalk through the workings at night.

The gentle ticking sound coming from mine timbers which a miner occasionally heard in the stillness led to the adaptation of the old English superstition of the death-watch tick. However, instead of a watch ticking to portend death, as in the legend, what the miner probably heard was a sound caused by an insect lodged in the timber. About two centuries ago, Jonathan Swift prescribed as follows for the recovery of a patient condemned by the death-watch tick:

> A kettle of scalding hot water injected
> Infallibly will die, and the sick will recover.
> The omen is broken, the danger is over,
> The maggot will die, and the sick will recover.

The scurry of rats on the mine floor was a familiar sound and occasioned no surprise except when they swarmed in large numbers in the direction of the shaft. This was a sure sign of impending disaster; and it is precisely for this reason that the presence of rats was regarded as a friendly omen. Some years ago one of the larger corporations issued an order that the rats in a certain colliery located in the west end of Schuylkill County should be exterminated because they were eating too much of the mules' feed. The order was not heeded.

Rats entered the mines with the hay that was taken down the slope or shaft for the mules. They took up quarters below, throve and increased rapidly, and grew to enormous size. They were bold and aggressive, and when attacked could turn on an enemy, whether man or beast, and fight to the death. No miner would deliberately kill a rat, believing as he did that that rat might some day be the means of saving his life. An aged miner told me that when, as a young man, he worked at the Ellengowan colliery near Shenandoah, his pet rodent snatched the lid of his dinner pail containing a cut of pie and scurried off with it down the gangway. The miner said that he chased the rat for some distance until he finally retrieved both lid and pie. Shortly afterward, the same rat returned and once again ran off with the lid and pie, and again the miner had to give chase. Believing that it was the pie that was tempting the rat, the miner ate it. However, the rat ran off with the lid a third time. My friend had lost his patience and vowed to kill the rat, but while he was away the roof caved in and many tons of rock and coal crashed down on the very spot where he had been squatting. "You see," he said, "that rat was trying in its own way to warn me and thus saved my life."

The popular myth, prevalent among people unfamiliar with mining, that mules went blind in the mines, was punctured at the start of the great anthracite strike of 1925. Of some fifty thousand mules brought to the surface, most of which had been underground many years, not a single one was found blind. This is easily explained. While the mines are dark, they are not wholly without light. The underground mule stables were always well lighted, and the turnout, to which were brought coal cars from many parts of the mine, fairly scintillated with incandescent lamps. The sudden change from the electrically lighted mines to daylight merely discomforted the mules, just as it would human beings. Incidentally, when mules were brought to the surface at the beginning of a strike it was regarded as an ill omen, and the people prepared for a long suspension. It was expensive to bring the mules to the surface, and they reasoned that the coal operators would not incur that expense unless the mines were to be idle a long time. Mules have virtually disappeared from the industry and in their place have come "electric mules," as the motor-driven locomotives are called.

If a miner on his way to the colliery were to meet a red-haired woman he would curse his luck and turn back in order to avoid the evil consequences. In some districts, this taboo embraced all womanhood, and so women remained indoors until their men had disappeared down the shaft. Of course, at no time was a mere female permitted inside a mine, for fear that she might lay a spell on it. It is interesting to observe, parenthetically, that this fear of woman's evil charms is a survival from the most primitive times of the human race, and still plays an important part in the daily lives of primitive peoples. Margaret Mead, the anthropologist, tells us that in British New Guinea the Melanesians have invented what they call the *Tamberan,* a fearful mythical monster, to frighten their women into seclusion when there is a man's work to be done. Savages believe that women possess magical powers for bringing men bad luck.

No miner would think of starting a new job, or moving, on a Friday.

Once he had put away his tools and had started home, a miner would not for any reason return to his breast. To do so would be courting death. Many cases were cited to me of miners being killed when they had violated this tradition.

Ascension Day has always been a day of idleness in the industry. This is not due entirely to the fact that it is a sacred holiday in the Catholic Church. It is a generally observed mining tradition, even in Protestant England.

The crumbs in a miner's dinner pail were believed to have marvelous curative properties. Old-timers have a vivid recollection of children stopping them when they emerged from the mine at the end of a shift to beg them for crumbs.

For a long time there was only one cure for whooping cough—powder smoke. A child suffering from this dread disease would be carried into the mine by its father. Its clothing would be opened at the throat to permit easier breathing, and then it would be exposed to the sulphurous fumes released by miners firing shots in the coal along a heading in quick succession.

Miners carried charms and amulets into the mine to ward off injury or death. Of course Roman Catholics had their crucifixes and holy images blessed by the parish priest. In the west-end section of Schuylkill County where the Pennsylvania Germans predominated, many miners carried a piece of paper on which a local powwower had scrawled the following charm, the name of the individual miner being written into the blank space:

Jesus walketh with ——.
He is my head,
I am His limb,
Therefore, Jesus walketh with ——.

If an injured mine worker were Catholic, his parish priest was summoned to give him spiritual comfort, while the local "wise woman" administered her home-made remedies and specifics. Among the Russians, the wise women were known as "znaharkhi," and among the Pennsylvania Germans "hex-women," or "powwow women." If a Pennsylvania German miner had been burned in an explosion, a "hex-woman" dressed his burns to the accompaniment of these lines from Hohman's *hexabuch,* and the usual invocation of the Holy Trinity:

Three holy men went on a journey,
They blessed the heat and the burning.

They blessed it that it may not increase,
They blessed it that it may quickly cease.

The "wise woman," by whatever name she was known, was an institution in every mine patch. Her remedies and specifics generally were concocted from roots, herbs, barks, and blossoms grown in the coal fields. These crones were essentially practical nurses who could dress injuries almost as well as the surgeons. They also had a knowledge of drugs. But they held the people's faith by their reputed possession of occult powers. The workers were still close enough to peasant lore to believe that disease and injury were caused by evil spirits which had to be exorcised by spells and incantations. The fear of the evil eye was general.

An insight into some of the primitive practices of wise women in a patch atop Locust Mountain during the seventies and eighties was given to me by one of its aged inhabitants.

A headache, he said, was believed to have been caused by a separation of the bones of the skull. The patient's head was bound tightly with a handkerchief until such time as the bones came together and the headache vanished.

A fallen palate was believed to be the cause of a cold. As the patient squatted on the floor, the wise woman inserted her middle finger under the palate and held the back of the head with her free hand. A cure was effected when the palate was restored to its normal position.

To cure a sore, feverish throat, the wise woman blew several times into the patient's mouth to cool it off.

If a speck of dust irritated a patient's eye, the wise woman would go into the adjoining room with a saucer. This she held before her as she muttered some spell. Suddenly the speck would leave the patient's eye and land squarely on her saucer.

The seventh son of a seventh son was believed to have the power to cure erysipelas, then a common disease. But the powers of posthumous children were even more miraculous, and they were anxiously sought when the wise woman had given up a case as hopeless.

Before the Civil War, when Welsh, English, and Scots were

in the majority, June 25 was observed as Mid-Summer Day. As twilight fell over the patches, bonfires were lighted on the hillsides. Girls came to watch the fires and imagined that they saw the faces of their future husbands in the crackling flames.

The legend associated with St. Swithin's Day was paralleled in the Feast of the Visitation of the Virgin Mary, known in the anthracite coal fields as "Mary goes over the mountain." The Feast commemorates the visit which the expectant mother of the Lord made to her cousin Elizabeth to see the newly born babe who was to grow up to be John the Baptist. The mining folk believed that if it rained on the day "Mary goes over the mountain" forty days of rainfall would follow.

It is interesting to observe how strikingly parallel were the superstitions and picturesque customs of the English-speaking miners and those of the Germans and the Slavs.

There was also a similarity between certain phases of Pennsylvania German *hexerei* and the superstitious practices found among Slavic miners. In view of this similarity, it was no surprise that the only hex murder in the history of the anthracite region was committed a few years ago not by a Pennsylvania German, but by a young Slav. He told the police that his victim, whom he described as "a widow witch," had so bewitched him as to deprive him of his peace of mind. "She appeared in my room at night in the form of a black cat with horrible green eyes," he said.

Irish keeners were known in the hard coal fields as "paid criers," and their counterpart among the Russians were the *plakalshchitsa.* In both cases these public wailers were gifted with eloquent tongues, and played skillfully on the emotions of mourners. They carried on a tradition that in their own countries went back for centuries. It was said that they had the power to wring tears even from a stone. The story is told of a "paid crier" near Pottsville who at a disreputable miner's funeral was so fulsome in her eulogy as to cause the widow to turn to her daughter and remark, "Mary, is there another caarpse in the room?"

THE PHILLIP GINDER LEGEND

It is told that Phillip Ginder, a German settler of the Mahoning Valley, was hunting on the summit of Sharp Mountain in 1791 when a sudden fall of rain caused him to direct his weary footsteps homeward, even though he had not shot any game. Plodding along, he accidentally stumbled over something hard which he kicked before him. Dusk was falling but there was enough light for him to see that it was black. Curious, he picked it up and examined it closely. Its surface washed by the rain, the stone gleamed, which reminded him of the rumor that coal lay embedded in the mountain. So he carried several specimens home and the next day showed them to Colonel Jacob Weiss, a former Philadelphian, who had retired to the frontier settlement that is now Weissport.

In the belief that they were really coal, Weiss took them to Philadelphia, where several capitalists confirmed his belief and authorized him to reward the German farmer for his discovery—provided he show where the coal lay. The simple Ginder declined a cash reward for an act which apparently he regarded of little significance. But he offered to take Weiss to the outcrop of the coal vein if he would obtain for him a warrant to a tract of land containing a mill-site in the Mahoning Valley which Ginder believed to be unclaimed. To this Weiss agreed eagerly. The following year Ginder took possession of the tract consisting of four hundred acres in Penn Township, part of the present Carbon County.

He lived to a ripe old age on this homestead which literally he had hacked out of the primeval wilderness. He loved his acres and expected to end his days on them. But fate intervened. One day a stranger appeared with papers showing that the tract was his by right of a prior survey. The heart-broken Ginder was forced to leave. Where he moved no one knows to this day.

Meanwhile Weiss had prepared a prospectus in which he represented himself as "the discoverer of a certain coal mine" and together with some capitalists had formed the Lehigh Coal Mine Company to exploit the coal; subsequently about ten thousand acres of unclaimed coal-bearing lands on the mountain were taken up.

However, with Philadelphia prejudiced against "stone coal," because of a lack of knowledge as to how to make it burn, and with transportation facilities from the source inadequate, the property was of small value at this time.

Philadelphia industries had been using "sea" coal from England, but the war of 1812 cut off the supply. This was anthracite's big opportunity. Colonel George Shoemaker, enterprising Pottsville innkeeper and pioneer operator, brought nine wagonloads of "stone coal" from his primitive mine near Pottsville, but so hostile was the City of Brotherly Love that he disposed of two wagonloads for a song and gave the rest away to those promising to burn it. Unable to burn the gift coal, some of the recipients ungratefully sought the colonel's arrest as an impostor and swindler. Luckily for him—and for the future of the industry—some of his coal had found its way into the furnace of a rolling mill, where it was burned successfully. Pleased with the results, the mill operators told the world about it through the medium of the press.

This led other mill operators to experiment with the new fuel from up state. Among them were two Quakers, Josiah White and Erskine Hazard, who owned a wire mill at the Falls of the Schuylkill. Their first cartload, which had been floated into Philadelphia on freshets of the Lehigh and Delaware rivers by means of crude arks, was wasted. A second cartload was bought and the mill workers spent a whole night trying to burn it. When dawn came they slammed the furnace door and went home in despair. A half hour later one of them returned to the mill for his jacket, which he had left hanging on a nail. To his amazement he found the furnace door red hot, and when he opened it, lo and behold! the coal was burning at a glowing white heat. He quickly called the other hands, who learned anthracite's secret: let it alone and it will burn itself.

HUDSONRYDER'S GHOST

There have been some shocking accidents at the Big Vein colliery in which many a good man has lost his life. And whenever a serious accident occurred, who in the Schuylkill Valley hasn't heard some old-timer remark, "Hudsonryder's curse is on them workin's still"?

It recalls a legend which goes back to the early sixties when Hudsonryder worked at the Big Vein, then operated by the Kaska William Coal Company. He was an atheist, and his church-going fellow miners ostracized him—avoided him as if he were a leper. This treatment hurt Hudsonryder and he vowed revenge.

One morning, while walking along the gangway on his way to work, he was halted by the fireboss who warned him that he had detected a feeder of gas in his working place.

"You'll find out whether there is a God or not if you go up there with that open flame," said the pious old fireboss sneeringly.

This stung Hudsonryder and, despite the danger, he strode on. As was to be expected, his lamp set off the gas and he was blown to pieces. His fellow miners gathered his shattered body in a canvas sheet and carried it down to the gangway where they placed it in a mine car. "Hudsonryder's gone at last!" cried one of the miners. "An atheist has met his retribution," said another.

Hardly had the latter spoken when a weird, unearthly cry pierced the stillness which petrified all within its hearing. A disembodied voice recognizable as that of Hudsonryder came out of the blackness hissing revenge.

"Hudsonryder is appearing!" yelled one of the men when he found his tongue. He and the others wanted to flee, but they were unable to budge their mule. It struck fire in the roof with its hoofs. The men concluded that the mule was seeing the ghost. So they unhitched it and quickly brought another mule in its place. But this one was every bit as balky as the other, and so a third mule was tried and it too balked at pulling Hudsonryder's remains.

In desperation the men got an old blind mule and hitched it to the car. Unable to see the ghost, it needed no prodding to drag the car up the slope. When the surface was reached Hudsonryder's remains were transferred to a straw-filled wagon and taken to the Hudsonryder cottage. The blood-stained clothes were thrown on a rail fence, which instantly went up in flames.

On the day of the funeral, an undertaker came from Middleport with a handsome hearse and two fine horses. But when the coffin was placed inside the hearse, the horses grew violent and worked themselves into a lather. And they refused to go forward. The mourners knew the reason soon enough as the shrill, unearthly cry of Hudsonryder's ghost filled the valley. Strong men quaked in their boots, and women and children ran screaming to their homes.

In the end, the undertaker's handsome hearse and fine horses were forced to return to Middleport without the remains, and the old blind mule, torn from its browsing in the fields, was again pressed into service. Hitched to an ash cart, it drew to the little cemetery along the pike all that remained of the atheist.

Before the sun had set that day, the miners of Big Vein felt the effect of Hudsonryder's revenge. Investigating the extent of the damage caused by the explosion which had killed Hudsonryder, the fireboss found that the vein had caught fire and was now crackling and hissing with a terrible combustion. All the primitive facilities then available for mine fire-fighting were used, but the flames defied all efforts to quench them; water accumulated, the mine was abandoned, and the poor miners were compelled to look elsewhere for a living.

Deserted, the colliery and its patch took on a ghostly appearance. The narrow-gauge railroad tracks in the yard became rusty and weeds filled the spaces between the ties; vegetation forced itself through the rock heap and the culm bank; brush obliterated all trace of human paths; most of the miners' shanties crumbled. The quiet air echoed the shrieks of catamounts, and wild game came down from Broad Mountain.

For about twenty years Big Vein Patch was deserted. Independent operators lacked the nerve to rest a pick on this accursed ground, even though they had the capital to reopen the mine. A big corporation finally took over the old workings and sank a shaft several hundred feet from Hudsonryder's white-ash slope. Far beneath the surface, a tunnel was driven to meet it so they could tap its stagnant water. This water was drained into the sump and from there was hoisted to the surface. When the last tankful of water had been removed there was rejoicing among engineers and mine officials. "This ought to put an end to the nonsense about the vengeance of Hudsonryder's ghost," they said.

The miners of the Schuylkill Valley, however, did not share their optimism, and stayed away from the Big Vein employment office. To convince them that they were wrong the company had hundreds of rats carried to the bottom and placed in gangways, headings, and breasts and in the deepest recesses of the mine. Not a rat remained. Instinctively they found their way to the bottom of the shaft and one by one clambered up its sides.

Unable to obtain the full quota of miners and laborers in the Schuylkill Valley, the company went outside for help. Evidences of Hudsonryder's spell are seen in the fall of timbers, the collapse of countless tons of upper strata, in gas explosions and in at least one disastrous flood, all taking a toll of human life.

THE DEVIL IN A STRANGE RÔLE

In the seventies there lived in Schuylkill County a stable boss who had forgotten God. His parish priest for many years had tried to win him back to the fold, but died without accomplishing it. His successor, a young man full of missionary zeal, heard of him on his first Sunday in the parish. Standing at the open sacristy window before mass he observed him plodding along the country road toward the colliery.

"Who's that going to work on the Sabbath?" he asked his sexton.

"That, your Riverence," replied the sexton, "is old Jack Boyle, stable boss of the slope, who is as hard as rock. He's on his way for to feed his mules inside."

"Does he always feed his mules on the Sabbath?"

"That he does, your Riverence, and it's the same he's been doing as long as I ever knew."

"He ought to give a thought to his Church, too," said the priest.

"The late fa-ather, may he rest in peace, often told the same to Jack but it didn't do no good. They say that the two of 'em had a diff'rence many years ago and Jack swore he'd never come inside the church again—unless driven by the devil. Jack's not the one to be shp'akin' about it, but I heard it 'tanny rate."

"A strange vow indeed," mused the priest.

The young priest, resolved to win the man's soul back to God, dogged his footsteps to plead the cause of the Church to him, but Jack remained obdurate and went his own way.

Months later his favorite daughter was to be married to a mine laborer. In giving the couple his blessing he warned that they must not have banns announced in church. That created a scandal. The bridegroom's people threatened to prevent the marriage. The young couple finally ran off and were married in the city.

This nettled the young priest, but remembering his mission he maintained a calm outward manner, exercising true Christian forbearance. However, he did take the occasion to warn the stable boss that he could not be buried in consecrated ground and expect salvation if he continued to live in such open defiance of God. Jack was impressed by the force of this warning, but still did not change his ways.

Some time later he was kicked by a vicious mule. At the hospital the surgeons gave him up for lost, and the priest administered the last sacraments of the Church. But to the surprise of the surgeons and to himself most of all, Jack managed to pull through. When he returned home the young priest called to congratulate him on his remarkable recovery.

"Your recovery was a miracle," said the priest. "Even the doctors at the hospital had said there was no hope for you. You ought to show your gratitude by turning a new leaf and coming back into the fold."

"I'm a lost sheep, I admit," Jack replied with a shrug of the shoulder. "But if God can do for me what you say he did, and me a sinner, well then, I'm just as well off outside the Church as in it, don't you think?"

The young priest had no answer. He took his hat and strode out, virtually giving up the stable boss for lost. There the matter stood until one Sunday morning when Jack Boyle had a strange experience. He was walking down the traveling way of the slope to feed his mules when he was startled by an apparition following him. He perceived it to be the devil. He walked faster but the devil kept pace with him. He started to run and—would you believe it?—the devil ran right after him, but was discreet enough to keep a few paces behind. When the bottom of the slope was finally reached, the devil let out a shrill, unearthly, and blood-curdling yell and disappeared into the depths of the mine. Jack gamely proceeded to the stable, but fed his mules with an unsteady hand.

When he was through, he turned his footsteps toward the village church. His face ashen, his body atremble, he knelt before the priest. "Your Riverence," he said, "I've just seen the devil and—and I reckon I want God now."

THE LEGEND OF THE BURNING MINE

It is not generally known that the Heckscherville Valley was once a mecca of seekers after the proverbial fountain of youth. Old residents point out the exposed roasted rock in an abandoned stripping on Broad Mountain at Coal Castle as evidence of the existence of the fabulous "burning mine." The last surviving link with that fantastic episode was James Moore, who died in 1932 at the age of eighty-six. His little home was at Thomaston close by.

He recalled how the valley lay under a barrage of smoke and steam, the heat so intense that it interpenetrated the rocky strata above it; caused great cracks in the mountain surface and the caving in of the earth. Out of these craters, hot sulphurous fumes and hissing vapors belched forth. The burned surface nevertheless retained its greenness, he said, even in the winter, when it was in striking contrast to the rest of the snow-covered valley.

The miners drank the thermal water and bathed in it, to regain their youthful strength and agility. The water not only healed the miners' ordinary cuts, bruises, and swellings, but cleared their skins of various eruptions and banished, as if by magic, the most severe rheumatic pains. Bent bodies and twisted limbs were restored to complete naturalness by the water.

The story goes that even a decrepit and wheezy old mine mule, turned loose to die in the pastures, drank the water in the marshy pool and returned to the mine as springy and graceful as a colt.

The fire is believed to have started one winter in the 1830's when mine workers were driving a drift on the great jugular coal vein. The water which dripped down from the surface through the timbering congealed in huge stalactites and lined the interior with brilliant glacial crystals, a magnificent spectacle which the practical miners, intent on getting their work done, regarded as a hindrance. So on a Saturday afternoon they kindled a fire under the walls and went home hoping that all would be melted over the week end. When they returned to work Monday morning they found the timbers blackened and charred and the coal vein itself burning fiercely and discharging volumes of sulphurous gases. Their livelihood endangered, they put up a valiant fight to extinguish the fire. But they failed and the mine was abandoned.

For many years the mountain continued to smoulder and hiss and belch like a volcano. The water that drained out of the burning mine naturally was hot, but it was not until about a quarter century later that the secret of the water's rejuvenating powers was learned. Workers in the employ of John McGuinness, a pioneer coal operator, were driving a slope under the burning level when the hot water from above penetrated their stout, waterproof boots. They cursed their bad luck until they took their boots off and then, to their amazement, found that the hot waters had washed away their corns and bunions, leaving their feet rested and soothed!

The subsequent miracles performed by this fabulous mine water excited the interest and curiosity of people everywhere. Travelers helped spread the news by describing how the mine workers went about with heads erect, singing and laughing as if they hadn't a care in the world. Miners began trekking to this modern Elysian field from all parts of the region in search of their lost youth. They trudged on foot or came on horseback or in crude wagons over rough roads and through a forbiddingly rough country. Each day scores of them, bringing casks, hogsheads, and barrels, poured into the narrow valley to take the elixir to their fellow workers back home. The supply seemed inexhaustible.

It was not long before people in distant cities—Philadelphia and New York included—flooded the valley with orders for hogsheads and barrels of the magical water. Some miners shipped it outside the region for profit, and at this the devout old Irish people shook their heads, for in their eyes this was a desecration. The Lord would be wroth!

The day came when their misgivings were realized. The snow no longer melted on the mountain in winter. Its water became like any other sulphurous mine water. The magic mine had grown cold!

Thus ended Heckscherville Valley's dream that it was the seat of the fountain of youth.

GHOSTLY MINERS

Jim never got over the shock when his only boy Mickey was killed by a premature blast in Number Seven Slope.

Jim's job was driving a gangway on the second level below the breast in which Mickey had met his death. It was customary in those early days for gangway men to start the work-week on Sunday night, which explains why Jim and his laborer, Tommy Leary, were the only human beings in their section of the mine at the time the following events took place.

Since Mickey's death, Jim always fingered his rosary beads and recited prayers for the repose of the boy's soul before starting to work. One evening, while lost in abstraction in the midst of the prayers, he was startled by a loud, muffled noise coming from above. It sounded like two men striking alternate blows on a jumper, a bar of steel used in those days as a rock drill. He knew that the men who occupied Mickey's breast on the day shift were not there, as he had met them lying on the village green when he was coming to work. But there was no ignoring the unceasing, eery sound. After listening for a moment he walked to the face of the gangway, where Tommy was making squibs.

"Phat do you make of it, Tommy?" he asked. But the frightened Tommy could not find his tongue.

"Phat do you make of it?" he repeated.

The laborer remained mute. When he ignored the question a third time, Jim grabbed him by the arms and demanded an answer.

"Two men hammering on a jumper!" Tommy finally said in a trembling voice.

"That's phat it sounds to me too," said Jim, releasing his hold; "I'm thinking it's me own Mickey and Paddy Ryan returned to clane up the job they was workin' at when they was blowed up."

"Saints above!" Tommy made the sign of the cross.

"I remember how the lad—be you listenin'?—I remember how the lad was bent on clanin' up that last length."

Jim sighed. The muffled sounds of ghosts at work overhead went on.

"Didja ever talk with ghosts, lad?" asked Jim earnestly.

"No."

"Well, it's me that's wishin' I knew how—ugh, I'm a-goin' up there."

He started to climb the monkey ladder leading to the breast, but Tommy caught him by the arm and refused to let him go. "Is it mad you are, Jim?" he said in a frightened, hushed voice. "Would you scare the lad away?"

"Guess you're right."

Jim thought hard for several moments. Then, cupping his mouth, he shouted up the manway:

" 'Lo, Mickey, it's me that's down here, your own fa-ather."

The words "Mickey" and "fa-ather" seemed louder than the rest of the sentence as the miner had stressed them. To poor Jim, in his excited mental state, they seemed to echo greetings from above, and he became electrified.

"Didja hear it, didja now?" he shouted at Tommy as he shook him. Tommy was petrified. "That's me Mickey's ghost. Sure it is. He's come back with Paddy Ryan for to clane up that last length."

As Jim nervously walked back and forth, alternately talking with Mickey's ghost and listening to the awful hammering above, not an inch of gangway advanced that night. At quitting time, he told the boss what had happened.

"Ah, come on, stop your kiddin', Jim," said he in a crushing, matter-of-fact way.

"So help me Jasus," Jim insisted as he made the sign of the cross. "Mickey and Paddy Ryan were in their breast last night. I'll swear to it. Why, it's me that talked with 'em, like I'm talkin' to you. They said they came back for to clane up that last length so's they wouldn't have anything on their minds in the other world. So if you please, have a keg of powder and enough cartridge paper for 'em tonight."

The boss shook his head ruefully. Jim had gone clean out of his mind.

THE DEATH-WATCH TICK

A miner was buried alive by a pillar of coal which he was robbing. After his body was dug out it was discovered that his watch was still in the mine. It was not hanging on a timber in the heading where he usually kept it but was buried in the gob, where it ticked away unseen.

It soon gave evidence of being the most amazing timepiece. Its chief function seemed to be to forecast the approach of death, and so uncannily accurate was it that miners feared it more than the devil. It flitted all through the mine, going from one working place to another and inflicting itself upon this miner or that, depending upon whom fate had marked for death. No one could learn in advance where or when it would appear. Always it announced its arrival by ticking. The ticking was slightly louder than that of an ordinary watch but marked by the same relentlessness. There was no use trying to smash it with one's pick, or to blow it up with a stick of dynamite. Sooner could one smash or blow up one's shadow. The death watch eluded all measures of force and merely mocked men's curses. It was as inevitable as death itself. There were stretches of weeks or months when it kept silent. Then with the suddenness of a fall of top rock, there would come the fateful tick-tock. . . .

One night, while on his accustomed tour of inspection, the fireboss was astounded to hear the death-watch tick. It sounded so weird and awesome in that empty mine! There were fear and pity in his heart for Jim Kelly in whose working place the watch was ticking.

When morning came, the fireboss was in his station along the gangway and waved Jim aside when he came up for his brass check.

"In the name of God, Jim, go back home," he said.

"What's the matter?" asked Jim.

"Now in the name of God, do as I tell ye. You'll be thankful to me later on."

But Jim, with seven hungry little mouths to feed, could not afford to miss a day, and for that reason insisted on knowing why he was being called off.

"Well, if I must tell ye, Jim, I heard the—the death-watch tick in your heading last night as plain as ever I heard anything. Don't go in there or it's kilt you'll be."

"The death-watch tick!"

Jim turned deathly pale. The dinner pail trembled in his hand. He turned back.

Now there was gratitude in Jim's heart for being spared the fate, as he thought, of so many of his fellow miners, and he knew of no better way to celebrate his defeat of the death-watch tick than by attending church. Looking at his watch he found that he could still make the eight o'clock mass and so hurried home to change his clothes. To reach the church from his home he had to go over a railroad grade crossing. When he got there he found the gates down. Rather than wait and take a chance of missing the mass, he ran across the tracks. But he was not fast enough. The 7:55 flyer mowed him down.

THE PEDDLER'S GRAVE

In the midst of a forest of scrub oak on a level stretch of the Mahanoy Mountain there is a lone grave. It lies just off the old Catawissa road opposite a reservoir built many years ago by a coal company to supply its local collieries with water. A slab of ground glass and cement, surmounted by a cross of the same material, marks the grave. It bears the following epitaph:

Jost Folhaber
Died August 20
1797

In the lower right-hand corner appear the initials "L. J. B." which belong to the man who conceived the memorial.

This is the peddler's grave, around which a pretty legend has grown in the Mahanoy Valley. The memorial was put up a quarter of a century ago by men of Jackson's Patch, the nearest mine settlement, who knew of the peddler only by tradition. Long before they reared this memorial, paths had been blazed through the underbrush leading to the solitary grave. Pilgrims from far and near came to view it. In those days the grave was marked by a rude, unsodded white graveled mound with small heaps of stone arranged at the head and foot.

Even today a spray of flowers occasionally may be found on it. In the summer, when children of the valley's mine patches go up the mountain to pick huckleberries, they pause before the peddler's grave to sing songs and strew upon it the wild flowers they have picked. On Memorial Day pilgrims come to this shrine from all parts of the Mahanoy Valley to bank the grave with fresh flowers and pay their respects to the memory of a poor peddler who met a gruesome death on that lonely mountain road many, many years ago.

That peddler's name was Jost Folhaber. Who was he? Where did he come from? How did he happen to be buried in this lonely retreat? A Schuylkill County history refers to him as a Jewish peddler, which, if true, would make him the first Jew in the anthracite region; this is not strange, as Jews were among Pennsylvania's earliest Indian traders, peddlers, and settlers. Another history states that he probably came from "Old Berks," which in 1797 still took in that area that now forms

Schuylkill County. There were thriving Jewish communities in Old Berks, and Folhaber might have used one of them as a base for his journeys through the wilderness. He was known to travel between Reading and Catawissa. He carried light wares for personal and domestic use, and his saddlebags were usually filled with old copper coins, the proceeds of his sales.

In his day most of the territory now included in Schuylkill County was still in a virgin state. South of the Broad Mountain, including the site of Pottsville, was a vast swamp known as "the Pine Swamp"; north of the mountain was a dense forest known by the Indian name of Shamokin. There were Indian paths through this wilderness and an occasional hunters' trail, but few roads. Traveling was done by horseback, and was difficult and dangerous. A few white men scattered through the wilderness lived by the game they shot and the fish they caught in the silvery streams.

Early on the morning of August 11, 1797, Jost Folhaber dismounted at a log tavern run by a German named John Reich in what is now Mahanoy City. The log structure was a way station on Mears' Road, later known as the Old Catawissa Road. Folhaber put the feed bag on his horse, and, taking his pack and saddlebags with him, entered the tavern for breakfast.

Sitting across the table from him was a thirty-one-year-old New Jersey adventurer named Benjamin Bailey, well dressed but empty of pocket. He had been a guest at the tavern for ten days, paying for his board and lodging with game that he shot in the vicinity. The jingle of coins in the peddler's saddlebags aroused his cupidity, and he decided to rob him. The unfortunate peddler, unaware of the young fellow's sinister motives, unwittingly allowed himself to be drawn out on those details which would aid Bailey in robbing him.

After breakfast Folhaber mounted his horse and rode off toward the mountain on his way presumably to Catawissa. Bailey remained behind long enough to avoid suspicion, and then, pretending that he was going hunting, set out for the mountain in pursuit of Folhaber.

Arriving at Waste House Run, a mountain spring, the peddler stopped to pick huckleberries and relieve his horse of pack and saddlebags. While strolling leisurely along the mountain road he was shocked to see Bailey coming out of the bush with a gun. He ran back to his horse, but before he could reach him a bullet from Bailey's gun had caught him in the back. He dropped to the ground with groans of pain and Bailey cleaved his head with a tomahawk. He dragged the body off the road into the bushes and nervously went through Folhaber's pack and saddlebags. He was stunned to find that the fortune he had anticipated amounted to only about five pounds in copper coins. He tied Folhaber's horse at a place in the woods where he could not be seen from the road. Before returning to the Reich tavern he washed his blood-stained hands in the spring and hid his blood-spattered coat and the peddler's pack and saddlebags, the latter still containing the coppers.

When he arrived coatless at the tavern, the landlord's wife asked him what had become of his coat.

"I lost it," he lied.

Three days later Bailey screwed up enough nerve to return to the scene of his crime. The horse was still there but when he attempted to mount it the animal, too weak from lack of food to carry him, caved in under him. Bailey thereupon shot him and struck him a blow with the same tomahawk with which he had finished his master. Before returning to the tavern, he hid such goods as he thought he could later carry away and buried the copper coins in a separate place.

He decided to flee—it was singular that he had not aroused suspicion up to this time—and went to the mountain again the next day, to search in vain for the copper coins. To his amazement the horse was still alive, and instead of putting him out of his agony with another shot, he abandoned him to his fate, and set out for Catawissa.

Folhaber's body was not discovered until August 26. Though decomposed, it was identified as that of the murdered peddler; the crushed skull and bullet wound were grim evidence of the gruesome manner in which Folhaber had been dispatched.

Justice moved swiftly even for those primitive times. Officers of the law set out to track the fugitive through the wilderness. They finally caught up with him in Easton, and when arrested Bailey not only denied the crime, but blamed Reich, the tavern keeper who had befriended him. This led to Reich's arrest on a bench warrant. Bailey was taken to Reading, Berks County seat, and locked up in the old colonial jail. He was indicted and tried before Judge Jacob Rush and a jury on November 9. The trial lasted twenty-four hours, and resulted in Bailey's conviction. The death sentence pronounced, January 8, 1798, was set as the date of execution.

Several days before the hanging, Bailey attempted suicide by cutting a blood vessel with a piece of glass. To prevent future similar attempts he was chained to the floor. Between midnight and two o'clock on the morning of the execution he made a complete confession of the crime, absolving Reich. He blamed evil companions for his downfall, pointing the finger at himself as a horrible example of the ruin that overtakes one who yields to "the wiles of the devil and the guiles of lewd women."

The hanging took place on the Reading Commons, now a public park, in the presence of seven thousand people. Drawn by morbid curiosity, the spectators, bringing lunch and liquor, had come from long distances on horseback and by team.

An execution was then regarded in the same light as a horse race or a militia drill and was a rowdy affair. Public hangings were finally abolished in 1834.

Bailey's last words on the scaffold were, "God be merciful to me, a sinner."

One day in August 1880, five boys were playing at digging up Indian arrows near the mule stables of Lawton's old slope, a short distance from Mahanoy City, when they unearthed green copper coins of pre-Revolutionary mintage. Great excitement prevailed as a result of the discovery—as great as that which followed the arrival of the first box-car of "hornless and tailless hunkies" from across the ocean. Lawton's Patch was literally turned upside down by treasure hunters, spurred by rumors of buried gold. But their yield was only the copper coins which Bailey had robbed from Folhaber's saddlebags and buried as he took flight after the murder.

OLD JOHN, THE PEDDLER

Many years ago a peddler, remembered as Old John, often came to the mine patches of the Panther Creek Valley. Unable to own a horse and buggy, he made his way about the mining countryside on foot, a pack resting on his shoulders. A bachelor, his appearance was anything but presentable; he had an unkempt gray beard; wrinkled, shabby clothes; his shirt was soiled and his shoes torn. He slept in miners' lean-tos, or in fields. If it were not for his honesty he would never have been allowed to enter miners' homes, so repulsive was his person.

Old John's customers were the wives and daughters of miners. Though he carried some articles for men, his stock interested the women more; there were undies, garters, stockings, house dresses, notions, and preparations guaranteed to exterminate the vermin that infested company houses. When he got to a house, the housewife would forget the beef stew on the stove and neglect her crying children to feast her eyes on the things he spread on the table. She would not have to hesitate to buy, for Old John sold on the book and collected on pay days. He was a simple, trusting soul, but some folks said that he was too trusting for his own good.

He had one consuming ambition in life—to marry and settle down To this end he proposed to many a miner's widow, but no one would have him.

One night while cooped up in a lean-to at Number Six Patch, and unable to sleep because of the cold, he listened to the seductive strains of a familiar Irish come-all-ye that floated through the crisp autumn air from a fiddle in the village *shebeen,* while the siren-like laughter and singing of female voices proved almost too alluring. It had been pay day at the colliery, and miners and their women were enjoying themselves; Old John himself had benefited as he collected many small debts. Just as he was debating with himself whether to abandon the lean-to and go to the *shebeen,* he heard a knock. It proved to be a young man sent by the *shebeen* keeper to invite him over "just to warm up a bit." He knew of course that a *shebeen* was a place where folks drank hard liquor illegally, and as a man of temperance he shunned liquor. But what was to prevent a body from sitting there just to keep warm?

"I'll come," he said.

A fiddler was scraping away at Irish tunes, and couples were swinging around the floor when the peddler, feeling timid and confused, edged over to a crude bench along the wall. The *shebeen* keeper winked to a boy who acknowledged the cue by raising his eyebrows and leaving the room. The peddler, his legs crossed, puffing away at his soiled cutty pipe, did not observe these signals. Presently a comely young woman wearing a shawl came into the house and Old John moved over on the bench and asked her to sit beside him, which she did with seeming reluctance. There was some winking and feminine giggling, but it all went over the peddler's head.

When the young woman had sat through several dances, the peddler felt the gallant thing to do was to offer to take her on the floor himself, even though he could not dance.

"Indade not," the young woman replied curtly as she spurned his offer. "I'm not dancin' as I'm after buryin' me man a short time ago."

The peddler stroked his beard as his eyes lit up with hope and anticipation. Another widow woman!

"Funny I never seen you before," he said.

"I'm not surprised, for I'm a stranger in these parts. I come from 'Chunk and am here on a visit."

The conversation became more intimate as the evening wore on, and soon the peddler was listening to a doleful tale of the plight of a widow left on her own resources in a cruel, cruel world. He was quick to step into the breach and offer the protection of his name. She would not hear of it at first, since she hardly knew him, but Old John was not going to let an opportunity like this slip through his gnarled fingers and so pressed his suit with all the persuasion that he could command. Finally, with some coyness, she nodded her head, after which he planted a discreet kiss on her forehead. He could not conceal his happiness and blurted out the news. The widow insisted that the wedding take place after her priest had announced the banns. But Old John, knowing from bitter experience how fickle was a woman's heart, pressed for an immediate ceremony, and he won the backing of the dancers. So a squire was brought in promptly and the marriage ceremony performed. The bridegroom was so overcome with joy that he opened his purse strings and invited all to drink at his expense as long as the money held out. There was no backwardness on the part of the group about accepting the invitation. For the first time since he took the Father Matthew pledge he tasted liquor—gulped would be the more accurate word—and was soon drunk. At the height of the festivity, the bride stole out of the house without the stupefied bridegroom. Presently he brought himself to his feet, staggered over to the *shebeen* keeper, and demanded to know the whereabouts of his bride.

"What bride?" countered the *shebeen* keeper, as he fought to keep a straight face.

"Why, the bride—what was her name?—the widow woman I was after gettin' hitched up to tonight," stammered the drunken peddler.

Boisterous laughter greeted this statement, and Old John, leaning with one hand against the sideboard for support, blinked his eyes.

"Hell, John," he heard the *shebeen* keeper say, "that wor no widow woman ye were hitched to."

"No?"

"Neh, that wor one of the beardless lads of the patch phat we dressed up in me daughter's duds. It wor all a game, John."

PRAYER IN THE MINES

There was once a young miner in Tremont who had lost his faith in God.

"Someday you'll change your mind," his minister warned him.

The young miner shook his head. Years rolled by, and still he wouldn't go to church. One day when he was working in a breast, he saw a pillar creep. He and his butty made for the heading below just in time to escape and were sealed up as in a tomb. With no light or air, they were doomed to a horrible death unless rescued in time. A long time passed—ages it seemed. They were hungry and thirsty and beginning to choke from breathing the foul air.

"Guess we're goners," whimpered the man who did not believe in God.

"No, somethin' tells me already we'll be saved," replied the other, who was religious.

"Oh! if there was the sound of rescue crews."

"Let's pray, mebbe that'll make 'em work faster."

"Nonsense."

"Can't you pray?"

"I've not led a Christian life already for many years and it's not in me to be cryin' to God now."

"The Good Book says that faith'll move mountains."

"It can't move this mountain of coal."

"Prayer will do it."

"Go ahead and pray if you want to."

The man of faith kneeled, clasped his hands, raised his head in reverence to Almighty God and moved his lips. In that position he remained for what seemed hours, and by the time the first tap-tap-tap of the rescue crew was heard he had keeled over. As the sound of pick and hammer became louder, indicating that the rescuers were getting nearer, the trapped miners were slowly suffocating. When an opening was at last made into their tomb, the man who had done the praying was dead, while the unbeliever was still breathing, though too weak to move. He was carried out and brought home. In time, with proper care, he recovered.

"It was a miracle you lived through it," he was told.

"It wasn't a miracle," he replied. "It was faith that done it—my butty's faith. He sacrificed his life to make me see the light."

That experience changed that man's whole attitude toward God. I ought to know—I was the unbeliever.

ARE THERE FAIRIES UNDERGROUND?

In the days when the Shoofly was a celebrated colliery there worked in one of its lower veins a miner named Jim O'Donnell. Jim was a hardworking, conscientious man, yet it was little enough he had with which to support himself and his large family. More than once he wished the fairies had come with him to the new world. For there was as much need of a lift from them on this side as on the rented farm back in Donegal.

One day after lunch Jim fell asleep in the heading. One of the good people alighted on his ample shoulder and whispered into his ear to go find a precious stone that would bring him fabulous wealth, the stone to be as big as the head of his little girl who had died a year ago. Jim awoke with a start, rubbed his eyes and peered for a sight of the fairy. But all he could see was the same old blackness.

That evening he told Mame, the sharer of his woes, of the fairy's visit.

"Ah, begone wi' you," she said. "Sure it's dreamin' ye were in place of cuttin' coal."

"To be sure, Mame darlin'," he replied. "But it's only in dreams that the good people can be talkin' with one."

Now and then Jim was beset by doubt whether he had had an idle dream or whether he had really been visited by one of the "good people." Though he said nothing to his fellow miners, he was determined to search for the precious stone just to put his faith in the good people to the test. Morning and evening for several weeks he scraped the gob with great care and poked into piles of loose coal. In time he excited the other miners' curiosity. Whenever they asked him what he was looking for, he would evade the question, or invent an excuse.

Two miners working in his section of the colliery lived in St. Clair, and to get to and from the colliery they passed St. Stephen's cemetery in Port Carbon. One morning before dawn they crept into the cemetery and borrowed a granite head of a child from a headstone and hid it in a pile of loose coal in Jim's working place.

"Saints above!" Jim gasped when he found it. He could not see the two miners hiding behind the pillar. "Can I belave me eyes? And me after doubtin' that the good people lived in the mines."

He wrapped the stone in his coat and started to climb down the manway.

"What is it you're after finding?" the disguised voice of one of the hoaxing miners shouted.

Jim was startled, but continued climbing down the monkey ladder.

To avoid the bosses to whom he would have had to explain his quitting work so early, Jim crawled to the surface through an old unused air hole.

"Mame, Mame, I'm just after findin' it!" he said excitedly when he reached home.

"Get your breath, man, and what in the name of God do ye have under your coat?" she demanded.

"The stone—the precious stone the fairy was after promisin' to lave me," he said in a hushed voice. "Sure, Mame darlin', it's me that can't belave me own eyes."

"The saints be thanked!"

They embraced and kissed each other, and Mame wiped a tear with the end of her soiled apron.

"Do ye think, Jim, that we ought to show the stone to Father Walsh onc't?" asked Mame, her womanly intuition asserting itself.

"Indade not!" he replied impatiently. "And phat, tell me, does a parish priest know about precious stones?"

Jim didn't go back to work that day. Borrowing Tom McGettigan's team, he drove down to the city to have the stone appraised with a view to selling it. As might have been expected, he was laughed out of the place. Nothing but common ordinary granite! The shock of this revelation almost drove him mad. And what was he to tell Mame? He would have risked a hundred dangers in the mine to be spared the ordeal of facing her.

"I guess," he observed as he revealed the sad truth, "fairies don't live in the mines after all."

THE STORY OF THE OLD STONE HOUSE

In the village of Donaldson, a mile off the state pike from Tremont, there is an old stone house that folks say is haunted. It is known as the Franklin House. I don't know about its being haunted, but it has a story and I'm goin' to tell you about it. The time goes back to a coupla years after the close of the War of the Rebellion. I was gettin' to be a young buck then. The central figger in the story was Davy Lomison, the landlord of this here Franklin House. He was tall, slim, and gettin' up in years. Old Davy had a quiet, dignified air about him. Never wasted a word, that feller. And he minded his own business and would not 'a' harmed a fly. A coal operator, a landlord, and the village postmaster, he was great shakes around here. But don't mistake me. He wasn't no plaster saint, for he could take a nip with the next feller and laugh at a naughty yarn like you and me.

Lomison, as I heard Dad say, came to Donaldson in the forties and was one of the township's first operators. His money helped build the Union Canal which used to carry the township's coal to Philly, and at the time of the fuss I'm a-tellin' you about, he was operatin' mines in different parts of the township either as a partner or on his own hook.

But in none of them money-makin' things did he take as much pride as in the little post office he kept in the Franklin House. He used to swell up with pride when a stranger would address him as "Mr. Postmaster." But most of the folks of the village just called him Davy. Ah! I can see him now of a summer evenin' dressed in white linen pants, a thin alpaca coat and a soiled straw hat a-settin' on the back of his head. The Pottsville stage had just come in, bringin' passengers and the mail. The whole township had turned out in the hope of receivin' a letter from the old home in England, Ireland, Scotland, or Wales, the miners having come from one or another of them countries. The arrival of the stage was the biggest event of the day and Davy used to make a regular ceremony of it. He didn't just pass the letters out. He called off every name with the care of a judge passin' sentence on a prisoner. After the mail was all distributed everybody retired to the tavern for a nip and a good time. Old Davy now played the rôle of host, and a more genial, open-hearted host you never saw. Well, in the crowd there was sure to be a fiddler, a singer or two and a lad as could spin a yarn. And many's the time I heard Bobby Burns's "A Cotter's Saturday Night" recited there, and the lad what could rattle that off was never wantin' for a drink on the house.

Lomison hardly ever tended bar himself. That he left to his housekeeper, a Dutchwoman from over the mountains by the name of Belle Yengst. And bless me, lad, she was twice the woman that Davy was man, and rougher and more loud-mouthed as a regiment of soldiers. One night I heard her brag that there wasn't nothing wearin' pants as could lift a bigger piece of ice into the ice box than her, and would you believe it, not one man took her up on it, though there was a quart bottle of rye a-waitin' on the bar for him as would. Nobody ever got fresh with that woman. No sir, for there wasn't no man in the township that she couldn't lift by the seat of the pants and throw out on the road. And it was her that Lomison took as helpmate when his wife died—but that's gettin' ahead of my story, I reckon.

About this time there was living in Tremont a man named E. Godfrey Rehrer. He'd moved up with his wife and children from Tamaqua-y. He was a minin' engineer, and while employed as super by the Tremont Coal Company had discovered a coal vein—the Buck Mountain, it was—that had never before been worked hereabouts. He threw up his job, took a lease on the property from his company and started developing it.

As an engineer he figgered out that the best way of reachin' the vein was to drive a tunnel. He started out with damn little capital himself and when he ran out of that he borrowed heavy from relatives, friends, and even the miners—my own Dad was hit up for a coupla hundred. And when he went through that he formed a company and took in as partners a friend named Smith in Tamaqua-y and Davy Lomison. It wasn't long before the partners decided that a better, less costly way of reachin' the vein was for to sink a slope. That's what they did. Their little colliery was in Donaldson, just a coupla hundred yards from my house. I worked in it myself. Dad ran the stationary engine. We'd been livin' over to Rausch's Creek, where Dad was tendin' an engine at workin's there, when Rehrer came to our shanty and offered Dad the job tendin' his engine, and Dad took it. Well, one day Dad was a-settin' at the engine when Rehrer came in. Without sayin' a word to Dad he walked around the engine three times. Then he jumps down into the drum pit sayin' "Now I know what's been wrong. The devil was inside the drum and now he's out—damn him!"

Rehrer was a medium-sized, well-built man. I remember his shock of curly hair. He walked with a quick, military step, and was soft-spoken.

One night the three partners, Rehrer, Smith, and Lomison, met in the company office located on Lomison's hotel property, several hundred feet from the colliery. It was one of their usual meetin's, called to talk over the affairs of the concern. They got into an argument, voices were raised in anger, harsh words passed from one to the other—and Lomison made a threat against Rehrer. The whole argument was heard outside, but the people paid little attention to it. For it was taken for granted that partners, like husband and wife, will have their spats now and then.

The next morning Rehrer got up early, had his breakfast and as he started from home told his wife that he was goin' to his office. And that was the last seen of Rehrer in Donaldson. The first coupla days of his absence caused little uneasiness except to his wife and children. But when a week rolled around and there was no sign of him, people became alarmed. Inquiries for him were made everywhere, but he couldn't be found. It was as if the earth had opened up and swallowed him.

Bear in mind that Rehrer was a mine operator in a minin' township; he couldn' 'a' stood out more prominent if he'd been the village banker. He was known to be a faithful husband and a good father. The slope that the company was sinkin' had almost reached the coal vein and when it had, it would 'a' made him rich. In a word, he had everything to live for. Do you wonder that his disappearance caused a fuss, the likes of which Schuylkill County never knew before or since? The whole township was turned upside down in search of him. There wasn't an able-bodied boy or man that wasn't in that mad hunt. We covered every inch of ground in the township, them mountains included. We combed the underbrush; climbed the trees; dragged the streams; dug deep into the ravines and the crop-falls. In them days we used to take our baths outdoors in them mine cave-holes up there in the hills. They were from twenty-five to thirty feet deep. How well do I remember how us lads would dive to the bottom and feel around in the hope of touchin' Rehrer's body. We didn't know what to think except that Rehrer had been murdered. This township became one great haunted place. We used to see Rehrer's ghost wherever we turned. It got to be after a while that it took guts to venture outdoors after lamplight. We were in an awful state of suspense. We couldn't sleep o' nights for thinkin' about the missing Rehrer.

When we made up our minds that Rehrer had been done away with, we cast around for a likely murderer, and Lomison was the man whom the suspicion fell on. People recalled the fight between the partners in the company office the night before Rehrer's disappearance, and remembered Lomison's threat. When everybody else in the township took it for granted that Rehrer was dead, Lomison said over and over again that he was alive. And in the midst of the whole fuss, he goes off and gets himself married to Belle Yengst, his housekeeper and barmaid, the last woman on earth a man like Lomison would think of tyin' up with under normal circumstances. "Why should he want to marry that hussy if not to shut her up?" people asked. It was assumed that she had knowledge of the facts.

The police investigation wasn't more than a day or two old when they found Rehrer's coat, hat, and pants—the very clothes that Rehrer had worn when he left his home the morning he disappeared. They were rolled up into a bundle and hidden in a bookcase in the company office. Here was proof that Rehrer had been in the office as he had told his missus that he would be. As I've said, the office was located close to the Franklin House which Rehrer must have passed. Was it unreasonable then to assume, as all of us did, that Lomison met Rehrer that mornin'? Yet old Davy stoutly denied that he had had even a glimpse of his partner.

The finding of Rehrer's clothes was the most valuable clue to come out of the investigation up to this point, and it raised hopes that a solution was near. Detectives came from everywhere, all eager to solve the mystery and carry off the glory. But they were up a tree, the same as us. It just seemed here was one mystery that the mind of man couldn't fathom nohow. In our desperation we turned to the black art. Even the detectives turned to it, consultin' with fortune-tellers, powwowers and such like. One of the investigators, Harry "Snapper" Reese of Shamokin, a well-known coal and iron constable, took to a Dutchwoman powwower, and begad, he put himself completely under her power. That he did. I remember well them two ridin' around the township in a buggy, a-snoopin' and a-smellin' to beat all hell, followin' up the lady's hunches. She told the Snapper that the man that murdered Rehrer could be identified because he still had the blood stains on his shirt. Since Davy Lomison was the only one in the township then under suspicion it was up to the Franklin House that the Snapper marched. The tavern was turned upside down in search of a shirt with blood stains on it. It was found, all right. When the Snapper screwed up his squint eyes and demanded an explanation of the blood stains, Lomison merely shrugged his shoulders and said that he had got them killin' a chicken for his dinin' table. "It's a damn lie and you know it, Lomison," the Snapper roared. "The law'll get you yet."

The Snapper was smart enough to know that there wasn't much sense pinchin' Davy before Rehrer's body was found. The trail got hotter than ever when he came across gore on the floor of a shanty in which the colliery's oil barrels were stored.

All he needed now was to find Rehrer's body. He told his powwow woman to get busy and find out where that body was. So she went off and consulted with the spirits of the dark world and then she came out with a statement that the body was hidden in the earth. The Snapper thought that that was a right smart lead and immediately set about pokin' into the culm banks and rock heaps. The long iron rods used in the pokin' were closely examined for trace of blood and smelt for the odor of decomposed flesh. But there was neither.

Then an elaborate system of ditches was dug for to drain the mine cave-holes. But that, too, was a misfire.

Then we went to work and pumped Marshfield slope, an abandoned slope a mile up the highway from Donaldson. That was the toughest proposition of them all. It was a pretty deep slope, runnin' near to three hundred feet underground, and all of it was filled with water. Did that discourage us? Not a bit of it, not a bit of it. We put up a pump for to throw the water out, but the blamed thing didn't work fast enough to suit us, or maybe we just plumb lost our patience. Anyway we threw it aside and got us a much bigger pump that took two boilers to run. We were gettin' along fine and I guess we had pumped out about half the water when the owner demanded to be paid. Most of us had had no money to start with, and them as had some had sunk it into this mad searchin' business. Well, we couldn't meet the man's bill and so there wasn't nothin' for us to do but let him have our pump. We were hoisting it up when the rope broke on us, and I'll be damned if it didn't fall back into the slope. And the gol darn thing is down there yet.

While all this was going on, didn't there blow a strange detective into town. It was rumored that he hailed from New Yawk or some such far-off place. As soon as he got out of the stage, he stepped into the Franklin House and demanded to see Davy Lomison—in private. That made us all a bit curious and so we waited around to see what was in the air. There was quite a crowd of men and boys around the place. The detective was in with Davy a long time and when he came out, what do you think he told us? That he had wrung a confession out of Lomison to the effect that it was he, his partner Smith, and a third man from Tamaqua-y that done the job of murderin' Rehrer—for business reasons. We were like a bunch of lighted squibs anyway, and when we heard that we exploded. "Let's hang him!" someone yelled, and the rest of us took up the cry and with that there was a rush for Davy. You gotta hand it to Davy. He stood his ground. He denied up and down that he had made any confession, but we were in no mood to believe him. There were tears in his eyes as he asked us, in that calm, quiet way of his, like a father would talkin' to his children, if we took a stranger's word before his'n. He asked us who had opened mine after mine in the township for to give us work; who had given us drinks on tick between pay days; and who had fed us during hard times. The answer he got from some of the hot-heads was to cut out the soft soap and admit he was guilty.

The soft talk touched some of us, and when they began dragging Davy outside for to hang him on the nearest tree—and they had the rope with which to do it—we put up a battle for him, but couldn't make no headway. So they dragged the old man outside, ready to string him up on a stranger's say so when the constables came rushin' up the road. "If there is any hangin' to do, the Commonwealth should have the pleasure," one of them said, and served a warrant on Davy. It charged him with Rehrer's murder. That was, as near as I can remember, a coupla weeks after New Year's in 1868.

They took Lomison to Pottsville and there threw him into the county jail like a common criminal. Smith and a suspect from Tamaqua-y were already locked up, also charged with Rehrer's murder. Public opinion in the county seat was all worked up against the three men, and the district attorney, to show what a big lawyer he was, boasted that he had enough evidence to hang the three of 'em. All he needed was to find even a bone of the missing Rehrer's body. But since he couldn't produce the body, old Judge Ryon set the prisoners free.

Davy came back to Donaldson, but with the cloud of suspicion still hangin' over his head. People just couldn't get out of their heads that the man was guilty. If they could find the body, they said, Lomison would swing.

A short time later, a boy was playin' around the mouth of Loux's Tunnel, an abandoned drift up in the mountains here, when he became curious and stepped inside the dark place. He wasn't in far when he stumbled on some bones. He ran into Tremont and told Squire Bechtel that he had discovered Rehrer's bones. Imagine what a fuss that created. Squire Bechtel, who was also a deputy coroner, called a coroner's jury which found that them weren't Rehrer's bones at all. They belonged to an old skeleton which for years had hung in Harry Bailey's drug store in Tremont. Since the skeleton was fallin' apart, Harry had two lads take it up into the drift, and the sulphur water had already eaten most of it away.

The people were too stubborn to admit that maybe they had Lomison wrong. Everybody kept away from the Franklin House. They even boycotted the post office; they just wouldn't write letters because it meant takin' 'em to Davy Lomison. If they had messages, they sent them with passengers travelin' on the stage. The miners who boarded at the Franklin House all left. Davy became bankrupt. His spirit was broken and so was his health. When he died he was unmourned and unsung, except by his own immediate family. His barmaid widow, Belle, sold the furniture, packed her few belongin's and crossed the mountain for to go back to her Dutch relations. She was done forever with Donaldson.

Through all these months, Rehrer's wife remained at her home in Tremont waiting with a woman's patience for her husband to come back. Then she gave up hope altogether, put on widow's weeds and returned to Tamaqua-y with her children.

What had become of Rehrer? Well, that question hung like a cloud over our heads, and many's the man that went to his grave not knowin' the answer. But they say that a Tamaqua-y coal operator, while in

Washington watchin' the parade at Grant's first inauguration, recognized Rehrer all rigged out as a sergeant of marines; dragged him out of the line and forced him to own up to being E. Godfrey Rehrer. The man is said to have sobbed out a confession that it was to escape the heavy debts he had contracted in tryin' to reach the Buck Mountain vein that he dropped out of sight. Forgiven by his wife, it is said, he left with her for the South to make a fresh start.

CHAPTER SIX

Injury and Death

A CODE of anthracite mine safety laws has been built up through the years. But shocking accidents continue to occur in the industry. After all, you cannot legislate against nature in the raw whether in the mines or at sea. The best that the laws can do is protect the miner from nature's ravages. Individual caution and honest enforcement must do the rest. The safety first movement has made great headway. Mines now have underground first-aid stations and safety crews, and comfortable ambulances in which to take the injured to state hospitals.

These modern methods of caring for the injured are a far cry indeed from the former makeshift, inhumane ways. There was a time when a miner was not considered really injured unless he lost an eye, a leg, or an arm.

When a miner was burned in an explosion he was brought to the surface, laid under a tree, and oil was poured over the burned surface. Instead of linen dressing which the law now requires, rough blasting paper was often used to cover burns. He would be taken home in the colliery ash cart if the man in charge of the boiler house could spare it. The homeward journey over a rough road was one long agony for the casualty in the jolting cart.

One day a miner who no longer could bear to see his fellow workers suffer for lack of a proper conveyance after an accident screwed up enough courage to approach General Pleasants, of the Philadelphia & Reading Coal and Iron Company, to see if there was not a more humane way of caring for the injured.

"There ought to be an ambulance kept ready at all times for such special purposes," General Pleasants agreed.

"Why not put your ideas on paper so I could use them?" the miner asked naïvely.

"No," replied General Pleasants. "It would cost my company a great deal of money to carry it out. It would not look well for me to be the prime mover in such a thing. Why not go to the Legislature and get a bill passed requiring all collieries to have such provisions made, then we would all be in the same position. I have given you the idea. Now you go and work it out."

The miner took the idea back to his friends, and a bill embodying the idea was framed and carried through the Legislature.

Painted black and drawn by black mules, the early ambulance was a somber affair, not much different in appearance from a hearse. Nor is the comparison inappropriate, as patients sometimes developed gangrene or bled to death on the slow ride to the hospital.

Nevertheless when the ambulance first made its appearance it was considered a novelty. Old-time miners tell a story about the first ambulance used in the Pottsville area.

It carried home the remains of a miner named Mike Ryan who had been crushed to death in a fall of rock.

"Don't drive in front of the house," the colliery boss cautioned the ambulance driver. "Keep the wagon around the corner and break the news to the widow gently."

The ambulance driver stopped his horses around the corner as he had been instructed, and then rapped on the Ryan door.

"Does the widow Ryan live here?" he asked softly of the little woman who answered his knock.

"No sir," she said, "but Mrs. Ryan lives here."

"No she don't," he contradicted as he raised his voice.

"Yes, Mrs. Ryan does live here, and it's me as ought to know who I am."

"But it's me as ought to know that it's the widow Ryan should live here," he said, his voice growing louder.

"If you say that, sir, then you're a liar."

"I tell you she does," he argued as his voice rose to a shout. "Sure, ain't I got Mike round the corner in a box?"

* * *

"The Avondale Mine Disaster" describes the anthracite industry's Black Hole of Calcutta. One hundred and ten lives were snuffed out in that big hole in the ground before an aroused public opinion forced the Legislature to outlaw such mines. It was sheer murder, as the defenseless men and boys, trapped hundreds of feet below the surface, had no chance to escape because there was but one outlet, a shaft built up into a rickety breaker. At the bottom of the shaft was a furnace to ventilate the mine. There you have the combination which caused the first great anthracite mine disaster. It shocked the world and started a flood of coins in the direction of little Avondale Patch. Even Queen Victoria contributed to this relief fund.

The fire started early in the morning of September 6, 1869, when the flue partition in the shaft caught fire. The flames roared up the shaft and fired the breaker. Men and boys, their only avenue of escape cut off, and the air currents stopped, fought a desperate battle against gases. Rescue work began immediately after the fire was extinguished. A box with a slot top containing a dog attached to a lighted lantern was let down into the shaft to test the air. While the dog survived, the light in the lantern was snuffed out by black damp.

However, the mere fact that the dog had come back alive held out a slender hope to hundreds of anxious people that their loved ones might still be alive. Volunteers went down the shaft, to return immediately gasping for air. Even after this experience, Thomas W. Williams of Plymouth and David Jones of Grand Tunnel—

> Two Welshmen brave, without dismay,
> And courage without fail,
> Went down the shaft without delay
> In the mines of Avondale.

When they reached the bottom they signaled for a pick and shovel, but died before using them. After the gases had been cleared, a crew descended to the bottom where they found the two heroic Welshmen, their bodies horribly bloated. Then, after several hours of groping through the recesses of that "blind prison," they finally came upon a barricade made of a turned-over mine car, powder kegs, and parts of clothing which had been thrown up by the workers in a desperate attempt to ward off deadly mine gases. Behind the barricade were found the bodies of sixty-seven men and boys—in some cases, fathers and sons—huddled in a gruesome heap. And when the final check-up was made, one hundred and ten names were on the death list.

The excitement caused by the accident had not yet subsided, nor had the grief been assuaged, when a ballad appeared which told the tragic story of the Avondale holocaust. Nobody knew whence it came nor who had composed it, though different names appeared on the penny broadsides, which sold by the hundreds. Everybody sang it—and wept for the poor widows and orphans. For a quarter of a century it was the most popular ballad. Its popularity spread far beyond the borders of the hard coal fields and has been found by folk song collectors as far away as Newfoundland.

It was among the first ballads I heard about when I began to collect folklore. Determined to find it, I interviewed Mrs. James Wylie, aged seventy-two, of Edwardsville, the only surviving widow of the disaster, but she recalled only a few stray lines. From there I set out for Avondale Patch and found John McKeon, the only man living there who had witnessed the fire. He too disappointed me. On my way back to the trolley two miles away, I met Joe Hillard, an elderly miner whose entombment five years before I had reported for the Wilkes-Barre *Record*. When I told him of my quest, he directed me to Jerome Lewis in Plymouth who, he recalled, had a copy of a broadside containing the ballad. When I finally held the yellowed, fragile sheet in my hand, I experienced one of my first thrills in ballad-hunting. It bore the by-line of one James Fox of Scranton, and the sixth and seventh lines of the second stanza had been worn away; when the ballad was published with the rest of my collection in the *United Mine Workers Journal,* one of its readers, Calvin Snyder of Shamokin, supplied the missing words. I have heard several variants in different parts of the region since then, but the original broadside version, used here, is still my favorite. David Rodden of Nanticoke sang the tune used here.

Recently a different ballad on the Avondale disaster was sent me on a faded and worn typewritten sheet by Floyd E. Wermuth, a young Nanticoke newspaperman. He wrote that he had received it from an elderly miner who had since died. Its title is "Avondale Disaster."

The incident described in "The Sugar Notch Entombment" occurred far below the surface in the Number Ten slope of the Lehigh & Wilkes-Barre Coal Company at Sugar Notch, shortly after midnight, April 23, 1879. As the night shift men were driving a new gangway, the overlying strata suddenly caved in and trapped five men and two boys in a lightless, airless and echoless tomb in which they were imprisoned for five days and nights.

The entombed were: Charles Hawkins, Edward Price, James and Patrick Green, brothers, Barney Reilly, William "Sult" Kinney, a young mule driver, and Johnny Clark, his thirteen-year-old patcher.

All but Kinney have since died. At seventy-six he lives in Ashley near the scene of the accident, and is made happy when asked to relate his experiences. He talks in a rambling manner, sparing the listener not the minutest detail.

The story is summarized here:

I was driving along the gangway with Johnny Clark, my patcher, when we noticed rats running toward the slope and feared something was going to happen. A couple hours later it did happen. We were hauling a trip of cars when suddenly I heard the cracking of timber, followed by a gust of wind so violent that it knocked Johnny and me off the trip and against the face of the gangway. Then came a thunder-like rumble as ton upon ton of rock and coal came crashing down in a cloud so thick I could not see my own hand.

Ordering Johnny to run to safety, I quickly unharnessed Harry, my mule, hopped on its back and sped away to spread the alarm while rock and coal continued to rain down on me. When I warned the last gang of men, they dashed away so fast they forgot to keep the door open for me. I got off the mule's back and started to run after them, but soon I met them coming back—the whole mine was caving in. All of us groped our way up to a far breast and when we counted noses, who do you think was there too? Little Johnny Clark. "I didn't want to leave you," he cried.

Well, sir, we put our lamps out to save oil and then stretched out. We slept, talked, sang, prayed, and waited—for death. For food some of us bit the barks off timber props. Some time during the entombment when we were near starvation, Jimmy Green said, "I could eat a mule."

I offered to get the mule ready if someone else would kill it, as I didn't have the heart to put away a faithful old pal like that.

"I'll kill the mule myself," volunteered Green.

"We'll help you," chimed in the others.

I tied the mule's head to a prop and then said, "Harry, you've pulled many cars along this gangway, but now your driving's at an end," as the tears rolled down my cheeks.

I handed a hammer to Jimmy Green, who hit the poor mule many blows over the head and soon killed him. When I cut the bridle rein loose, Harry fell over on his side. I chopped his head off with an axe and then all of us chopped up the body and stored the pieces in a tool box where the rats couldn't get at them. We built a fire with our lamps. Some of the meat was chopped up in seven small pieces—one for each of us—and we boiled them in water collected in our dinner cans from the roof. But we were so starved we ate the meat half raw, not willing to wait until it had been fully cooked.

Thus we lived in that tomb. Of course we had lost all sense of time and imagined we had been imprisoned for weeks instead of days. We never lost hope that ultimately we would be rescued. But when? The suspense and the stillness and the waiting, waiting, waiting nearly drove us mad.

Then the great moment arrived! We heard the muffled sound of voices, and listened breathlessly, hoping that this time we would not be imagining. The voices came nearer and nearer until we were able to recognize them as belonging to Smith, the mine super, and Williams, the mine inspector. They had tunneled through a great barrier of coal and rock and shattered timber to reach us.

Saved at last!

Sung to the same melody as "The Avondale Mine Disaster," and written in the same metre, "The Mines of Locust Dale" tells the story of an accident which occurred at the Potts colliery in Locust Dale, Schuylkill County, about six years later—November 18, 1875, in which four miners lost their lives.

Barney Kelly, seventy-eight-year-old mine worker, who wrote out this ballad for me from memory, has a vivid recollection of the accident.

"I was then fifteen years old and working in the Potts breaker," he said. "All of a sudden the machinery came to a halt and the colliery whistle blew. We knew what that meant all right. We breaker boys made a dash for the head of the slope and saw people come running from all directions for to see the men fetched up."

Anthony Ferguson of Merriam Patch, Northumberland County, was a witness to the accident described in "Charley Hill's Old Slope." The accident occurred at Mine Hill Gap near Pottsville "three days after the assassination of President Lincoln." In his seventies when I interviewed him in 1925, he had a vivid recollection of the mine tragedy; he was working in the breaker at the time and the Ferguson mentioned in the ballad was his father.

"A mine car carrying nine men and boys was climbing up the slope," said Ferguson. "When close to the surface it suddenly jumped the tracks, stood for a few seconds and, the haulage chain broken, tumbled back into the mine. The news spread pretty quick and soon the whole patch was at the slope, the children bawling for their daddies, and mothers and wives screaming and tearing their hair in anguish and despair.

"There was a team of horses at the slope; one of the horses was named Lion. Mike Laffee, who had come up the slope on an earlier trip, unharnessed Lion and rode him at breakneck speed to Minersville where he called Father Malone, our parish priest.

"Right at Laffee's heels was Ned Casey, another miner who had run all the way from the patch on the same errand as Mike.

" 'Come on, fa-ather,' said Ned all out of breath. 'They're all murthered in Hill's ould slope.'

"With that he dropped exhausted to the floor. Father Malone and his housekeeper, Lizzy Shore, lifted him to a couch and covered his sweaty body with a comforter. Then they left for the slope in the priest's buggy.

"They found Shannon, one of the victims, with his brains oozing out on the ground near where the car had jumped the tracks. The priest pushed the brains back and begged Lizzy to cover the hole in the head with his white handkerchief as he took the dying man's confession. This was a little too much for her and so in her Kilkenny brogue she screamed, "Fa-ather, this is ver-ry quare."

"Get off with ye," said the priest, "this man would make a confession with his head cut clean off."

"Charley Hill's Old Slope" was sung for me in Wilmington by Patrick Brislin, a former anthracite miner, who had learned it from his father.

Nobody knows how many miners were lost in the great Twin-Shaft colliery squeeze at Pittston early on the morning of June 28, 1896. The number of dead has been estimated variously between sixty-five and one hundred and thirty-five. None of the bodies was ever recovered.

The rock between the fifth and sixth levels had been working for several days when these men were ordered down to the sixth level to timber in to prevent a cave-in. They made the mistake of entering the section where the overlying strata pressed hardest, instead of working toward it from a place where they might escape, as custom and common sense dictated. While they were groping their way around, the Susquehanna River, finding a weak spot in the fifth level, broke through with a great roar. Down went the roof with a thunderous crash, and the men perished under an avalanche of river water, sand, rock, and coal. During the vain search for their bodies, and as the whole region waited tensely for news of possible rescues, a young mule driver, Harry Tempest, in the Turkey Run mine at the other end of the region, groped for words to express the emotions that the tragedy had stirred in him. Scribbling on rough cartridge paper under the dim light of his lamp, he wrote the ballad, "The Twin-Shaft Mine Squeeze," which I obtained from him in 1925.

Several years ago, I was a guest at a reunion of the Markle family in a grove near Orangeville, Columbia County. As many of those present were from the anthracite region, particularly Hazleton, I made an appeal for mining ballads. Only one response gave promise of being fruitful. Oddly enough, the volunteer was a farmer, George Markle of Orangeville. He said that he once sang a ballad about a mine disaster in Pittston which he had learned thirty to forty years ago when a Pittston woman, singing in the Jonestown Methodist Church, had first brought it into the neighborhood. In a shaky voice—he was past sixty years of age—he began to sing it for me, but he didn't seem to be able to recall more than a few lines of it. Apologizing for his failure, he promised to stir his memory and send it to me. He was as good as his word, for not long afterward I received a copy of the ballad from him which is headed, "The Miners' Fate." It sings of the same accident as "The Twin-Shaft Mine Squeeze." On September 4, 1935, Le Mon and I drove through a heavy downpour of rain to his farmhouse where he made a record for us.

There was still a third ballad on this accident. It was entitled "The Twin-Shaft Disaster"and was composed by John A. Murphy of Dickson City, who was also the author of "The Driver Boy."

When John J. Curtis was blinded in an accident in the Morea mine in May, 1888, he was helpless. Joseph Gallagher, Lansford balladist, wrote a ballad for him of which broadsides were printed by the Lansford *Record*. Led by a Scranton boy, Curtis roamed all over the region singing or reciting the ballad "John J. Curtis," and selling the broadsides for a livelihood. That mine workers were sympathetic was shown in Curtis' case. When he wrote the ballad, Gallagher did not set it to music, but somewhere along his peregrinations Curtis picked up the present tune which Andrew Rada of Lost Creek sang for Le Mon and me.

"The Miner's Doom" is an old Welsh ballad popular in the Panther Creek Valley. It was obtained from Thomas Jones, of Seek, Schuylkill County.

This chapter would not be complete without a word concerning the heroism displayed by anthracite miners at the time of a mine accident. From the very nature of this hazardous occupation, merely to work inside a mine is to take one's life in one's hands, but when disaster strikes a colliery, heroism in its highest form comes to the surface. The two Welshmen who gave up their lives during the rescue work at the Avondale mine were typical of the courage found among anthracite miners. Heroism is so commonplace in the industry that no roll of honor is kept of those who sacrifice their lives for their fellow mine workers. Yet, long indeed would be such a roll if heroes of labor were recognized and appreciated as are the heroes of the battlefield. Some of the noblest deeds of man have been performed by workers in the anthracite industry.

THE AVONDALE MINE DISASTER

Transcribed by Melvin LeMon

Good Chris-tians all, both great and small, I pray ye lend an
ear,— And lis - ten with at - ten - tion while The
truth I will de - clare; When you hear this lam - en -
ta - tion, It will cause you to weep and wail,— A -
bout the suf - fo - ca - tion In the mines of A - von - dale.

On the sixth day of September,
  Eighteen hundred and sixty-nine,
Those miners all then got a call
  To go work in the mine;
But little did they think that day
  That death would gloom the vale
Before they would return again from
  The mines of Avondale.

The women and the children,
  Their hearts were filled with joy,
To see the men go work again,
  And likewise every boy;
But a dismal sight in broad daylight,
  Soon made them turn pale,

When they saw the breaker burning
  O'er the mines of Avondale.

From here and there, and everywhere,
  They gathered in a crowd,
Some tearing off their clothes and hair,
  And crying out aloud—
Get out our husbands and our sons,
  Death he's going to steal
Their lives away without delay
  In the mines of Avondale.

But all in vain, there was no hope
  One single soul to save,
For there is no second outlet
  From the subterranean cave.
No pen can write the awful fright
  And horror that did prevail,
Among those dying victims,
  In the mines of Avondale.

A consultation then was held,
  'Twas asked who'd volunteer
For to go down this dismal shaft,
  To seek their comrades dear;
Two Welshmen brave, without dismay,
  And courage without fail,
Went down the shaft, without delay,
  In the mines of Avondale.

When at the bottom they arrived,
  And thought to make their way,
One of them died for want of air,
  While the other in great dismay,
He gave a sign to hoist him up,
  To tell the dreadful tale,
That all were lost forever
  In the mines of Avondale.

Every effort then took place
  To send down some fresh air;
The men that next went down again
  They took of them good care;
They traversed through the chambers,
  And this time did not fail
In finding those dead bodies
  In the mines of Avondale.

Sixty-seven was the number
  That in a heap were found,
It seemed they were bewailing
  Their fate in underground;
They found the father with his son
  Clasped in his arms so pale.
It was a heart-rending scene
  In the mines of Avondale.

Now to conclude, and make an end,
  Their number I'll pen down—
One hundred and ten of brave stout men
  Were smothered underground;
They're in their graves till the last day,
  Their widows may bewail,
And the orphans' cries they rend the skies
  All round through Avondale!

AVONDALE DISASTER

Come, friends and fellow Christians, and listen to my tale,
And as I sing, pray drop a tear for the dead of Avondale;
The sixth day of September, in eighteen sixty-nine
We never shall forget the day until the end of time.

One hundred and eight men went in the mine as I am told,
Not thinking that before the eve in death they'd all lie cold.
And some there were with snowy locks and others in their prime
And children in their tender youth were working in the mine.

They left their friends and homes so dear that morning cheerfully
And worked along till half past ten when the fire fiend they did see.
It quickly passed up through the shaft as though propelled by fate.
It was then they tried to save their lives, but alas, alas, too late!

What they then said, or what they done, no one on earth can know,
No one can tell their horror, their agony or woe.
The breaker burned above them and though their friends were brave,
It was madness then to try to help, no hand but God's could save.

The news of the sad accident the valley soon went round
And quick their brother miners came flocking to the ground,
Where the miners' little children, their darling wives likewise
The hills all around they did resound with sad and mournful cries.

To hear the women weeping and note the stifled moan
Would cause your eyes to fill with tears, if your heart was made of stone;
Crying, "Husband, dearest husband, indeed I am bereft.
Since you have gone from this bright world, in sorrow I am left."

And children in their innocence as through the crowd they roam
Saying, "Tell me where is my father, why does he not come home?
What makes the people gather round and mama drop her head?"
But little thought their father dear was numbered with the dead.

They worked along right manfully all night and the next day
But the furnace like a sentinel of fire barred the way.
Their friends and fellow miners to save them they did strive
And amongst them Jones and Williams who nobly lost their lives.

The bodies were all found at last as on the ground they lie
All clustered there together in company to die.
And amongst them aged fathers with children in their arms
As if through death's cold valley they'd shield them from all harm.

I never shall forget the sight as through the shaft they came
And weeping friends stood waiting by, their cold remains to claim,
While their souls may have ascended up to God who gave them breath
To plead against the Company whose greed has caused their death.

The widows and the fatherless our sympathies they crave
While weeping for the loved ones, now silent in the grave.
May the Lord in pity look on them nor let His mercy fail.
Be a father to the orphans and a friend to Avondale.

THE SUGAR NOTCH ENTOMBMENT

It was in the month of April in eighteen seventy-nine
When seven men came to Sugar Notch to work down in the mine.
The night shift was before them and honest they began—
The driver came and told them that the mine was caving in.

They walked in the gangway and then sat down,
They held a consultation and the talk went all around;
Pricey held the safety lamp and Reilly he was last,
Hawkins put up his hand and shut off all the gas.

The rocks stood on their edges up against the roof,
And all of them sat quiet, afraid for to make a move.
Some were very hungry and some were very weak;
Says Johnny Green, "Let's kill the mule and have a jolly feast."

So Bill Kinney went and got his mule and tied him to a prop,
The tears came rolling down his cheeks saying, "Harry, you must drop."
On picking up the hammer, Johnny Green found it to be dull,
He hit the poor old mule ten times on the head before he cracked his skull.

Then Kinney said, "Harry, you're dead and gone; your life is gone astray,
But many a hundred cars of coal you've pulled out of this gangway,
Many a driver's drove you, but now your driving's at an end."
They hauled him in and shared him fair between the seven men.

THE MINES OF LOCUST DALE

(AIR: *The Avondale Mine Disaster*)

Oh, come all you tender Christians,
I pray you will draw near,

It is of a sad disaster
  I mean to let you hear.
And if you will pay attention
  To my sad and mournful tale,
Of an accident that happened
  In the mines of Locust Dale.

It was the eighteenth of November
  In the year of seventy-five,
Four honest sons of labor
  That day did lose their lives.
Oh, an accident that happened
  To those so young and hale;
It was an explosion of powder
  In the mines of Locust Dale.

The names of those unlucky four
  I will to you explain,
There were Mordecai Jones and Alfred Steele,
  John Durkin and Robert Payne.
Down in the gloomy mines
  They were confined, as if in jail,
To try and earn their daily bread
  In the mines of Locust Dale.

Oh, how little did those heroes dream
  As they went to work that morn,
That soon they would be carried
  Back all shattered up and torn.
Or that soon their dearest friends
  Would o'er their shattered bodies wail—
That they were doomed to perish
  In the mines of Locust Dale.

While sitting on the powder box
  Amid the smoke and damp,

The powder was ignited
  By a spark from off the lamp.
Oh, a sudden flash and a deafening sound
  Like a heavy storm or gale,
Which perished those four miner boys
  In the mines of Locust Dale.

There was soon a rush to their rescue
  But alas! that fatal hour;
It was all in vain, for they were past
  The help of mortal power.
But to hurry and to let them out
  I am sure they did not fail,
For they saw that they were dying
  In the mines of Locust Dale.

All mangled and disfigured
  And the hair burned off their heads;
Likewise the clothes from off their backs
  And the flesh hung down in shreds.
Oh, it would make you cry
  To hear them so mournfully bewail
As they were taking them away
  From the mines of Locust Dale.

Oh, beseeching and lamenting
  With piercing cries of woe,
Which caused their fellow miners
  Their sympathy to bestow.
And soon the fatal news was spread
  Through valley, town, and vale
Of the accident that happened
  In the mines of Locust Dale.

So now kind friends, all breathe a prayer,
  For those that met their doom,
Stricken down so instantly
  All in their youthful bloom.

Oh, to be stricken down so instantly!
So kind friends, do not fail
To breathe a prayer for those who died
In the mines of Locust Dale.

CHARLEY HILL'S OLD SLOPE

Come all ye true born Irishmen wherever you may be,
I hope you'll attention pay and listen unto me;
It's of those true-born Irishmen that left their native clay,
To seek their destination here in Americ-a.

It was on the eighteenth day of June when flowers were in full bloom,
The small birds hopped from tree to tree and sweetly chimed their tune,
To my surprise, I heard a noise that gave me a fatal stroke,
When I heard of that sad accident at Charley Hill's old slope.

In future time this cruel crime to you I will explain;
Nine upright men ventured their lives to ride upon a chain.
When near the land it made a stand the chain it quickly broke,
Which caused many a widow to mourn her loss at Charley Hill's old slope.

There was Michael Hunt and Ferguson, they met their fate that day,
While Jimmy Sharp and Billy Hughes in their bloody gore they lay,
Though Shannon's brains lay on the plane, a few doleful words he spoke,
Saying: "Th' Almighty King, may our sowls bring this day from Hill's ould slope."

It would grieve your heart with pity for to see those miners' wives,
All looking for their dead husbands with heart-rending cries,
Their children's cries, raised to the skies, abandoning every hope;
Saying: "Our daddies dear, no more we'll see; they're lost in Hill's old slope."

Jane Sharp she stood upon the spot with a sad and mournful cry,
Her orphans round, all on the ground, their tears I did espy,

With bitter cries she wrung her hands and her coal black hair she tore,
For her husband and two of her loving sons lay bleeding in their gore.

A lady fair stood weeping there, Mis' Donahue was her name,
With bitter cries and dismal sighs she sorely did complain,
All pressed with grief without relief, with trembling lips she spoke:
"Will they ever bring my husband out of Charley Hill's old slope?"

It would grieve your heart with pity to see the number of the dead,
Some with their legs and arms broken, some more with shattered heads,
Nine of those doomed lay in one room—what a dreadful sight was there!
May the God of Light, this blessed night, hear each widow's prayer!

Now to conclude and finish, I have no more to say,
May God look on the fatherless and poor orphans here today!
May God look on the fatherless this blessed night, I hope!
And may God have mercy on their souls who died in Hill's old slope.

THE TWIN-SHAFT MINE SQUEEZE

One Sunday morning early just before the break of day,
Pealed forth an awful warning of ninety brave souls passed away,
Ah! little thought those happy ones who slumbered in their bed
That those who toiled so hard for them were numbered with the dead;
The news flashed out like lightning through those peaceful village homes,
Which rent the air with sorrow from sad mothers' weeping moans,
Down in a dusky coal mine five hundred feet or more,
Fell those true and honest men to rise again no more.

CHORUS

Then let's ne'er forget this sad fate they have met,
Let us pledge them our strongest of love—
Every man give a hand by the poor widows stand,
And pray God to protect from above.

Around the mining shaft there stood ten thousand souls or more,
Gazed at the Twin-Sister colliery which held the loved ones they adored,

Such sighing and such crying it would make your blood run cold,
To see those little children and gray-haired mothers old:
"Oh God! bring back our husbands," was their sad and mournful cry,
"Our homes they are so lonely," as the tears cours'd from their eyes,
The scene is one I'll ne'er forget if I should live for years,
Of those ninety miners brave who left their homes in tears.

Now many days have since gone by, not one single soul they found,
They're lying crushed and mangled in that cavern underground,
With the rocks there piled upon them to mark their resting place.
Oh! God have mercy upon their souls and bless them with thy grace,
For He who ruleth over all, His blessings we must ask;
And when our lives are ended, to Him we go at last,
When the trumpet it will sound to mark the Judgment Day,
We all will be united there upon that blessed day.

THE MINERS' FATE

At just three o'clock in the morning
As the whistles gave the death sound,
One hundred brave men that were mining
Were buried alive in the ground.
O, what can we do now to save them—
To rescue their bodies at least?
O, help us, Great Father, we pray thee,
One poor soul to rescue at least.

CHORUS

O, we ne'er can forget that sad morning,
When the whistles all loudly blew;
And the people all ran to their rescue
To see what there they could do.

One woman stood weeping and wailing,
Her cries were heard far around;
They told her they could not be rescued—
She fainted and fell to the ground.

O, Father of love and of mercy,
  Protect us forever from harm,
And help us to trust thee forever,
  And forever to lean on thy arm.

Soon widows and orphans were screaming
  Their voices were heard far around,
On account of the cave-in in the morning,
  Just before the break of dawn.
Great Father in Heav'n, we pray thee,
  Assist us this Sabbath day,
And help us to rescue our husbands
  Who so lately from us passed away.

Far down in the coal mines at Pittston,
  Five hundred feet underground,
There lie our sons and companions
  Who were buried alive in the ground.
But now they rest from their labors,
  Their toils and trials are past,
But we hope and trust in the future
  To meet them in heav'n at last.

Some sisters were left without brothers,
  And mothers without a son,
And help us to say, O Father,
  Not my will, but thine, be done.
Far down, far down in the coal mines
  Where fathers and brothers must stay,
Till Gabriel shall blow his trumpet
  On the Resurrection Day.

THE TWIN-SHAFT DISASTER

(AIR: *The Cumberland Crew*)

Kind friends draw nigh and give me your attention,
  And a sad story to you I'll relate,

It's of a disaster that occurred down in Pittston,
  Where eighty brave miners met a sad fate.
The pride of the valley were those brave manly fellows,
  That fatal morn ended their sorrows and joys,
Let each good Christian shed a sad tear of pity
  When he thinks of the fate of the poor miner boys.

On the twenty-eighth of June about three in the morning,
  The news was received that the men were entombed,
The message was brief but it told us all plainly,
  That every poor man in that death trap was doomed.
At the call of the company the white slaves responded,
  To save the old mines that threatened to cave,
Face danger or starve, was the choice of the miners,
  But now their poor bodies lie in a deep grave.

On a calm summer's evening they left friend and kindred,
  And went down the shaft with a smile and a cheer,
With a kiss to the wife and each one of the children
  Or a hasty good-bye to the friends they loved dear.
They marched to the place where the danger was lurking,
  The squeeze was affecting the pillars of coal,
When down with a crash came the roof that was working
  And buried the victims in that dismal hole.

Inspector McDonald, what will be your answer
  When you face the Almighty upon Judgment Day?
You were fully aware that the mine was in danger,
  You neglected your duty I am sorry to say.
The lament of the widows and fatherless children,
  Will sound like a death knell where e'er you go;
For the sake of the gold which you treasure so highly,
  You caused all this desolation and woe.

Kind friends, don't forget the poor widows and orphans,
  O, give them assistance which they need so bad.
Remember that God loveth a cheerful giver,
  And a kind word at least will make their hearts glad.

And think of the true-hearted heroes that's toiling
In the midst of great danger their comrades to find,
May each gallant rescuer wear a halo of glory,
When he leaves the cares of this sad world behind.

O, when will the laws be made for the poor miner?
What mockery is this in the land of the free!
For although we are miners remember we're human,
And a worm that is trod on will turn to get free.
But a day will yet come when the haughty mine owners
Will humble themselves to the slaves they now own!
So drop a few tears when you think of the victims
And the friends they have left in this world all alone.

JOHN J. CURTIS

Transcribed by Melvin LeMon

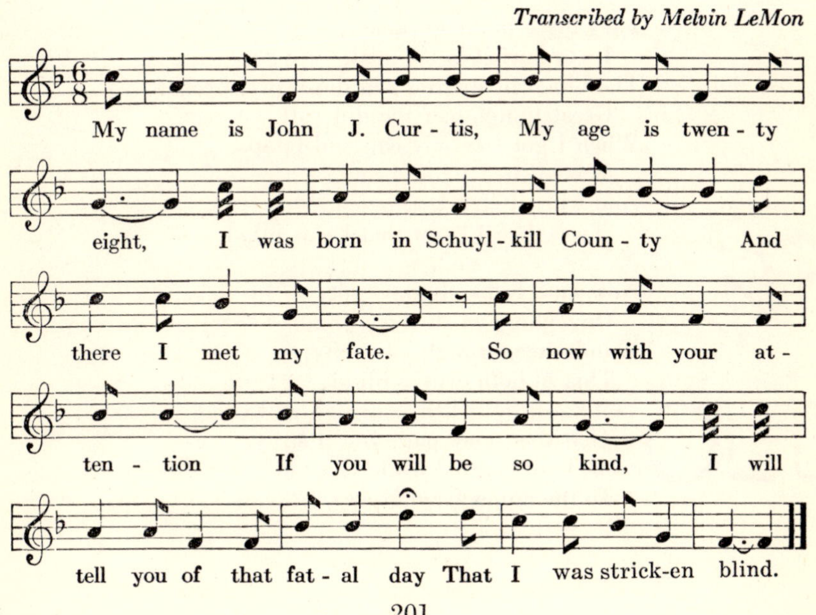
My name is John J. Cur - tis, My age is twen - ty
eight, I was born in Schuyl - kill Coun - ty And
there I met my fate. So now with your at -
ten - tion If you will be so kind, I will
tell you of that fat - al day That I was strick-en blind.

It was on a bright May morning,
  As the sun peeped o'er the hill,
The little birds sang loud and sweet:
  I seem to hear them still;
My heart was filled with purest joy
  As to the mines I did stray,
To earn an honest living
  In the colliery of Morea.

At eight o'clock I climbed the pitch,
  And to my work did go,
I drilled two holes and loaded them—
  Touched one and fled below.
It soon went off; I then went back
  To the one that did remain,
When by its mouth it too went off
  And blew me down again.

I lay there in the darkness;
  I was buried in the coal,
The blood in streams ran down my cheeks;
  Great lumps o'er me did roll.
When I got free, my cap and lamp
  Was all that I could find,
And when I struck a match,
  'Twas then I knew that I was blind.

Now kind folks, do have pity
  On whom you chance to find
Wandering through your city,
  That in both eyes is blind;
You know not when your day will come
  That this same path you'll stray,
So be kind-hearted while you can
  To the miner from Morea.

THE MINER'S DOOM

(AIR: *Adieu to Dear Cambria*)

At five in the morning as jovial as any,
The miner doth rise to his work for to go,
He caresses his wife and his children so dearly
And bids them adieu before closing the door;
And goes down the deep shaft at the speed of an arrow,
His heart light and gay without fear or dread,
He's no thought of descending to danger and peril—
That his life is depending on one single thread.

His wife is his queen and his home is his palace,
His children his glory, to maintain them he tries,
He'll work like a hero; he faces all danger,
He'll deprive his own self their bare feet to hide.
Now his day's work is o'er, he's homeward returning,
He thinks not how the change in an hour will be,
But he thinks how his wife and his children will greet him—
But his home and his children he'll nevermore see.

Now his wife had been dreaming of her husband so dearly,
She had seen him in danger—"God help me," she cried;
Too true was the dream of the poor woman's sorrow:
The rope broke ascending; her dear husband died.
Their home that morning was as jovial as any,
But a dark cloud came rolling straight o'er their door—
A widow, three children are left for to mourn him;
The one that they ne'er will see any more.

At the day of his funeral the great crowds had gathered,
He was loved by his friends, by his neighbors, by all,
To the grave went his corpse, by his friends it was followed,
The tears from our eyes like the rain they did fall,
And the widow, lamenting the fate of her husband,
Broken-hearted she died on the dear loved one's tomb,
To the world now is left their three little children
Whose father had met with a coal miner's doom.

CHAPTER SEVEN

The Strike

THE anthracite miner is a peculiar creature. As an individual he is unknown. Only collectively does he make his presence felt. Many miners are seriously injured or killed underground in the course of a year without our hearing of it, but when a big explosion tears a mine asunder, taking a heavy toll of life, they make the front page—in numbers. Let a strike threaten our winter comfort and we become acutely aware of him again, but only in the mass.

This is the miner's tragic destiny. Civilization itself may rest on his shoulders, yet for civilization he exists only as a collective unit. Perhaps this is because tradition has assigned him a place low in the social scale. It seems but a short time ago, as time is measured, that the world's mines were worked by serfs, slaves, and convicts.

The miner understands his position well, and so is strong for organization. Bitter experience has taught him that if he has rights to preserve, or wrongs to adjust, or economic security to win, or happiness to attain, he can achieve them only as a collective unit. Hence he worships his union as a religion. A union button restores his self-respect, revives his self-confidence and gives him the feeling that he really belongs in the society of civilized human beings—a society that doubtless would shun him but for the respect it holds for his collective strength.

"Only a miner" is a common expression reflecting society's opinion. We pity a human being who of his own volition gives up fresh air and sunlight to work in a dungeon hundreds of feet underground. Yet there is no other work that the miner would or could do. He may not be articulate about it, but there is a strong appeal for him in the familiar gloom of the mine, despite its hardships and hazards, to which he early becomes inured. He fights as does no other class of workers for the improvement of his lot, and for what he believes to be a more equitable share of the profits for his labor. And his weapon is the union. As one commentator has observed, "These people with tired hands and weary feet have modest longings in their hearts that are never satisfied. The union has been the means of bringing into their lives some of the beautiful and the good that our material civilization has to offer."

Almost from the beginning of the industry, mine workers thought hopefully in terms of unionism. But not until 1849 did a union dare to rear its head. Organized by an English miner named John Bates, who lived in St. Clair, it struck for higher wages, shorter hours, abolition of company store orders, and removal of other grievances. The strike failed, however, and the four thousand strikers went back to the pits without an organization.

Its successor, the Workingmen's Benevolent Association, popularly known as the W. B. A., was chartered in 1868 with John Siney, also of St. Clair, as president. The W. B. A. received its baptism of fire in a strike originating in the Schuylkill Valley. The strikers marched all over the valley closing colliery after colliery and adding to their ranks. Thus augmented, they crossed the Broad Mountain into the Mahanoy Valley, where they succeeded in calling out hundreds of workers and shutting down several other collieries. The hills rang with their songs and shouts as they pushed on triumphantly into the Wyoming Valley, where they paralyzed Wilkes-Barre and Pittston production.

The W. B. A. had come into existence during the post-war period which was characterized in the nation by gigantic industrial expansions with financial titans fighting ruthlessly for control of natural resources, railroads, and key industries; a period in which rampant rugged individualism was paralleled by great strikes, riots, and bloodshed among the nation's industrial workers.

This period—the late sixties and the entire decade of the seventies—also saw the anthracite industry experience its greatest expansion. To insure themselves a steady supply of coal to feed their expanding facilities, the anthracite-carrying railroads plunged into the purchase of coal-bearing lands in their respective territories and began producing themselves, forming subsidiaries for that purpose. Wherever they could, they took advantage of the financial embarrassment of individual operators, especially during the depression of 1873, and bought them out or obtained control of their properties by means of loans.

Of course labor trouble frequently had broken out long before the railroads captured control of the anthracite industry. But never was it so intense, nor marked by so much violence. The independent operators, while not always seeing eye to eye with their workers, nevertheless had been close to them and had understood their problems. Hence they had been inclined to compromise more often than the impersonal, absentee-controlled corporate monopolies.

At the mercy of the law of supply and demand, the industry suffered its most severe headache from unstable markets. Hard times had much to do with this instability, but the industry's own weaknesses were also an important factor. Cutthroat competition between the railroads on the one hand, and between the operators on the other, brought on overproduction. This led to falling prices, wage cuts, and unemployment. All added up to suffering among the miners, and the 1873 panic intensified it.

Conditions the miners complained of and fought to alleviate included starvation wages, inhumanely long hours, unreasonable dockages for impurities in the coal they sent up to the breaker; dishonesty of company checkweighmen, compulsory purchases at the company "pluck-me" stores which overcharged them; payment in scrip by those companies chartered to issue their own paper; and favoritism and discrimination at the mines by petty bosses cloaked with a little authority.

The leading factor in the industry was the Reading Railroad which, with its coal and iron subsidiary, had undisputed mastery of the middle and southern fields; and the dominant voice was that of its young president, Franklin B. Gowen. It is no mere accident, therefore, that "the company," as the Reading was referred to, and Gowen appear so frequently in these ballads.

Gowen was an able, daring, and aggressive industrialist who made use of histrionic gifts to keep himself in the limelight. Essentially a superb showman, he did things in the grand manner. A "rugged individualist," he was intolerant of opposition whether it came from stockholders, competitors or employees.

Before his election as president in 1869—he was thirty-four at the time—the Reading, through conservative management, had attained the strongest possible position as one of the nation's largest and most prosperous corporations. Yet Gowen departed from this conservative policy the moment he took office when he conceived the grandiose scheme of buying up all the coal-bearing lands served by the company, and the properties of hard-pressed individual operators in the same territory.

Between 1871 and 1874 he succeeded in purchasing one hundred thousand acres—many of the tracts at inflated prices—and organized a subsidiary, the Philadelphia & Reading Coal and Iron Company, to administer the holdings and mine the coal. To pay for this vast acreage and for new mine equipment proved too great a burden for the Reading Railroad, and an orgy of borrowing ensued. Gowen went to London for most of his capital, and British financiers obtained control of the company, keeping it until the eighties. By his large-scale purchases Gowen had created a great reservoir of coal traffic for his railroad, but he was unable to control economic conditions which, in the seventies, made it difficult to handle this traffic profitably. Hence he was in constant trouble and was kept busy trying to explain mounting losses, and passed dividends to the company's stockholders and bondholders. He was able to stave off disaster until 1880, when the company was finally forced into receivership.

Gowen's pet obsession was trade unionism. The W. B. A. was in the ascendancy when he became the Reading's president, and by word and deed he showed that he was determined to crush it. For the company it was an expensive fight, involving the use of the blacklist, coal and iron police, labor spies, and the importing of contract labor. The ballads in this chapter and the next paint a vivid picture of the relentlessness of this campaign of repression, and of its effect on the mining population. Gowen was actuated primarily by two motives—to remove the threat to his one-man control of the company's labor policies, and to keep the wage bill down to a minimum. However, his critics charged that in seeking to destroy the union he was moved by a desire to redeem himself in the eyes of his stockholders and bondholders, most of them British, who protested continued losses.

In 1869 the W. B. A. ordered a suspension, obeyed only by the mine workers in the southern field, to allow surplus coal to be disposed of. It came to an end with a joint agreement, the first in the industry, signed by the W. B. A. and the Anthracite Board of Trade, recently created for the purpose of dealing collectively with the union. This agreement provided for a sliding scale to regulate wages in accordance with the rise and fall of average prices at Port Carbon, then the head of the Schuylkill canal. The basis for calculating monthly percentages was three dollars a ton, the miners to receive a five percent increase for every twenty-five cent advance in the market price above three dollars. When the price fell below the basis, a suspension would go into effect until the market had adjusted itself.

The miners had accepted the sliding scale in good faith as a means of stabilizing relations with their employers. Only a few months later, however, when market prices took a tumble, the Anthracite Board of Trade put into effect wage cuts which the men refused to accept, maintaining that they were in violation of their agreement. Consequently they were locked out and remained idle for about four months until they had accepted the so-called "Gowen's Compromise," which called for a two-and-a-half-dollar basis and a percentage of eight and a quarter on or off the basis.

"The Sliding Scale" bears evidence of having been inspired by Gowen's Compromise. It illuminates the lighter side of the device which drove miners daft trying to keep account of their earnings in the face of market fluctuations. The ballad was composed by Thomas Morgan, a St. Clair miner, who sent a copy to Gowen in his neatest handwriting and received in return a crisp new ten dollar bill, but no comment. It was sung for me in 1938 by Mrs. Bridget Monahan, a miner's widow aged eighty-three, at her St. Clair home. Another variant was used in my previous collection.

"What Makes Us Strike?" which appeared during the seventies gives the miners' philosophy of the strike as a weapon. I found it in the archives of the Historical Society of Schuylkill County.

The coal operators' viewpoint is set forth in the ballad "W. B. A." Directed against the Irish miners, it was ironically cast in the Irish dialect. It was circulated as a broadside in Schuylkill County in 1871, shortly after being printed in the Pottsville *Miners' Journal.* Caustic and downright insulting, it must have stirred the miners' ire. Having more potent weapons, the operators rarely employed balladry in their battles with the workers, which makes this ballad of especial interest. I copied it from one of the broadsides.

The W. B. A. resisted substantial wage cuts, even during the '73 panic, because the operators could not get together long enough to forget their own bitter rivalries. However, Gowen succeeded in uniting them late in 1874 on a wage-slashing scheme that affected the entire industry.

Protesting the cut, the W. B. A. went on strike, though against the advice and pleas of some of its leaders who feared the united strength of the operators. Heretofore strikes had been local or sectional in scope, with one field profiting from the strikes of the other. This 1875 strike started with production suspended everywhere. However, in a few weeks the northern men gave up the struggle by accepting a cut, and thus abandoned their fellow strikers in the southern and middle fields. To add to the latter's misfortune, some of their own men began to desert. Stigmatized as blacklegs, they were scorned by the strikers.

"The Blacklegs," written by Patrick Johnson, a Schuylkill County bard then working as a blacksmith at the Eagle Hill colliery, attempts to explain the motives of these men.

"The Long Strike," which appeared in the Panther Creek Valley in the second month of this struggle, seems to have been inspired by these defections. Obviously its aim was to buoy up discouraged hearts, and it must have acted as a tonic to the strikers whose morale was weakening through cold, hunger, and persecution. I obtained the ballad from the late William Forgay of Lansford who had been one of the strikers. He recalled the words without much trouble as he had sung them many times during those trying months.

As the strike wore on, suffering increased, especially among women and children. The strikers offered to return to the pits if the W. B. A. would be given a voice in the settlement. They had wanted so desperately to save their union! Many of the independent operators were willing to settle on this basis, but not the big corporations. Seeing a chance to break the union, they held out for a fight to the finish. The strike dragged on till June when it fizzled out. When the men returned to work they were weakened in body from long privation, humbled in pride and broken in spirit, their union smashed. And Gowen reported to his stockholders that "the company had rid itself of the last vestiges of trade unionism."

If conditions were bad before "the long strike" of 1875, they became infinitely worse after it, as told in the ballad, "After the Long Strike." Purporting to be a letter from one Schuylkill County miner to another who had returned to his home in England, it was published in a Pottsville paper in 1878. The paper endorsed it as "a just portrayal of conditions existing in the region."

"The Hard Working Miner" and "A Stranger at the Scoop" throw additional light on those sad, sad seventies. They were composed at the time by a miner, Patrick J. O'Neill, who became better known as "Giant" O'Neill, bard and minstrel. He sang both ballads for me in the back room of an Atlantic City chop house during the 1925 season. Between ballads and schooners of beer, he gave me and the customers who had gathered around us a demonstration of the jig dancing which long had endeared him to his fellow miners of the anthracite region. The last stanza of "A Stranger at the Scoop" was added during the 1902 strike. As O'Neill explained, "Conditions were then still the same as in the seventies."

The destruction of the W. B. A. did not improve the Reading's financial condition. It continued to show a loss every year from 1876 until it was forced into receivership four years later. Being human, the mine workers derived no little satisfaction from the knowledge that Gowen was having troubles of his own, and when he committed suicide in a Washington hotel in 1889 they believed that he had done it out of remorse, though the real reason was not revealed.

Gowen's costly failure to reach the Mammoth seam at East Mines, near Pottsville, gave them cause to laugh, as reflected in the mocking ballad, "The Big Hole in the Ground." Warned by engineers that the Mammoth at this point lay 2,600 feet deep, rendering it impracticable to mine, Gowen nevertheless persisted in sinking a shaft. Not until he had dropped a fortune in that big hole in the ground and its echo in England had caused a great uproar among British security holders did he abandon the venture.

Gowen had not stamped out trade unionism, as he believed. He had merely driven it underground. The W. B. A. was still warm in its grave when a new union made its surreptitious invasion of the industry. This was the "Noble Order of the Knights of Labor," a vertical union which was known locally and secretly as the "Five Stars." Its motto, borrowed from Solon, was, "That is the most perfect Government in which an injury to one is the concern of all." Its first district assembly was instituted at Scranton in July 1876.

Its activities cloaked in secrecy, protected by codes and passwords, the Knights of Labor spread rapidly through the industry. Its necessary secrecy, however, drew sharp criticism in a region that had not yet recovered from the violence of the Molly Maguires, who also had moved in darkness and secrecy. This proved a serious handicap.

It was at the height of its power when, in December 1887, engineers and trainmen of the Port Richmond branch of the Reading were discharged for refusing to haul goods for a shipper on the union's blacklist. The railroaders called a strike which quickly spread to the anthracite mine workers, who had grievances of their own. The strike, however, was ill timed. The northern miners continued working, and disunity broke out in the strikers' own ranks. In three months the strike was over and the Knights of Labor joined the W. B. A. in the limbo of the anthracite miners' lost causes.

"The Knights of Labor Strike" preserves the memory of that struggle. It was one of several ballads by John Hory of Ashland which I obtained from him.

Number Six Patch in the Panther Creek Valley stood the full brunt of the Knights of Labor strike, as its men left for other parts, chiefly the northern anthracite field, to find work to tide them over the struggle. When they returned and began drawing pay at the colliery again, the patch resumed its normal way, as told in Joseph Gallagher's balled, "Number Six Picks Up Again," which he sang for me.

One of the strike breakers during this struggle was a Pat Mullaly, who earned the doubtful honor of having a ballad sung about him. I picked up these stray lines thirteen years ago from a railroader in Carbondale who had learned it as a boy in Avoca, Luzerne County.

In 1890, anthracite workers were heartened by reports that a new union, the United Mine Workers of America, had been formed in the bituminous coal fields. In 1894 the young union sent its first emissary into the anthracite region. He was John

Fahy of Columbus, Ohio, a fearlessly eloquent young man with dark hair, drooping mustache, and eyes as dreamy as a poet's. Fahy led coal and iron police a merry chase through the mine patches, and after several months succeeded in organizing his first local union at Forrestville, Schuylkill County. He continued his activities all through the middle and southern fields. After the 1902 strike, when the region was divided by the union into three districts, Fahy was elected president of No. 9 with headquarters at Shamokin. Ten years later, his job completed, he returned to his Ohio home.

The union's president, thirty-year-old John Mitchell, made his entrance in 1899. Wearing a long black coat and clerical collar, soft spoken and matter of fact, with deep-set burning eyes, Mitchell appeared more like a missionary than the conventional labor leader. So moved was he by the plight of the mine workers—one hundred and fifty thousand of them—that he resolved to do his utmost to free them from their economic serfdom. No one knew better than Mitchell the tremendous odds he faced; on the one hand the powerful financial groups that controlled the industry, and on the other the disunity among the mine workers; sectional rivalries and jealousies; distrust between the English-speaking workers and the Slavic group they called "Hunks" and "Roundheads."

Mitchell spent a hard year organizing the miners into a disciplined body. He crowned his year's work with a call for a convention, where a set of modest demands was drawn up. He then invited the coal operators to meet him. When they ignored him he issued a strike call on September 17, 1900. Fortunately for the miners this strike came in the midst of the McKinley-Bryan presidential campaign. Mark Hanna, Republican Party boss, urged J. P. Morgan, head of one of the two money combines controlling the industry, to settle with the workers to avoid the development of an issue of social injustice. Mitchell called another convention at which the miners' demands were modified to make it easier for the operators to settle. The latter refused to meet the men around the conference table, but quietly posted notices on their bulletin boards abolishing the sliding scale and granting the men a ten percent increase in wages to April 1, 1901. Since these were among their major demands the miners joyfully regarded this as a victory for the new union. The strike was called off officially on October 29 and the jubilant miners established the date as Mitchell Day, an annual holiday that is still observed. The victory inspired Henry Carey's ballad "Break the News to Morgan."

April 1901 rolled around almost too soon for comfort, and Mitchell sought to negotiate a new agreement. The operators announced they had renewed the scale for another year.

As April 1902 approached, the fear grew that a showdown between operators and miners could be avoided no longer. Mitchell, desperately aware that he was not yet prepared for a real test of strength, sought mediation. Instead of granting the union a few concessions, the operators actually drove the workers into its arms by their arrogance. Mitchell, still pursuing a policy of conciliation, invited the operators to a conference in February of 1902. While they did not ignore him this time, their replies were uniformly unsatisfactory to Mitchell and his followers. A tri-district convention of miners was called at Shamokin during which Mitchell sent the operators telegrams offering to mediate the men's demands. Again he was rebuffed. The convention thereupon voted a temporary suspension on May 12, 1902. One hundred and forty thousand men and boys responded. Two days later another convention was called at Hazleton to consider making the suspension permanent. Mitchell was still hopeful for peace and so were many delegates. Hazleton took on a holiday appearance with bunting and flags flying and bands serenading the delegates. Some of the men from remote mine patches had brought homing pigeons in pasteboard boxes ready to fly back home with the news to the anxious womenfolk. Good news did not go back. After a bitter debate on the floor, the convention, by a narrow margin, authorized Mitchell to call a strike.

The Slavs worried Mitchell. How would they stand up in this fight? Undisciplined, illiterate peasants, would they remain loyal to the union? When he first came into the region Mitchell saw clearly that if he were to succeed in his mission to organize the industry, racial and national barriers must first be broken down. He made this one of his first objectives. All races, creeds, and classes he addressed with this gospel: "The coal you dig is not Slavish coal, or Polish coal, or Irish coal. It is coal." At every opportunity he urged the Welsh and Irish miners to be tolerant toward their Slavic brothers. It took time and much persuasion to dissipate the mutual hatred and distrust existing between these groups. Gradually he accomplished his purpose, and Slavs mingled with English-speaking fellow workers at mass meetings, picnics, and parades on terms of equality. The Slavs grew to love Mitchell. When he finally issued the call to strike, there was no doubt in his mind as to where they stood. The ballad, "Me Johnny Mitchell Man," in the Slavic-American dialect, which was sung throughout the region, had reassured him. It was composed by Con Carbon, whose sister, Mrs. James Sheerin of Wilkes-Barre, gave me version A. Jerry Byrne, Buck Run fireboss and minstrel, sang version B.

The mine workers and their families at first took the strike in holiday spirit. Flags were hoisted over homes. Women dressed up and went visiting while the men puttered around the house or in the tiny garden performing chores they had neglected when they were employed. Before long, however, the specter of industrial war hung over the region. The first sign of the operators' stiffening attitude appeared when mules were brought out of the mines and turned loose in pastures. Workers living in company houses received quit notices. Strike-breakers were brought in to augment the few thousand miners who had refused to strike, thereby enabling the partial operation of some workings. Collieries were fortified with electrified moats and stockades and with garrisons of coal and iron police. Mounted National Guardsmen appeared in the towns where they were joined by State troopers and local police. Mitchell and the priests urged the men to be peaceable and remain sober. They obeyed.

Release from restlessness was found by miners and their families in parades through villages, towns, and cities. Led by bands and bugle and drum corps and carrying home-made banners which bore such legends as "We are slaves now but Mitchell will soon set us free," these poorly clad processions went on singing, laughing, and cheering. They stopped to serenade the home of every man still working. There were daylight parades, before-breakfast parades, and parades after midnight. Effigies of strike-breakers were hung everywhere, and at one point fifty of them dangled from one telegraph pole. There was one effigy of a man dressed in mining clothes and hob-nailed shoes which bore a placard "J. P. Morgan." As the summer wore on and no sign of an early settlement appeared on the horizon, there developed an hegira for the big cities of the East where strikers sought work to tide them over until peace came. Having no money they departed on freight trains, which were jocularly known as "Johnny Mitchell specials," celebrated in the ballad "On Johnny Mitchell's Train." Some of the younger men, more free to move than the married workers, struck out for the Klondike. "When Jim Gets to Klondike" originated during the strike. Dennis P. Coyle of Wilkes-Barre and David E. Fuge of the same city sang variants of this ballad. "On Johnny Mitchell's Train" was supplied by Jerry Byrne.

For the vast majority of strikers there was no alternative but to stick it out at home. With the passing of summer, want and suffering became acute. Thousands of families subsisted on little more than bread and water until relief came from the cities. Despite the apparent hopelessness of the cause, Mitchell, still idolized everywhere, was comforted by the thought that the men were sticking. Public opinion was with the strikers, and most of the country's newspapers supported them. One of the breaks came late in the strike when George F. Baer, operators' spokesman, wrote a letter, duly printed and derided in the newspapers, in which he intimated that the operators were doing God's work.

The country was beginning to see the specter of a coalless winter with its attendant suffering. Merchants in the mining towns were being ruined as banks refused to carry them longer. Public opinion, in and outside the region, raised a clamor for an end to the strike. Mitchell as usual was ready to arbitrate, but the operators remained obdurate until Theodore Roosevelt, then President, threatened to take over their properties if they still refused. A White House conference was followed by the appointment of a Board of Arbitration, and the strike was at an end on October 23, 1902. Out of arbitration emerged a permanent Board of Conciliation which still functions.

Thus came to a close the greatest strike in American history.

Mitchell is still the anthracite mine workers' greatest hero, and a monument to his memory stands in the courthouse square at Scranton. It was dedicated by John L. Lewis in 1924.

WHAT MAKES US STRIKE?

"How far to Pottsville?" Stranger, did you say?
I guess it's 'bout a dozen miles away,
Straight out in that direction—o'er the hill.
"Do any Mollies lie in wait to kill?"
Oh, no. You're south of the mountain,
And murdering Mollies, sir, you needn't count on.
You see we're civilized on this side,
And do not deadly weapons hide
As do, I hear, the men on th' other;
Here we're good and kind to one another.
"A miner?" Yes, sir, I work in the coal.
But some men treat you as though we had no soul,
You see these big bugs look down on the miner,
They're better—more educated—finer.
That's what they think; but I think th' other way,
And think myself as good, sir, any day
As any man that walks upon this earth,
No matter what his name or place of birth.
I wouldn't bow my knee to General Grant,
Never did—nor could—and what is more, I shan't.
What's that you say? What makes us strike?
Well, now you've hit a subject which I like
To talk upon to strangers, for you'll understand,
A very wrong impression fills the land—
That we are lazy, bloody, reckless men,
Who live beneath the ground, in cave and den;
And come out once a while to get the light
To burn a breaker, kill a boss, or fight—
That miners ain't like other folks do be;
All is wrong which I will let you see.
We're men like you, though not so finely clad,
Some of us are good, and others very bad,
Just as you'll find in any other set
Of men who work their daily bread to get.
A pretty independent lot we are likewise,
And will allow no boss to tyrannize,

We hate that like the Devil hates the water
Blessed by the priest—and so we oughter.
Besides all this, you see the work is hard,
We oft get hurt, and sometimes lost, pard;
And consequently we good wages like,
And when we can't get that, why, sir, we strike.
That's how it comes—I don't see we're to blame,
For any other men would do the same.
But don't think, Stranger, we make all the strikes,
There's Mr. Gowen makes one when he likes.
To him they don't say bah about the thing;
But see the difference—he's a Railroad King!
And then again, this Mr. Gowen's sly,
And makes the people think the reason why
The mines have stopped is that the men have struck
For higher wages—darn the fellow's luck!
He always makes believe we're in the wrong,
And draws his pictures of us pretty strong.
He says he is the workman's great admirer,
While we, in turn, say he's the great conspirer
Against our price, our liberties, our rights,
And the instigator of one-half our fights.
But I think I've said enough to you, a stranger.
Good-bye, that's the way—there's no danger.
"Have a drink?" Well, no, I think I won't;
Some miners like their whiskey, but I don't.
In fact, to tell the truth, I can't afford it
Since corporations stepped in here to lord it
O'er us poor devils, who have got to poke
In dust all day—I'll take a smoke.
Good-bye, Stranger; hope I'll see you again,
And mind, tell them we're like other men.

W. B. A.

An' fwat ar yez wantin' Paddy from Cork;
An' fwat is the fuss anyhow;

An' fwy are yez all afther stoppin' yer work;
  An' raisin' a Kilkenny row?

Shure the wages is betther nor iver yez got
  In yer d——d little "Gim of the Say";
Yez have a foine cabin, a cow and a lot,
  And whiskey, tobaccy and tay.

Troth a shillin' a day wud hev done for yez thin;
  An' thankful ye'd bin for that same;
One wud think to hear now, how yez slutther at tin,
  Yez wuz raised upon paches and crame.

Yez talk of the resk, workin' undher the ground,
  Away from the light of the day,
There's divil a wun would be there, I'll be bound,
  If ye'd git at aught else, the same pay.

Go back to yer work, me broth of a boy,
  An' shtop all yer strikes an' yer fuss.
Or divil a wun will get any employ,
  An' ye'll soon all be shtarvin' or wuss.

It's d——d little minin' yer doin' at all;
  There's others work betther nor you.
Yer fit but for ditchin' out in the canawl,
  Or workin' wid some railroad crew.

If minin' don't suit yez, why go till the Wist,
  Or anywhere's out of the way;
'Twouldn't grieve uz at all if yez all were at rist
  'Neath the sod of yer bog in the say.

So shtart or be off—(we're wanting no such)
  An' lit those min who want to work, be:
We've miners enough, both English and Dutch,
  An' in your place we'll get the Chinee.

THE SLIDING SCALE

Come all ye jolly miners who love to hear a song,
I will unfold a circumstance which to us all belongs;
It's of those operators as I do tell the tale—
How nice they pull down the price upon the sliding scale.

REFRAIN

To meetings they did go; to meetings they did go
They tried all means and laid all schemes to keep the poor man low.

And thinking that the scale would turn the men did work along
Expecting for the coming month to have eight and a quarter on,
But when the twenty-fifth did come, it was the same old tale
To have eight and a quarter off, me boys, upon the sliding scale.

So now those operators themselves begin to slide
And just take notice of my word, they have a noble guide,
One-half the coal mines that's around I'm sure will be for sale
To pay the interest of their debts upon the sliding scale.

Success to Gowen, I do say, to carry out his plan,
To purchase all the Schuykill mines and elsewhere if he can.
And you hear those operators with a loud and mournful tale
Saying, "All we made is gone at last upon the sliding scale."

If anyone shall ask you who did compose this song,
Tell them it was Thomas Morgan composed it right or wrong.
And in the basis of '69 in a tune he told the tale
How the operators would be fixed upon the sliding scale.

THE BLACKLEGS

Curiosity caused me one evening to ramble,
It's down by the Shoofly I chanced for to stray.
I espied two old ladies in great conversation—
In silence I waited to hear what they'd say.

Says one to the other: "Poor people's ruint
  If the basis ain't settled in a day or two;
Bad luck to thim blacklegs, I wish they were vanished.
  And good union men would get somethin' to do."

"Don't shpake so cruel," replied her companion,
  "For the blackleg's proven that he is a wise man;
He's a hard-hearted father who'd see his child starvin'
  And no one on earth to lend him a hand.
It's thim as has plenty can live ver' da'nty,
  And thim as is poor for employment must push.
There's an old maxim since I was a baby—
  'A bird in the hand is worth two in the bush.' "

"Then if it be true," said one to the other,
  "There's a great many men workin' well able to stand;
But no, they must keep their few dollars together
  To take advantage of their fellow men.
It's dead was our heroes when our own states was in trouble?
  They quickly rebelled when John Bull taxed the tea!
It was none o' your blacklegs signed the Declaration—
  If it was, sure this country would ne'er be free."

"If ye examine that cent'ry, I'm sure you'll find plenty
  Of blacklegs, as well as there is in our day.
Then there was leaders; they was no deceivers;
  When men went into battle did not them betray.
No doubt, me good lady, your leaders was honest;
  Thim levies they made, they kept 'em I'm sure—
This is th' country for good edjicashun;
  The lesson ye l'arn, for it ye pay dear."

"What if this union was forsaken forever,
  And poor men made slaves as they've been before?
To make matters worse, they must work for small wages;
  They ne'er can pay their bills that they owe in the store.
If they had been united and pulled all together,
  And kept politics within their own bounds—

But when they were elected, the poor was neglected;
  They sold the men's freedom to Franklin B. Gowen."

"I see it's but folly, to talk to ye, Molly,
  But mind what I tell ye: on no one depend.
It's well I remember, one day last November,
  When me pocket was empty I lost me best friend."
"When the men go back to work, they must all be determined
  To prepare for a struggle in some future day.
This is me road, I must bid ye good evenin'—
  The childer's alone, I must be away."

THE LONG STRIKE

Come all you jolly colliers, wherever you may be,
I pray you will attention give and listen unto me,
I have a doleful tale, and to relate it I will strive—
About the great suspension in eighteen seventy-five.

In eighteen hundred and seventy-five, our masters did conspire
To keep men, women, and children without either food or fire.
They tho't to starve us to submit with hunger and with cold,
But the miners did not fear them, but stood out brave and bold.

Now two long months are nearly o'er—that no one can deny,
And for to stand another month we are willing for to try,
Our wages shall not be reduced, tho' poverty do reign,
We'll have seventy-four basis, boys, before we'll work again.

And when we get the basis, boys, we'll work again with joy,
We'll never mind them blacklegs named peddlers or decoys.
May the world all frown upon them, for such traitors they have been!
And may each miner think of them whene'er we do begin.

So come all you jolly colliers, that appreciate good times,
And never mind them blacklegs I have mentioned in my rhyme,
They are a disgrace unto their race, wherever they may be—
Traitors to their fellow miners, likewise society.

AFTER THE LONG STRIKE

Well, we've been beaten, beaten all to smash,
And now, sir, we've begun to feel the lash,
As wielded by a gigantic corporation,
Which runs the commonwealth and ruins the nation.
Our "Union" lamp, friend John, no longer shineth:
It's gone up where the gentle woodbine twineth;
A great man demonstrated beyond a doubt
The miners would better fare without
Any such thing; trade unions were a curse
Upon God's fair creation, nothing worse.
It died, because the miners did neglect it;
And he declares they shall not resurrect it.
And thus the matter stands. We do not dare
To look a boss in the face and whisper "Bah,"
Unless we wish to join the mighty train
Of miners wandering o'er the earth like Cain.
And, should you wish to start upon a tramp,
O'er hillock, mountain, valley, plain and swamp,
Or travel as the pilgrim of John Bunyan,
One talismanic word will do it, "Union."
Just murmur that, and all the laws of state
Or Congress will not save you from your fate;
They'll drive you out, forfeit your goods, degrade you,
Just as the British did in old Acadia.

Our wages, John, grow beautifully less,
And, if they keep on growing thus, I guess
We'll have to put on magnifying specs,
To see the little figures on our checks.
The sliding scale which once some comfort sent us
Is now declared to be non compos mentis.
To curse it dreadfully we are incited,
Because, somehow, it works so darned one-sided,
It suffers from a bad disease, "decline,"
And pines away right down to twenty-nine.

It's nothing strange to find on seeing the docket
We've worked a month and still are out of pocket.
It makes a man feel dirty cheap, you bet,
To work a month and then come out in debt.
And now, friend John, in fewer words I'll state
What I've been trying to communicate:
Lest anything herein you misconstrue,
In Anglo-Saxon plain I'll say to you—
If in exchange for the labor of a day
You wish to have an honest fair day's pay;
If you do wish to have just rights among
Those of freedom of action, speech and tongue,
If you do wish to have a fair supply
Of wholesome food, be buried when you die
With decent rites—by this I mean at least
Sufficient to distinguish man from beast,
Stay where you are, or, if you must go hence,
Go East, go North, go South, no consequence.
Take any one direction; you'll be blest
Sooner with what you seek than coming West.
In short, if you wish to enjoy God's bounty,
Go anywhere except to Schuylkill County.

THE HARD WORKING MINER

(AIR: *I'm a Man You Don't Meet Every Day*)

I'm a hard working man, you can see by my hands,
  Although I am friendly and free.
A dollar a day is a very small pay
  For a man with a large family.
I didn't come here, boys, to boast or to brag,
  But just for to tell you my troubles,
I work day and night and the world I must fight
  And load coal with my pick and my shovel.

THE STRIKE

CHORUS

I work in the mines where the sun never shines
  Nor daylight does ever appear;
With my lamp blazing red on the top of my head,
  And in danger I never know fear.

Just think of the poor man who works in the mines
  With the mules and the rats underground;
Where the smoke is so thick you can cut it with a stick,
  And can weigh it on scales by the pound.
My face it is black from the dust of the coal,
  Though my heart it is open and free;
I would share my last loaf with the man that's in want,
  Though I earn it hard you can see.

Now, my kind friends, I will bid you good-bye;
  I cannot stay here any longer,
I'll pick up my pack, throw it o'er my back,
  And I think I will make my road shorter,
I have a wife and small family at home in the house,
  And to meet me I'm sure they'll be glad,
They will stand at the door when I'm on my way home,
  And they'll say to their mama, "Here's Dad."

A STRANGER AT THE SCOOP

(AIR: *The Man at the Top Does All the Work*)

I came to this country a stranger unknown,
I hadn't any friends to give me a home;
My pockets were empty, I hadn't a stamp,
So I thought I would work, boys, before I would tramp,
I went to the boss, he had a lamp in his hand,
He said, "I'll engage you, you're a strong looking man,"
I said, "My good boss, I want none of your taffy,
You can give me a job but you mustn't laugh at me."

CHORUS

I work for the company and Franklin B. Gowen,
From the top of the shaft with a rope I'm let down,
I travel in the gangway to the face of my work;
I'm surrounded by danger in the bowels of the earth.

The first thing you'll do, boys, you'll pick up your drill,
You will then sound the top and your car you can fill,
If the top it is bad, drill in a long hole,
Give it powder and tampin' and blow lots of coal;
You will then break the lumps, throw them into the car—
Wipe the sweat off your face—I tell you it is hard.
When your legs you must bend and your back you must stoop,
You will curse the first man who invented the scoop.

There's one thing I'll tell you and don't you forget,
That your back with the droppers is all wringing wet,
Your clothes they're soaking; your shoes are wet through,
Oh! never be a miner whatever you do.
The man who is outside his life it is safe,
If an accident happens he has time to escape,
But the poor weary miner that works underground,
If the top it should fall he would never be found.

I wish that the company would give us a chance,
Our hours they would shorten and wages advance,
I ne'er would grumble for that would suit me;
And I'm sure with that same all the rest would agree.
On three days a week, boys, our living we make,
And we work like mules for the bit that we eat;
But now we have a union let them say what they may;
We will strike for more wages than a dollar a day.

We can boast of our leader, a man of great fame,
He is loyal to the cause, John Mitchell is his name;
He will never betray us, for gold he don't care,
He's a man God made to be honest and fair.

There's three more I'll mention; their names are well known,
John Fahy, John Siney and our beloved Mother Jones,
They built up our union and it's here now to stay,
And we'll strike for more wages than a dollar a day.

THE BIG HOLE IN THE GROUND

(AIR: *The Irish Washerwoman*)

Draw near to me, friends, form a circle around,
And join in the chorus with music compound,
To the song that I sing which will fully expound
Poor Franklin B. Gowen's big hole in the ground;
Some nine years ago Mister Frank had a dream,
And when he awakened he loudly did scream,
"Skim milk for John Tucker, but I'll have the cream,
For I'll sink a big shaft to the great Mammoth seam."

Repeat first stanza for chorus.

How to undermine Tucker and give him a shake
Some lessons in mining he thought he would take
From dirty stock gamblers or any old rake,
No matter from whom so he was on the make;
And how he succeeded is well understood.
Tho' he didn't prove much to the company's good,
But now that they have him 'tis fair that they should
Pay fully enough for their foolhardihood.

'Twas a great undertake for a limb of the law,
And a poor one at that, for he's nothing but jaw,
But by tricks and deception he thought he foresaw
How that we might play him a second John Law;
The far south sea bubbles were greatly renowned,
And a plausible scheme John Law thought he had found,
But the schemes of this upstart are such all around,
As his wonderful hole—the big hole in the ground.

Frank thought himself clever and very discreet,
And choosed for his foreman a regular beat,
Who said he could sink him a shaft all complete,
And bottom the vein at fourteen hundred feet,
And this great engineer with his pictures profound,
And level and compass went bobbing around,
But the great Mammoth vein not yet has been found,
In Franklin B. Gowen's big hole in the ground.

And now for the sequel I think I might pull,
By telling a tale that is quite wonderful,
How Frank succeeded in pulling the wool
O'er the eyes of our big-belly'd cousin John Bull;
Now John for his money will roar I'll be bound,
And his army and navy will soon be around;
But his forces we'll sink with his ten million pound,
In Franklin B. Gowen's big hole in the ground.

THE KNIGHTS OF LABOR STRIKE

(AIR: *The British Grenadiers*)

We're brave and gallant miner boys
  That work in underground,
For courage and good nature
  None like us can be found.
We work both late and early,
  And get but little pay
To support our wives and children,
  In free Americ-a.

Here's to the Knights of Labor,
  That brave and gallant band,
That Corbin and old Swigard
  Is trying to disband.
But stick and hang brave union men;
  We'll make them rue the day

They thought to break the K. of L.
  In free Americ-a.

If Satan took the blacklegs,
  I'm sure 'twould be no sin,
What peace and happiness 'twould be
  For us poor workingmen.
Eight hours we'd have for labor,
  Eight hours we'd have for play,
Eight hours we'd have for sleeping,
  In free Americ-a.

Corbin, Cox and Swigard,
  What will you have to say
When you meet our Master
  Upon the Judgment Day?
With a frown He will confront you,
  And show you the other way,
Saying, you have starved my children,
  In free Americ-a.

They're trying to run the Keystone,
  Assisted by Adam Knapp,
Bill Davis at the bottom,
  And Bill Raudy at the top.
But stick and hang, brave union men!
  We'll show them Yankee play,
And drive them off to blazes
  In free Americ-a.

When this strike is at an end,
  And we have gained the day,
We'll drink a health to our miner boys,
  Both near and far away;
And our brothers on the railroad
  In free Americ-a.

NUMBER SIX PICKS UP AGAIN

(AIR: *Annie Laurie*)

Old Number Six is brisky, she has risen from the dead,
When the boys get full of whiskey, they paint the town bright red;
They paint the town bright red, no home till the bottle goes dry,
For old Number Six, my birthplace, I'd lay me down and die.

We've a poll to cast our vote at, a club room to pass our time,
We're out of sight wi' the ladies, especially those that's blind;
Especially those that's blind, for a glimpse at our figure they sigh,
For old Number Six, my birthplace, I'd lay me down and die.

How well do I remember the games we used to play!
When I was young and tender, it seems like yesterday;
It seems like yesterday, those good old days gone by,
For old Number Six, my birthplace, I'd lay me down and die.

PAT MULLALY

There's Pat Mullaly who never kept tally,
He would work a mule's work to get two men's pay.
Let us all get together and write him a letter,
The quicker the better to get him out of the way.

CHORUS

We'll combine, the union join,
And work eight hours a day;
And keep the market clear of coal,
And then they'll raise our pay.

BREAK THE NEWS TO MORGAN

(AIR: *Break the News to Mother*)

When monopolists were trying to satisfy their greed,
The miners they were struggling their families to feed,
When a call from brave John Mitchell: "Come, boys,
Your tools throw down and drive those slavery days away."
"We will," the miners shouted. "We'll shake them off or die,
Shake them off but stay united;
It is an honest cause, we cannot fail,
And some day we'll have the abolition of the sliding scale."

FIRST CHORUS

Just break the news to Morgan, that great official organ,
And tell him we want ten percent of increase in our pay.
Just say we are united and that our wrongs must be righted,
And with those unjust company stores of course we will do away.

From that great and glorious Mitchell, our national president,
To all the corporations an invitation went,
To attend a joint convention to be held in Hazelton
And there our grievances arbitrate.
But when they ignored his message, he said: "I'll call a strike
And have our wrongs adjusted in that way."
We struck and were successful, so then a scale was formed,
Agreeable unto the first of May.

SECOND CHORUS

It came from J. P. Morgan, that great official organ.
He said, "I'll give you ten percent of increase in your pay."
He saw we were united, that our wrongs must be righted,
And now for brave John Mitchell, we will give three cheers, hooray."

ME JOHNNY MITCHELL MAN

A

Now you know Mike Sokolosky—
Dat man my brudder.
Last night him come to my shanty,
Un me tellin': "V'at you cummin' fer?"
Him tellin' 'bout tomorra dark night,
Every miner all, beeg un shmall
Goin' fer on shtrike.
Un him say t' me: "Joe, me tellin' you
Dunt be 'fraid or shcared fer nottink, nevair, nevair do."
"Dunt be shcabby fella," him tellin' me again.
I'm say, "No sir! Mike, me out o' sight—
Me Johnny Mitchell man."

CHORUS

Me no 'fraid fer nottink,
Me dey nevair shcare,
Sure me shtrike tomorra night,
Dats de biziness, I dunt care.
Righta here me tellin' you—
Me no shcabby fella,
Good union citizen—
Johnny Mitchell man.

Now me belong t' union, me good citizen.
Fer seven year me livin' here
In dis beeg America.
Me vorkin' in de Prospect,
Vorkin' Dorrance shaft, Conyngham, Nottingham—
Every place like dat.
Vorkin' in de gangway, vorkin' in de breast,
Labor every day, me nevair gettin' rest.
Me got plenty money, nine hoondred, maybe ten,
So shtrike kin come, like son-of-a-gun—
Me Johnny Mitchell man.

THE STRIKE

B

Transcribed by Melvin LeMon

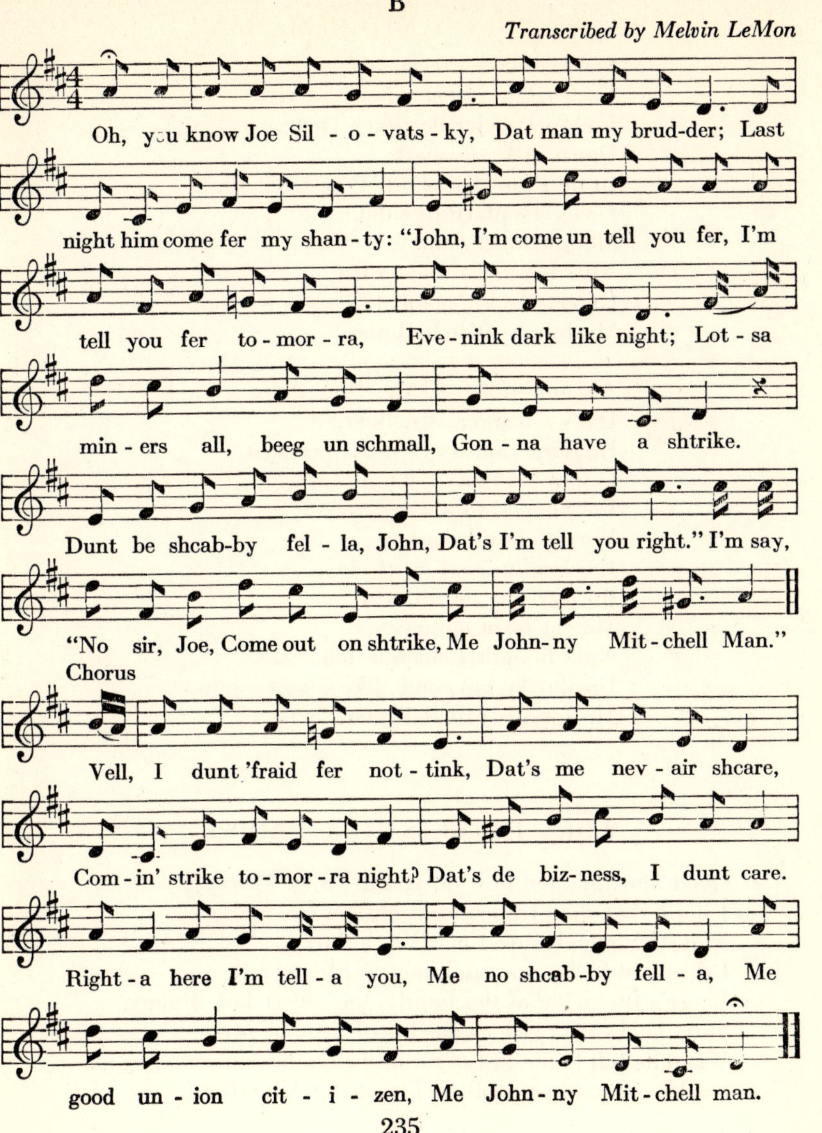
Oh, you know Joe Sil - o - vats - ky, Dat man my brud-der; Last
night him come fer my shan - ty: "John, I'm come un tell you fer, I'm
tell you fer to - mor - ra, Eve - nink dark like night; Lot - sa
min - ers all, beeg un schmall, Gon - na have a shtrike.
Dunt be shcab-by fel - la, John, Dat's I'm tell you right." I'm say,
"No sir, Joe, Come out on shtrike, Me John-ny Mit-chell Man."
Chorus
Vell, I dunt 'fraid fer not - tink, Dat's me nev - air shcare,
Com - in' strike to - mor - ra night? Dat's de biz- ness, I dunt care.
Right - a here I'm tell - a you, Me no shcab -by fell - a, Me
good un - ion cit - i - zen, Me John - ny Mit - chell man.

Vell, me belong fer union,
Me good citizen,
Seven, mebbe 'leven, year,
I'm vorkin' in beeg, beeg 'merica;
I'm vorkin' fer de Black Heat',
Down in Lytle shaft,
In de Pine Hill shaft, Pine Knot shaft,
Un every place like dat.
Me got lotsa money,
Nine hoondret mebbe ten,
Un shtrike kin come, like son-of-a-gun,
Me Johnny Mitchell man.

Ah, son-of-a-gun, Mr. Truesdale,
Dat's a bugger, Mr. Baer,
He dunt vantsa gib it ten per zent,
Cripes a'mighty dat's no fair.
I'm vorkin' in a gangway,
Vorkin' in a breast,
I'm loadin' coal every day,
By jeez, me nevair rest.
Me got lotsa money,
Nine hoondret, mebbe ten,
Un shtrike kin come, like son-of-a-gun,
Me Johnny Mitchell man.

WHEN JIM GETS TO KLONDIKE

Good mornin', and how do you do, Mrs. Murray,
I hope that the old man and childer are well,
Alas! for mesel' sure I'm all in a flurry,
I dropped in this mornin' me troubles to tell.
There's the pride of the family, me oldest lad, Jimmy,
Sure, he'd earn twice as much as Darby or Mike,
When he left home last night in his clothes not one penny,
Sez he, "Good-bye, mother, I'm off for Klondike."

Bad cess to the strikers for 'twas they that started
Me own darlin' Jim on this dang'rous trip;
He left his poor mother behind broken-hearted,
Faith, broken it was when he gave me the slip.
Me Jim was a hero, he was, Mrs. Murray,
Sure he said he'd not work or he'd not go on strike
When he left home last night, an' sure I cannot blame him;
He'll be makin' his fortune 'way out in Klondike.

And also bad cess to the men they call sojers,
Sure they are the boys keeps the workin' man down,
At the first sign of strikin' their bayonets they'll shoulder,
Like bees in a hive then they'll swarm through the town.
Sure ye can't say a word or you're shot like a h'athen,
They run the whole town and they do phat they like,
Then it's queer to me that there ain't more men l'avin',
Like me own darlin' Jimmy, 'way out to Klondike.

When Jim gets to Klondike, some money he'll send me,
They say that out there it's picked up on the strate;
I'll pay all me bills and I'll buy for young Huey
A bicycle, faith, and another for Kate.
I'll shake this ould driss I have on, Mrs. Murray,
I'll buy a fine silk one you'll ne'er see the like,
Then I'll say au revoir and I'll l'ave in a hurry,
To me own darlin' Jimmy, 'way out in Klondike.

ON JOHNNY MITCHELL'S TRAIN

(AIR: *Molly Durkin*)

I'm an honest union laboring man,
  And I'll have you understand,
I'll tell you just the reason why,
  I left the minin' land.
It was Baer and Morgan done it,
  And for it they'll repent,

For I don't intend to work a tap,
  Till I get the ten percent.

FIRST CHORUS

There's no use for Mr. Durkin,
In the coal mine to be workin';
We were a little shaky,
  But no longer we're in pain.
So what's the use o' kickin',
When the top and bottom's stickin'?
I'll pack me grip and make a trip,
  On Johnny Mitchell's train.

I struck a place called Coatesville,
  A flourishin' iron town,
Where politics were very strong,
  And candidates goin' around.
I was invited to a party,
  He says, "Phat are you doin', Dan?"
I says, "I'll tell you plumb and plain,
  I'm a Johnny Mitchell man."

When I landed in New York City,
  I a friend of course did meet,
I axed him if he would show me
  The place they call Wall street.
I met several operators,
  Assembled in a mob,
Along with a Morgan prisidint,
  I think they called him Schwab.

The small operators they were pl'adin',
  And they wanted to give in,
And recognize the union—
  But Baer said that's too thin.
So it broke up in a wrangle,
  Put Baer near insane,

Then I took a side-door Pullman car
   On Johnny Mitchell's train.

SECOND CHORUS

I'll bid you all adieu now,
Let you bid me the same,
The strike is nearly o'er,
   With joy I'm near insane.
Here's health unto the union,
Which is very strong they say,
Likewise the conductors
   On Johnny Mitchell's train.

CHAPTER EIGHT

The Molly Maguires

THE origin of the name "Molly Maguire" in Ireland is lost in legendry. There is the story of a poor widow named Molly Maguire who was evicted from her cottage by a landlord's agent. So severely abused were she and her daughter that their neighbors were roused to anger, and in future evictions in that district resistance was offered with the cry, "Remember Molly Maguire!" Another story has it that the secret order held its first meeting at the home of the woman who gave it its name. The most common legend is that it came from an Amazon who led gangs of young Irishmen, dressed in women's clothes and wearing fantastic masks, who harassed landlords' agents.

It is impossible to establish exactly when the name was first applied in the anthracite coal fields, but it is known that warnings to mine bosses signed "One of Mollie's children" were being received a decade before the Civil War. However, in those days the name generally whispered was "Buckshots." Not until after the Civil War did "Molly Maguire" come into widespread usage. This secret order had no central authority, but controlled and worked through several county divisions of the A. O. H., principally Schuylkill, Carbon, and Northumberland. It was less active in the other counties. For nearly a quarter of a century the anthracite region was, as Conan Doyle described it, "a valley of fear," the result of systematic violence attributed to the Molly Maguires. They were accused of assaulting and murdering mine bosses, and occasional fellow miners; also of firing breakers, blowing up bridges, and dynamiting railroads. Their principal motives were intimidation and revenge.

Though more than sixty years have passed since the Molly Maguires were destroyed, opinion regarding them is still to be crystallized. A movement has set in of late to interpret them in the light of present-day economic and sociological thought, and this is giving them a "break" heretofore denied them.

In an endeavor to make up my own mind concerning them, I have interviewed many elderly people who lived in that tragic era. One of those with whom I talked on the subject was a very old man living in Philadelphia who, the source of several ballads in the present collection, volunteered the information that he had been a member of the Schuylkill County division of the secret order, and had fled to Philadelphia when the region became too hot for Mollies. There was no attempt on his part to apologize for his Molly Maguire association, and his reaction was surprisingly jocular, as if he had taken part in a lark.

The Molly Maguires, for all their noise, were a small minority among Irish mine workers. Irish old-timers whom I interviewed did not overlook or condone their violence, but some held the opinion that a few Mollies were railroaded to jail or the gallows in the hysteria. Not infrequently, union leaders were tarred with the Molly Maguire brush by coal operators to discredit them or to get them out of the way—a practice made much of by the Molly defense lawyers.

Vigilantes sprang up in different localities under a variety of picturesque names, such as "Modocs," "Sheet-iron gangs," and "Chain-gangs," while one powerful group functioning in Carbon and Schuylkill Counties called itself the "Committee of Safety."

Virtually all the old-timers, Irish and Welsh alike, agreed that the economic and political oppression practised by the coal operators of the period, and the persecution and discrimination suffered by Irish mine workers, provoked and goaded the Mollies. The general opinion expressed was that the Mollies found fertile ground for a reign of terror because of the weakness of the miners' union to cope with the powerful buccaneers who ran the industry in those early days.

The Mollies' routine was somewhat as follows. First, a secret warning was given to an offender by means of an anonymous note illustrated with rude drawings of coffins and pistols. Known as a "coffin notice," it bore a threat of property damage, personal injury, or death, if a certain grievance was not removed. In case the coffin notice was disregarded, it was followed with a threat by a stranger from another colliery, or county. If the offender still refused to heed the warnings, he might be ambushed and riddled with lead, or called out of bed at night and shot before his family. Major crimes were nearly always entrusted to strange Mollies and arranged on a barter basis between two county bodymasters. Thus many crimes were not solved until long after their commission, if at all. From a town or patch it was but a few steps to the mountains where Mollies fled on their way to a hideout. Not until the Pinkerton agent, James McParland, alias Jim McKenna, had come into the region and joined the order were its secrets revealed.

The Mollies moved in an air of secrecy. To communicate with one another in public, a series of signs, toasts, quarreling toasts, general passwords and night passwords known as "the goods," were created and were changed every three months. Thus, if two Mollies got into an argument in a saloon, one would recite the current quarreling toast as, for example, "You seem to be getting vexed," the reply to which was, "Not with you, sir." Then the one Molly would place the tip of his right forefinger to the hole of his right ear and the other would do the same with his left forefinger and left ear, thus proving to each other that they were fraternity brothers.

Two Mollies meeting in a lonely place on a dark night would identify each other by one saying, "These nights are fine," and the other replying, "Yes, we shall have a fine harvest."

The general password for this particular quarter was:

Here's health to every Irishman
That lives in Ireland,
To assemble round in Dublin Town
In memory of Great Dan.

The response:

When born, he found our country
In chains and slavery.
He labored hard to set her free
But he's now in the clay.

McParland, a legendary figure in the anthracite coal fields, is remembered by old-timers as a glorified labor spy. He gallivanted up and down the region, making love to miners' daughters, drinking, dancing, gambling, and fighting—simulating the character of a wild, dissolute fellow always in pocket because of the "queer money" he was counterfeiting. He was of slender wiry build and medium height, and had a ruddy complexion, hazel eyes, and auburn hair except for his beard and mustache which were of a darker shade. His Irish brogue was thick and picturesque, as was natural in an immigrant from Ireland. He knocked about the mining country in a slouch hat, brown trousers, and a mildewy coat of the coarsest shoddy.

After sparking a young woman for the sake of the Molly secrets he might wheedle out of her, he would drop into a saloon to mingle among the boys. He had the reputation of a prince of good fellows, so he always received a warm welcome. In addition to having money to "set 'em up" he had wit and a genial disposition that disarmed even those who were suspicious of him. He won everybody by the turn of a graceful jig, by a yarn, or by singing a ballad which evoked memories of the ould sod. In other words, he acted the rôle of strolling minstrel. One must admire the consummate art with which he kept his secret, and admire too his uncanny ability to communicate information to his superiors daily, and his downright agility in getting out of situations which might have led to his premature exposure and possible death.

Characteristically it was with a non-indigenous Molly Maguire ballad, "Pat Dolan," sung by him in the barroom of Pat Dormer's Sheridan House in Pottsville, one November night in 1873, that he made his début among the Mollies. It was afterward printed in the Pinkerton book.

Meanwhile little dramas were being enacted which never reached the newspapers—dramatic episodes which reflected the struggle among a majority of Irish mining folk, aided by their priests, to keep from being drawn into the Molly Maguire maelstrom. One such episode, told to me by one who had witnessed it, took place in Centralia.

Rev. Daniel I. McDermott, its central character, was only twenty-six years old at the time. He was tall, slender, with chestnut hair and blue eyes. Able and fearless, he was a man of engaging personality and of great moral courage. Although young in years, he was well-equipped to deal with conditions as he found them in the region. He denounced the Molly Maguires, but also cried out against the coal corporations' brutalizing tactics which drove mine workers into their ranks. Some years later, as pastor of the Pottsville parish, it was he who prepared the condemned Mollies in the Schuylkill County prison for their doom.

And now here is the story:

In the spring of 1869, Father McDermott of the Philadelphia diocese came to Centralia to establish a new parish. He was in town only a short time when he began to feel the insidious presence of the Molly Maguires. Though he suspected some of his parishioners were members, it did not keep him from denouncing the secret order. His outspoken manner did not increase his popularity, many people fearing that the Mollies might retaliate against him. The people of Centralia were accustomed to talking about the Mollies in hushed voices.

One evening the young priest was in his rectory reading the evening office out of his breviary when a rap on the door interrupted him. On opening the door he saw one of his parishioners, a middle-aged woman, standing before him with her face buried in her hands, weeping. He asked the cause of her distress.

"Oh Father," she exclaimed, "help me get me lad back."

"Come, tell me, what's up with Patrick?"

"It's the Mollies. Last night they got him into a shebeen, filled him with poteen, and while he lay drunk on the floor they gave him the oath of the Molly Maguires. Ochone! Ochone! It's a murtherer they're after wantin' to make out o' me flesh and blood."

The blood rushed to the young priest's face, and he fought to control his anger.

"Bring Patrick here," he ordered. An hour later, as the frightened boy stood before him, the priest wrung from his reluctant lips all the harrowing details of a Molly initiation, and the names of the men responsible for it.

The next Sunday Father McDermott thundered his challenge to the secret order. Centralia, he solemnly warned, was too small to hold Molly Maguires and the Church of Jesus Christ. One or the other must go, he warned.

"The Church never yields to the forces of evil," he declared, "and I am here to see that it shall not in this crisis. Next Sunday you will hear from my lips the names of the cowards who are trying to tear boys from their mothers and God in order to administer to them the oath of a foul and wicked society."

Strong words, they struck consternation in the parish. The fight was now out in the open, and no one dared predict what the consequences might be. Older men in the parish who themselves were not Mollies shook their heads ruefully. They feared such recklessness would deprive the struggling young parish of a brave rector. Men who blow up bridges, fire coal breakers, and shoot bosses certainly would not hesitate to do away with a fledgling priest who they thought had spoken out of turn.

The week that followed the flinging of his challenge was the darkest, the most horrible that Father McDermott had experienced, as Mollies tried desperately to deter him from carrying out his plan. Disguised voices shouted warnings through his window at night. Coffin notices were slid under his door. Shadows lurked behind him as he walked in the evening, Mollies slinking away when he suddenly turned his head. He spurned his parishioners' offers to guard him, saying it would be glorious to die for Mother Church. And all the time he prayed fervently for strength to withstand the ordeal.

The next Sunday the little church was filled to capacity. The air was tense. At the conclusion of the Mass, Father McDermott changed his vestments for a solemn black stole. In a voice resonant with deep feeling, he reviewed the local acts of violence committed by Mollies since his coming into the parish, and recalled that he had repeatedly warned them from his pulpit to change their ways.

"They have not heeded my words," he exclaimed, "and now they shall have action."

Whereupon he called out the names of two men upon whom all eyes were turned as they stood up. Pointing an accusing finger at them, Father McDermott demanded to know if they were not members of the Molly Maguires. "No," they both replied. He then demanded to know if they had not enticed young boys into shebeens and forced the Molly oath on them while they were drunk. "No," they answered again.

Having obtained their names directly from victims, the young priest was amazed at their effrontery.

"Do you declare before God and man in this sacred house of worship that you are not guilty of these grave charges?" he thundered.

For the third time they denied their guilt.

Father McDermott then quenched the altar candles and pronounced a curse upon their heads. As he spoke, women sobbed, and tears rolled down the cheeks of hard-boiled miners.

"If you are innocent, as you swear you are," the priest said in a trembling voice, "this curse will turn into a blessing. But if you are guilty, may God have mercy on your souls."

One of the men soon after was crushed to death in the mines, while the other murdered a man in a saloon brawl and served a long term in prison.

From the crown of the hill on which sprawls the Odd Fellows' cemetery just west of Tamaqua, one may see a small clearing on the slope of Sharp Mountain. Near by runs a spring known by local tradition as Kerrigan's spring. A stone shaft might appropriately be raised here and upon its face inscribed some such legend as the following: "This marks the spot of Kerrigan's folly which led to the destruction of the Molly Maguires."

Early on the morning of September 3, 1875, Jimmy Kerrigan, bodymaster of the Tamaqua division, and two accomplices, Mickey Doyle and Ed Kelly of Mount Laffee, had murdered John P. Jones, a Lansford mine boss, on his way to the colliery. Being familiar with the rough mountainous country, Kerrigan had led his accomplices through the back roads of Lansford and Tamaqua, eluding scouts sent out to intercept them. When he came to the mountain spring southwest of Tamaqua, force of habit overcame Kerrigan's judgment. Had he led Doyle and Kelly only a few miles further west, to Tuscarora, then a notorious Molly Maguire stronghold, they would all have been safe. Doyle and Kelly could then have been put on a train to Pottsville, and the Jones murder might never have been solved. But the fugitives, mine workers by occupation, were so accustomed to opening a dinner pail at noon that when they reached this spring they stopped to eat. Believing Doyle and Kelly safe, Kerrigan, who lived near by, left them while he set out for his house to fetch food and whiskey. That act of hospitality, innocent in itself, was probably the most crucial mistake ever made by a member of the Molly Maguires.

While Doyle and Kelly were resting in the bush, a young law student named Sam Beard, who had witnessed the murder at the Lansford railroad station, had returned to Tamaqua with the tragic news. Excitement in Tamaqua rose to fever pitch. Men and boys brought out guns and stalked the streets bent on killing someone to avenge Jones's murder. Young Beard went to Lawyer Conrad Shindle's office, where he worked as a clerk, but the face of the martyred Jones haunted him and he paced the floor restlessly. There was no question in his mind that this had been another Molly Maguire outrage. Revolving in his mind the possible suspects, it occurred to him that he had not seen Jimmy Kerrigan on the streets of Tamaqua for several days, and he decided to keep watch over his house. Taking along field glasses, and accompanied by a trusted friend, he proceeded to Kerrigan's house at the western end of town. The pair arrived in time to see Jimmy leave his house with a small bundle under his arm and a flask protruding from his back pocket. After shadowing him part of the way toward Sharp Mountain, they climbed the Odd Fellows' cemetery hill, from which vantage point Beard followed Jimmy through his field glasses as the little miner climbed the mountain-side. Suddenly he saw him wave a handkerchief, in response to which two men emerged from the bush. The three figures then were seen to walk a short distance and squat down by a spring which ran down the mountain.

This gave Beard the opportunity he sought. Leaving his friend to stand watch, he raced to town, gathered a posse and surrounded the fugitives who, after throwing away their arms, gave themselves up without a struggle. They were marched into Tamaqua and thrown into the town lockup. When the frenzied mob threatened to lynch them, they were transported under heavy police guard to the Carbon County prison at Mauch Chunk.

With the arrest of Kerrigan, Doyle, and Kelly, people began

to feel that the end of the long Molly Maguire terror was approaching. The indictment by the Carbon County Grand Jury was the first against Mollies that had a chance of bringing a conviction. The cases were severed and Doyle was the first of the trio to stand trial. The evidence produced by the Commonwealth seemed so preponderant, especially in intimate details, that the elaborate alibi defense prepared by Doyle's able lawyers fell to pieces. It appeared plain to Molly leaders that the testimony spread on the record had come out of the innermost recesses of the order. Who was the traitor in the ranks? Who was the informer guilty of the highest crime in the Molly ethics? Up to that time they had not yet suspected McParland, the Pinkerton agent, and the onus of suspicion fell on poor Kerrigan and resulted in his being ostracized in the jail by the other prisoners. Kerrigan felt the unjust accusation deeply, and resentment led him to unloose his tongue. He reasoned that as he already bore the brand of the informer he might just as well make use of it to save his neck. Before the end of the Doyle trial he made known to the District Attorney that he wanted to turn state's evidence. His offer was promptly accepted, and the remarkable confession which poured from his lips brought Doyle, Kelly, and later Alex Campbell within reach of the hangman's noose.

Kerrigan immediately became known as "the boss squealer." The talk of the whole region, he seemed to relish his notoriety. His mind relieved of its terrible burden, his conscience cleared, sure of escape from the gallows, he found it easy to relax. Vain, cocksure, and quick at repartee, he kept the jail amused with his wisecracks which injected a rather grim humor into an atmosphere surcharged with impending tragedy. Jimmy was not satisfied with merely a confession that would be buried in court records. There was posterity to be considered. His untutored mind occupied itself in casting the confession into a ballad,

"Jimmy Kerrigan's Confession," which he gave to a Mauch Chunk reporter who used it in his paper. There I found it.

Doyle was convicted and sentenced to be hanged. McParland, still under cover, reported to his superiors that news of the conviction came on the secret order like an earthquake on a quiet village. It carried dismay into the ranks of the Mollies and shocked the nerves of their leaders. Mollies in the courtroom sat mute with terror as the jury announced its verdict.

"Doyle's Pastime on St. Patrick's Day" was the first of three ballads which Doyle composed before his execution. It was inspired by a St. Patrick's Day parade which passed his jail window. Not since his conviction did he feel so low in spirits, and it did not buoy him up to recall that only a year ago he had proudly carried the flag in the St. Patrick's parade at Mahanoy City. The ballad was printed in the Pottsville *Evening Chronicle,* April 1, 1876, where it bore the line, "Written by M. J. Doyle for Turnkey Madara."

Doyle's second composition was on the Centennial Celebration, and his third, the ballad, "Michael J. Doyle," where he expresses a pathetic longing to see once more his beloved Mount Laffee, which, alas! the law denied him.

Kelly was the second accomplice to stand trial, and he too was found guilty and sentenced to the gallows.

Testimony thus brought out caused the arrest and indictment of Alex Campbell, a saloon keeper at Storm Hill. Though he held no office in the secret order, he dominated the Carbon County Mollies by sheer force of will. The Commonwealth's lawyers were aware, of course, that Campbell was not at the scene of the murder, but they sought to convict him as an accessory before the fact on court testimony that he had hired Doyle and Kelly to murder Jones. They felt sure that with the conviction of an alleged accessory, proof would be given to all Molly leaders that they themselves and not merely their tools could be brought to justice. Since the stakes were high the Commonwealth decided to play its trump card, which had been carefully concealed at the Doyle and Kelly trials. Jim McKenna, darling of the Molly Maguires, at last put aside his mask and appeared in his true identity as James McParland, Pinkerton detective. We may well imagine the shock to the Mollies when they saw him take the stand for the first time and with his own lips expose the details of the plot against Jones, many of which he had gleaned while courting the lovely and vivacious Mary Ann, Jimmy Kerrigan's sister-in-law. In addition he brought to light the darkest secrets of the order—all the signs, passwords, toasts, and trades among county bodymasters for the lives and property of enemies.

When McParland completed his remarkable testimony, the conviction of Campbell seemed inevitable, and he too was sentenced to be hanged. But Campbell vehemently protested his innocence.

Several months later, when his appeals for a new trial had been denied by the higher courts, Campbell heard the sheriff read his death warrant. Then he rose to his full height—he was a big, powerfully built man—and declared: "It's hard to die innocent, but I shall not be the first to die thus. God knows that I am innocent of any crime, and the people know it, and the Commonwealth knows it."

More months passed and then came the dawn of Black Thursday—June 21, 1877. Campbell was up early that morning and as he fingered his rosary his lips moved in prayer. He dragged his ball and chain closer to the oblong-shaped chink in the wall representing a window, and with weary eyes sought to catch a last fleeting glimpse of the patch of blue beyond.

In the jail corridor there was a murmur of hushed voices—many spectators had assembled for the hangings.

Suddenly the heavy cell door was opened with a clang. It was the sheriff. The zero hour had arrived. As the door stood partly opened, Campbell caught sight of the scaffold in the narrow, somber corridor, and a shiver must have run up and down his spine.

As the sheriff approached him, Campbell said brokenly, but with evident deep sincerity, "I am innocent. I swear I was nowhere near the scene of the murder—"

And then, as if to impress the sheriff with the truth of his protest, Campbell bent over, ground his right hand in the dust on the cell floor, and dragging his ball and chain with him, took a long stride toward the wall. Then stretching himself to the full height, he smote the wall with his large hand.

"There is the proof of my words," he shouted. "That mark of mine will never be wiped out. There it will remain forever to shame the county that is hangin' an innocent man."

They hanged Campbell that morning, but the imprint of his hand stood out from the wall like truth itself. In vain did the sheriff try to remove it. Succeeding sheriffs also failed. Campbell apparently was right.

The conviction of Doyle, Kelly, and Campbell was received with relief in the region, and the general opinion was that the power of the Molly Maguires had at length been broken.

However, there were many people not previously sympathizers of the Mollies who were drawn to them out of disgust for Kerrigan's confession, contempt for McParland's testimony, and out of a feeling that mob hysteria, whipped to a frenzy in Carbon County, had influenced the course of their trials. This sentiment is reflected in "The Doom of Campbell, Kelly and Doyle," which made its appearance soon after their convictions. According to the last verse it was composed by Michael Reddy of Yorktown,

Schuylkill County. The Commonwealth's lawyers mentioned in the ballad were Judge F. W. Hughes and General Charles Albright of Schuylkill County, and the defense counsel was Daniel Kalbfus of Carbon County. The reference to Mrs. Murphy and her buttermilk concerns an incident which occurred while Doyle was lingering in Lansford before the Jones murder. Mrs. Murphy testified at the trial that Doyle had obtained buttermilk from her at her home in Number Six Patch, thus establishing his presence in the vicinity of the murder and shattering his alibi.

While Campbell, Kelly, and Doyle were awaiting their doom in Mauch Chunk, Hugh McGeehan, convicted of murdering Policeman Benjamin Yost in Tamaqua, was a prisoner in the Schuylkill County prison at Pottsville. Testimony at his trial bore out the Commonwealth's charge that the murder of Boss Jones was the result of a barter under which Carbon County Molly Maguires murdered Yost and in return for which Doyle and Kelly of Schuylkill County invaded Carbon and took Jones's life.

During McGeehan's trial, a local newspaperman caught a touching domestic picture in the courtroom:

> Mrs. McGeehan, a bride when her husband was torn from her arms and thrown into prison, sits by his side, apparently happy in his presence, hardly realizing his position. Young and pretty, small in figure, with auburn hair and fair complexion, decked in her wedding finery, she does not seem ever to hear the testimony being given by the witnesses on the stand. Her husband gazes proudly upon her whilst she, fondly clasping his hand, or when wearied, leaning upon his breast, has thrown aside the memory of past misery, has discarded fear for the future and only feels that in the present she is with him.

McGeehan was in his early twenties when arrested. He did not swear or drink and, until his initiation into the Molly Maguires, his life had been exemplary. Like many other Mollies, he claimed to have been discriminated against at the mines. McGeehan is believed to have composed the ballad "Hugh McGeehan" while he was awaiting trial in 1876. Perhaps its greatest significance is that it refers to Franklin B. Gowen's breaking the miners' union, thus directly connecting the Molly Maguire riots with the labor unrest of the day.

A Schuylkill Valley man, who for many years has advised me on Molly Maguire lore which he acquired at first hand in his youth, gave me the three ballads, "Hugh McGeehan," "Michael J. Doyle," and "The Doom of Campbell, Kelly and Doyle."

The bravery with which the Mollies met their death on the gallows is told in "Thomas Duffy." This Molly was convicted as an accomplice in the Yost murder and was among the six hanged in the Schuylkill County prison courtyard. He was twenty-five, handsome and sturdy. With his dark hair and swarthy features, he looked more like a Latin than a full-blooded Irishman. He was a man of few words, sullen and unemotional, but a competent, steady miner. "Thomas Duffy" came to me two years ago under the following circumstances. Barney Kelly, an aged Ashland minstrel, had a friend write the ballad down many years ago. His friend scrawled it on a letter form headed as follows: "Germantown, April the 2, 1881, thommas Duffy song." During one of my calls on the minstrel he showed me this original copy and, seeing my enthusiasm, permitted me to borrow it. Though over half a century had passed since it was written, it was still in a fairly good state of preservation, thanks to the care that Kelly had taken of it.

Michael "Muff" Lawler, who acquired his nickname from breeding mufflers, a fine strain of gamecocks which found their way into many of the cockpits of the region, was once Shenandoah's leading Molly. He was tried in the Schuylkill County courts as an accessory after the fact in the murder of Thomas Sanger, a mine foreman, and William Uren, a miner, at Raven

Run. When the jury disagreed he was retried and convicted, but saved his neck by turning state's evidence. As an informer he drew a storm of jeers upon his head and the ballad "Muff Lawler, the Squealer" appeared to mock him. While I have heard several variants, the one used here, which was published in my previous volume, is, I think, the best. I obtained it in 1925 from a self-exiled Molly in Philadelphia. I shall never forget the mocking tone and the trembling voice with which that man sang it for me. The tune used here, however, was sung by Thomas Hill of Tucker Hill, Schuylkill County.

Ten Molly Maguires were hanged on June 21, 1877—four in the corridor of the Carbon County jail at Mauch Chunk and six in the prison courtyard at Pottsville; there was another execution on that day, in Wilkes-Barre, but it had no connection with the Molly Maguires. The mass hangings were intended by the authorities to prevent an uprising and at the same time to serve as a symbol of the doom of the Molly Maguires.

Recently I asked an elderly miner's widow if she remembered the day of the hangings.

"Indade I do, sir," she replied mournfully. "Will I ever forget it! A sad day it was in the hard coal fields, sir. When the hour of the hangings arrived for them poor Irish lads, the world suddenly became dark and we had to burn our lamps. It's Black Thursday it was, sir."

PAT DOLAN

Pat Dolan, it's my Christian name,
Yes, an' my surname too, sir;
An' oft you've listened to me sthrane,
I'll tell you somethin' new, sir!
In Cavan-town, where we sat down,
Our Irish hearts to inspire,

There's bould recruits an' undaunted youths,
  An' they'r led by Mollie Maguire!

CHORUS

With my riggadum du, an' to hell wid the crew
  Wouldn't help to free our nation;
When I look back, I count 'em slack,
  Wouldn't join our combination!

Said Mollie to her darlin' sons,
  "What tyrant shall we tumble?
That filthy tribe we can't abide,
  They rob both meek and humble;
There is one Bell, a child of hell,
  An' a magistrate in station,
Let lots be drew an' see which av you
  Will tumble him to damnation!"

The lot's now cast, the sentence passed,
  I scorn to tell a lie, sir!
I got my chance, it wur no blank;
  I wur glad to win the prize, sir!
To swate Bill Cooney's I did repair,
  To meet the parson, Bell, sir!
At his brain I took me aim,
  Sayin', "Come down, ye fin' o' hell, sir!"

Those Orangemen, they gathered then,
  An' swore they'd kill us all, sir,
For their frien' Bell, who lately fell,
  An' got a terrible fall, sir!
But Mollie's sons, wid swords an' guns,
  Wid pikes—pitchforks—glancin',
Those bold recruits an' undaunted youths,
  Stepped into the field just prancin'.

Those Orangemen, they all stood then,
  To fight they thought it a folly;

They'd rather run an' save their lives,
  An' leave the field to Mollie!
Altho' I'm in a foreign land,
  For the cause I'll ne'er retire,
May heaven smile on every chil'
  That belongs to Mollie Maguire!

One night as I lay upon me bed,
  I heard a terrible rattle;
Who wur it but Bell, come back from hell,
  To fight another battle!
Then at his brain I took me aim—
  He vanished off in fire—
An' as he went the air he rent
  Sayin', "I'm conquered by Mollie Maguire!"

Now I'm in America
  An' that's a free nation!
I generally sit an' take my sip
  Far from a police station!
Four dollars a day—it's not bad pay—
  An' the boss he likes me well, sir!
But little he knows that I'm the man
  That shot that fin' o' hell, sir!

CHORUS

Wid me riggadum du, an' to hell wid the crew,
  Wouldn't fight to free our nation,
When I look back I count 'em slack—
  Wouldn't join our combination!

JIMMY KERRIGAN'S CONFESSION

You know I am that squealer they talk so much about,
And sure you know the reason, of which I have no doubt.
If not, I will tell you as nearly as I can,
So please in kindness listen to Jimmy Kerrigan.

I fought for my country as you will plainly see,
And I always did my duty when we met with General Lee.
Indeed, on many a battlefield we saw the rebels flee,
I and my comrades marching 'longside me.

And when the war was over and I at home again
Had married and settled down in a comfortable way,
Carroll, Donahue and Campbell did lead me astray.
And it's them that I may thank for where I am today.

On the first day of September in eighteen seventy-five,
Returning from my work, at Carroll's I did arrive
To take my beer, as usual, but did not get a fill,
When Carroll said, "Kerrigan, here are men for Summit Hill."

Says I, "Why, Carroll, I have got to work, with them I cannot go."
"Kerrigan, you know better, and what you say is not so."
So lastly I consented and fixed myself in style
To lead, as he requested, young Kelly and Michael Doyle.

We arrived at Alex Campbell's at half-past nine or ten.
When Campbell did accomp'ny us from there to Summit Hill
Saying, "Hugh, these are chaps we've talked about, and who have left
their homes
To satisfy the rest of us—to kill the hated Jones."

Hugh got the pistols ready to see if they were free.
Then handed one to Doyle, young Kelly and to me
Saying, "Take these, boys, we'll arrange the rest all right,
If you'll but try to have it done against tomorrow night."

On Thursday we had a glance at Jones but failed the deed to do.
The command "Thou shalt not kill" once more appeared in view.
But Campbell he insisted and the following day we went
And did the bloody deed over which we now repent.

And when we were arrested that day about noon,
All of us were in life's full bloom.
Kelly, I think, a little past nineteen
Led astray, as it was thought, by a chap named Jerry Kane.

When Doyle was tried and I saw it was no use
For me to hold my tongue, I resolved to let it loose;
I told the whole story from beginning to end
And think that since I have told it the country's on the mend.

I had one to assist me who was both good and true
To religion and to country, nor less to me and you:
His name was James McParlan; he's a credit to his race.
A clever chap, still young in years, and honesty's in his face.

That this society was a shame to Irishmen you know,
Though outside the coal region I learn it is not so.
For there they do their duty and churches they supply
To teach the way of holiness and fit all men to die.

But not so in the coal fields where by church they are accursed,
And excommunicated, which still made matters worse;
They craved to be admitted into her fold, you know,
Through those notorious criminals—Tom Fisher and Kehoe.

Tom Fisher and Kehoe were county delegates
For Schuylkill and for Carbon; but now they have pale pates,
For crimes which they encouraged and sent vile men to do,
And though they now would squeal on them, their squealing will not do.

MORAL

And before I do lay down my pen, I'll address these words to ye,
Abstain from drinking liquor, and from all bad company;
For if you don't, you will it rue unto the day you die,
And with this I shall leave you, and bid you all good-bye.

DOYLE'S PASTIME ON ST. PATRICK'S DAY

It was early on this morning,
  As on my bunk I did sleep;
I was awakened by the brass bands
  A-playing on the street.

So I did rise and rub my eyes,
  No more this day to sleep;
And when I thought the day it was,
  I jumped up to my feet.

FIRST CHORUS

Saying, can I walk or can I talk,
  Or can I anyone see? No!
But closed up in a dismal cell
  In hopes of liberty.

And when I came to myself,
  And in my cell did hear
The music that the band did play,
  It gave me good cheer.

And when the tune was finished,
  And the band it ceased to play,
I passed remark upon myself,
  And on them these words did say:

But shortly after that,
  Before a half hour passed,
The turnkey he came in,
  And gave me my breakfast.

SECOND CHORUS

Can I walk or can I talk,
  Or can I anyone see? No!

But this one thing I can do—
   Is to eat my grub pretty free.

When he was about to go,
   After I got my coffee and bread;
I spoke some words to him,
   And these are the words I said:

So then I sat down,
   My breakfast for to eat,
For, when a man is in good health,
   I tell you it goes sweet.

Now to conclude and finish,
   With one more thing to say,
This is a nice way to be
   On St. Patrick's Day!

MICHAEL J. DOYLE

Mount Laffee, oh my happy home! Of thee I love to sing,
No spot on earth's more dear to me than to which my heart doth cling.
For to cross the old school house hill 'twere my joy to roam,
And call to mind the happy hours I spent at father's home.

When Mike Keely and I would go home at night, our day's work bein' done,
We would have a talk and take a walk to where we would find some fun.
At nine or ten we would return again to the parents at our homes,
And there we would find them and with them enjoy a poem.

Let others speak of where they will, perhaps their own glorious home.
But give me sweet Mount Laffee still, my birth, I claim my own.
Where all the people, both great and small, kindness have in store,
And with the help of kind Providence, we will see them all once more.

Of all the scenes that's passed there is one before my sight,
When we was leaving home the sun was shining bright,
Each heart was then free and light and gentle in every tone,
And pleasant were the words we spoke, when we was leaving home.

We made the train in hit of time, to look for work was our design,
It's little we thought that day our troubles to meet at noon,
When a crowd of men did us arrest with p'inted guns in their hands and a revolver with every man,
But we not knowing what was wrong to them ourselves we did resign.

A hearing for to undergo they marched us over through the town,
Unto the station house there for everyone that wished to look on,
Some would say, "Those are the men," whilst others would nod their head;
One woman she came in, which my quick ear had overheard:

"I can swear those ain't the men," but in a very short time she left again.
Next comes in Mauch Chunk police and in this manner they did begin:
"First bring out the biggest man until we get the handcuffs on."
And when they had our three hands bound they marched us o'er the town.

Around the town like all pell mell until we reached this dismal cell,
Which by experience I can tell is not much short of an earthly hell;
This cell is like a graveyard vault to which I do declare,
It's better for to live in hopes than die in dark despair.

Can I walk or can I talk or can I anyone see?
No! but locked up in a dismal cell in hopes of liberty.
So now to conclude and finish my verses, I hope to the company I've said nothing wrong;
My name is Michael J. Doyle, I was born in Mount Laffee, and I am the poet of this little song.

THE DOOM OF CAMPBELL, KELLY AND DOYLE

Kind-hearted Christians, I pray you give attention,
It's of a young man, down in jail he doth lie,
For the shooting of the boss, John P. Jones,
A murderer's death he is doomed for to die.

They say Doyle and Kelly committed the murder,
And that it was plotted by some cruel gang;
And likewise Jimmy Kerrigan that weak-hearted creature
That told all about it, 'fraid he would hang.

In years after this when he will be at his freedom,
When people will see him their blood it will boil.
They will say, "There goes that weak-hearted creature
That swore away the lives of Campbell, Kelly and Doyle."

The Commonwealth lawyers have done hard against them;
The ones that have done it are Hughes and Albright.
They say that the Hibernians are a great band of criminals
That go about robbing and murdering at night.

Now Hughes and Albright, stop throwing your slander
When the whip is in your hand; don't crack her free
Lest early some morning or late in the evening
You may trip on a brick and come down on your knee.

Now bad luck to Mrs. Murphy that speaks of her buttermilk,
She's the woman can swear without toil,
As brave as a lion she stood quite defiant
To swear away the lives of Campbell, Kelly and Doyle.

Here's success to brave Kalbfus, that noble defender,
He done his endeavor their lives for to save,
But the opposite party had plead hard against him,
Which leaves Doyle to fill up a murderer's grave.

So now to conclude and finish my verses,
I hope to the company I have said nothing wrong;
My name is Mike Reddy, I still live in Yorktown
And I am the poet of this little song.

HUGH McGEEHAN

Come all ye true-born Irishmen wherever you may be,
I hope you pay attention and listen unto me.
For if ever you do get in jail, you'll surely rue the day,
And curse the hour when you first set sail all for Americ-a.

Just think on poor Tom Munley, all in his mannerly prime,
He is sentenced to be hung for an atrocious crime.
The jury found him guilty and the Governor says he must die,
So now poor Tom is sentenced to be hung which seals his destiny.

It would break your heart to listen as he sits in the jail,
To hear his wife and children at his cell door weep and wail.
He kisses his little children and through the iron door
Sayin', "Adieu, my little ones, farewell to ye evermore."

Just think, James McKenna, the detective, has gained himself a name,
And in the detective agency has risen to great fame.
He said he came amongst our people in November 'seventy-three
Which leaves many's the wife and babe to mourn and curse his memory.

He came amongst our people in a very quiet time,
He was the foremost plotter of that atrocious crime.
He should be tried for murder, condemned he ought to be,
And along with his poor victims, die on the gallows tree.

That's not half of what he done as unto you I'll tell,
He plotted other murders and that you know full well.
Himself and Jimmy Kerrigan says they done it up in style,
While in Mauch Chunk they swore away the lives of Campbell, Kelly and Doyle.

One day up in Tamaqua he met four or five men,
James Carroll and James Roarity with Boyle, Duffy and Hugh McGeehan.
He spent his money freely and great joy he did maintain,
And with his good behavior their confidence did gain.

By this villain, like Judas of old, they were sold for cursed gold, their lives he did betray.
It's for Franklin B. Gowen of high renown he drove us to the range;
He broke down our glorious union, upon us did hardship bring,
And in every paper now you read he is styled our Railroad King.

My name is Hugh McGeehan, I am scarcely twenty-four,
I was born in the County Donegal, on Erin's pleasant shore.
I left my foster parents there, like many of my race,
But now I'm held in durance vile, bowed down with sore disgrace.

The first place that I worked a shift was in the Jeddo mine,
And there the men can testify how well I served my time.
The day I left my native land I took a solemn oath,
That liquor vile of any kind should ne'er go down my throat.

So now I still am keeping it until the day I die,
Let it be on a bed of roses or on the gallows high.
So now I am accused of murder and the same I do deny,
And when my trial will come on, the traitors I will defy.

By the Holy Virgin Mary, I'll tell to you what's true,
I never knew Jimmy Kerrigan, or any of his crew.
I never kept his company and that he knows full well,
But to save his guilty neck he would swear a saint to hell.

THOMAS DUFFY

Come all ye true-born Irishmen, wherever you may be,
I hope you will pay attention and listen unto me,
Concerning ten brave Irishmen all in their youthful bloom,
Who died in Pennsylvania on the twenty-first of June.

Thomas Duffy and James Carroll as you can plainly see,
They were murdered by false perjurers all on the gallows tree.
Thomas Duffy on the brink of death did neither shake or fear,
But he smiled upon his murderers although his end was near.

He took his brother by the hand and kissed him o'er and o'er
Saying, "Farewell, my faithful brother, I shall never see you more,
Till your spirit from this world has fled to that celestial shore
Where perjurers can't enter to shake loving hearts any more.

"Take my advice, dear Patrick, and follow in my wake.
Let perjurers do all they can, my heart they will never shake."
He scorned his prosecutors although he stood alone,
As did many a gallant Irishman before England's king and throne.

He said, "We are not defeated; up or with our banner high,
Although our parents were treated we will show them how to die."
He mounted on the scaffold with a firm and steady tread,
Resembling a young nobleman a-going up to bed.

He looked upon the circle that stood around him there,
And smiled upon his brother whose heart was in despair.
"Give me your hand, dear Patrick, fret not for my sad fate,
But before I will bid this world adieu, the truth to you I'll state.

"I never saw James Kerrigan, the truth to you I'll tell,
Save once at Carroll residence where I treated him right well.
I never asked James Carroll to shoot a man for me,
Nor offered him ten dollars, as my God I hope to see.

"I bear no living creature the slightest hate or spite,
But as I am going to face my God my conscience it is light.
But why should I tarry longer in this dark world of woe?
My faith was never stronger and I am longing for to go."

The rope was dropped around his neck and the warrant to him read,
And in twenty minutes after, brave Duffy he was dead.
God rest his soul; he perished there to friends and country true,
And he kept his secrets to the last as Irishmen should do.

Bright angels thronged the jail yard until they saw him dead,
And taking a last look at him his spirit with them fled.
Tom Duffy was as true a man as ever blessed our sod,
And now we hope his soul's at rest with Mary and with God.

MUFF LAWLER, THE SQUEALER

Transcribed by Melvin LeMon

When Muff Law - ler was in jail right bad did he feel,
He thought di - vil the roost - er would he ev - er heel,
"Be - ja - bers," says Law - ler, "I think I will squeal."
"Yes, do," says the Judge to Muff Law - ler.

It was down in the office those lawyers did meet,
"Come in, Mr. Lawler"; they gave him a seat.
"Give us your whole history and don't us deceive."
"Be jabers, I will," says Muff Lawler.

"There are some o' thim near," he says, "and more o' thim far;
There are some o' thim you'll never catch I do fear."
"If they are on this earth," he says, "we'll have them I'm sure."
"Yes, but be jabers they're dead," says Muff Lawler.

"It's the live ones we want, not the dead ones at all."
"If you want the whole history, you'll have to take dead ones and all."

"Come out with your history or quickly we'll plant
You back in your cell, Mr. Lawler."

"Now I'll commence," he says, "me whole story to tell,
When I go back to Shenandoah, I'll be shot sure as hell."
"We'll send you to a country where you're not known so well."
"Be jabers, that's good," says Muff Lawler.

CHAPTER NINE

A Miscellany

"ONCE a miner and twice a breaker boy" is an old saying in the anthracite industry. It recalls the custom of employing old miners to pick slate in the breaker alongside boys, after a lifetime underground. This sop from the industry kept them from becoming public charges. But since mechanical slate pickers have displaced manual picking, there is no longer any place for old men in the breaker or, for that matter, anywhere else in the industry. Many of my best sources have been very old miners. One of them has lost his sight; others are suffering from miner's asthma, and their lungs sound like the blacksmith's wheezy bellows; nearly all of them have bent backs from dodging low roofs in the mines and are pale from many years spent in darkness. My heart was saddened at the plight of many of them during the depression, especially before Federal relief came into existence. Despite their condition they found the heart to be patient with me and to share with me their precious memories of anthracite's golden age of minstrelsy.

"The Old Miner's Refrain" is one of the most popular anthracite ballads and one of the oldest in the present collection. There the old miner sees his whole career summed up—his dreams, his hopes, and his thwarted ambitions. He looks back on a lifetime of back-breaking labor in the mines, and what does he find staring him in the face at the end of the road? Poverty and the threat of the poor-house.

Aside from its intrinsic value, "The Old Miner's Refrain"

will always be close to my heart as it was one of the first three ballads to come to me when I began collecting back in 1925. It was sent by B. I. Curran, a Centralia school teacher. The present tune was sung by his fellow townsman Daniel Walsh in 1935.

"The Miner's Life" must have enjoyed a measure of popularity in its day. I first heard of its existence in Carbon County, picked up a copy in Northumberland County and traced it to its source in Luzerne County. It was composed by Jack Johnson in 1884. I copied the present version from the balladist's original manuscript at the home of his son, Jack Johnson Jr., a mine superintendent at Drifton in 1925.

The best-known miner's ballad is "Down in a Coal Mine." Once sung all over the nation, it has at last found its resting place in the anthracite coal fields. Its popularity was so widespread and of such long standing that I believed it to be an indigenous product. As a matter of fact, having been molded so long by anthracite miners it does have the spirit and flavor of an anthracite ballad, and one has a difficult time convincing the average old-timer that it isn't native. However, it was originally a stage song composed by one J. B. Geoghegan in 1872, when it was published by S. Brainard's Sons. First sung for me by the late James Walsh, Pottsville veteran miner, it appeared in my former collection. The tune used in this chapter was sung by Daniel Walsh of Centralia.

The story of coal bootlegging is too well known to require reiteration here. "My Wee Coal Hole" by William Keating was composed in 1932 as a protest against the ruthless suppression of the illegal industry in its earliest days, when bootlegging was still in the hands solely of starving unemployed mine workers. Their attitude of mind is vividly set down in the ballad. It is authentic, as Keating drew upon a personal experience as a bootlegger, or "independent miner," when he wrote it.

The present version of "The Battlefields of France" was copied from a piece of paper lent me by Edith Patterson, who had received it from an elderly miner. However, I have heard other variants, one of which Professor Le Mon and I recorded. "The Battlefields of France," which purports to represent the anthracite miners' attitude toward the World War, was composed by Patrick J. "Giant" O'Neill when he was living in St. Nicholas, a Schuylkill County mine patch. It was published on December 28, 1918, and copyrighted by O'Neill.

"A Miner's Son," another O'Neill ballad, is a popular piece. O'Neill himself sang it at the first Pennsylvania Folk Festival at Allentown in 1935.

"I Love My Miner Lad" betrays its origin by allusions to Newcastle town, Durham City, and Auckland, and particularly so in the last verse by references to a castle, the nobility and royalty. Yes, it is an English mining ballad, brought over by Mrs. Elizabeth Megann, aged seventy-four, of Zerbe, Pa. when she immigrated to this country in 1925. I recorded it with Professor Le Mon on May 10, 1936, when she sang the song for us at the home of Joseph P. Zerbe, a retired mine boss, in Zerbe Patch.

Mrs. Megann explained that she learned the ballad while a little girl in her native West Cumberland, in the heart of the English mining country. Although she hadn't sung it for many years she had no trouble recalling it, and despite her advanced age her voice was steady and clear.

The next four pieces do not bear the stamp of the traditional miner's ballad. They were obtained directly from printed sources, and I have no knowledge of their tunes, if they ever had any. Their contents, however, fit into the theme and setting of this volume.

I found "The Miner Lad" in "a general geological, historical and statistical review," edited by Eli Bowen and published in Pottsville, 1848.

"Sing Ho! For Miners" and "Sing Ho! For Anthracite" were copied from a thin volume entitled *Trevaro and Other Poems* by Alpha Lyra, published in Pottsville in 1853. Hiding behind the nom de plume was squib manufacturer Samuel Harries Daddow of St. Clair.

"The Old D. & H. Gravity" was originally printed in a Carbondale newspaper in 1902, a clipping of which had been carefully preserved by I. W. Osborne, a carpenter employed at the Powderly colliery of the Hudson Coal Company at South Carbondale. While ballad-hunting through the Lackawanna Valley in 1925 my path crossed Mr. Osborne's, and he permitted me to make a copy of the clipping. Having once worked on the old gravity, he assured me that the verses preserved an authentic factual and spiritual record of that pioneer phase of coal transportation. The ballad bore the by-line of John McComb and had the following preface: "Verses written to commemorate the doings of the men who gave loyal service to their employers when the old system of handling coal was popular and profitable."

The ballad describes the Delaware & Hudson gravity railroad which for many years carried Lackawanna Valley coal to the head of the D. & H. Canal at Honesdale; the empty cars were brought back to the mines by steam on another track. The famous Ashley Planes and the Switchback were similar devices.

The fragments which wind up this chapter are of miners' ballads which I could not complete.

A MISCELLANY

THE OLD MINER'S REFRAIN

Transcribed by Melvin LeMon

I'm get - ting old and fee - ble and I can work no

more; I have laid the rust - y min - ing tools a - way—For

for - ty years and o - ver I have toiled a - bout the mines,

[Chorus :𝄋:] *Where*

But now I'm get - ting fee - ble, old and gray. I

are the boys that worked with me in the break - er long a -

start - ed in the break - er and went back to it a -

go? There are ma - ny of them now have gone to rest; Their

gain, But now my work is fin - ished for all time; The

cares of life are o - ver and they've left this world of

on - ly place that's left me is the alms - house for a

[fine.]

woe; And their spir - its now are roam - ing with the blest.

home, That's where I'll lay this wea - ry head of mine.

[:𝄋: to Chorus]

In the chutes I graduated instead of going to school—
  Remember, friends, my parents they were poor;
When a boy left the cradle it was always made the rule
  To try to keep starvation from the door.
At eight years of age to the breaker first I went,
  To learn the occupation of a slave;
I was certainly delighted, and on picking slate was bent—
  My ambition it was noble, strong and brave.

At eleven years of age I bought myself a lamp—
  The boss he sent me down the mine to trap;
I stood in there in water, in powder smoke and damp;
  My leisure hours I spent in killing rats.
One day I got promoted to what they called a patcher,
  Or a lackey for the man that drives the team:
I carried sprags and spreaders and had to fix the latch—
  I was going through my exercise, it seems.

I next became a driver, and thought myself a man;
  The boss he raised my pay as I advanced:
In going through the gangway with the mules at my command,
  I was prouder than the President of France.
But now my pride is weakened and I am weakened too;
  I tremble till I'm scarcely fit to stand:
If I were taught book learning instead of driving teams,
  Today, kind friends, I'd be a richer man.

I next became a miner and laborer combined,
  For to earn my daily bread beneath the ground.
I performed the acts of labor which came in a miner's line—
  For to get my cars and load them I was bound.
But now I can work no more, my cares of life are run;
  I am waiting for the signal at the door;
When the angels they will whisper, "Dear old miner, you must come,
  And we'll row you to the bright celestial shore."

THE MINER'S LIFE

(AIR: *The Little Old Log Cabin in the Lane*)

I am a poor old miner, my race of life is nearly run,
Like many of my comrades my mining days are done.
My strength you see is failing me, old age is coming fast;
The only thing that is left for me is a picture of the past.

When I went to the breaker first I was very young,
My mother was left with a family and I the only son;
My father he was taken, I hope his soul's at rest—
He was crushed to death by a fall of coal while working in his breast.

If father had been spared to us, as you may understand,
I might have had education and been today a different man.
Like many other mining boys, my parents they were poor;
I was compelled to go to work to keep hunger from the door.

When I left the breaker I went down the slope,
To become a miner it was my brightest hope.
First, tending door was all I had to do:
Open it and shut it when the drivers they passed through.

The boss came to me one day and said, "My little man,
I'm going to promote you, I'll put you blowing fan,
Away in the gangway where they are driving the airway,
And if you do your duty I'll advance your pay."

I next became a patcher, from that to driving mules—
I was graduating here instead of in the school.
Then became a laborer, the coal car for to fill,
Then became a miner boy to use the pick and drill.

You can talk about the railroaders, the danger they go through,
Warriors and sailor boys, I know it's very true.
They have good air to work in, for the roof they have the sky:
There's no one braves the danger like the poor miner boy.

They have bad air to work in, shattered pillars and bad top,
They don't know the moment when a fall on them might drop,
A little lamp to show them light—that is their brightest hope,
See the danger they go through coming up a shaft or slope.

When a miner is at work in a gangway or a breast,
His mind is never easy if he sits down to rest,
For fear some careless comrade the gas he might ignite
And cause a great explosion, and then you would see a sight.

There are other dangers poor miners often dread:
Water in abandoned slopes, perhaps not far ahead.
There are instances where they struck it they hadn't time to fly,
Brought death and destruction to the poor miner boy.

Way down in the coal mines, in the bowels of the earth below,
Where the sun it never shines or gentle wind does blow;
If you went there it would make you stare and fill your heart with dread,
To see the dangers they go through to earn their daily bread.

Little I thought when I grew old and mining could do no more,
I'd go back to the breaker where I spent my days before.
This world is full of trouble, hardship, care and strife,
It's twice a boy and once a man, is a poor miner's life.

DOWN IN A COAL MINE

Transcribed by Melvin LeMon

I am a jo - vial col - lier lad, and blithe as blithe can
be, For let the times be good or bad they're all the same to
me; 'Tis lit - tle of the world I know and care less for its
ways, For where the dog star nev - er glows, I wear a - way my
[Chorus]
days. Down in a coal mine, un - der - neath the
ground, Where a gleam of sun - shine nev - er can be
found; Dig - ging dusk - y dia - monds all the sea - son round,
Down in a coal - mine, un - der-neath the ground.

My hands are horny, hard and black with working in the vein,
And like the clothes upon my back my speech is rough and plain;
Well, if I stumble with my tongue I've one excuse to say,
'Tis not the collier's heart that's wrong, 'tis the head that goes astray.

At every shift, be it soon or late, I haste my bread to earn,
And anxiously my kindred wait and watch for my return:
For death that levels all alike, whate'er their rank may be,
Amid the fire and damp may strike and fling his darts at me.

How little do the great ones care who sit at home secure,
What hidden dangers colliers dare, what hardships they endure;
The very fires their mansions boast, to cheer themselves and wives,
Mayhap were kindled at the cost of jovial colliers' lives.

Then cheer up, lads, and make ye much of every joy ye can;
But let your mirth be always such as best becomes a man;
However fortune turns about we'll still be jovial souls,
For what would America be without the lads that look for coals.

MY WEE COAL HOLE

While the woes of unemployment were increasing,
While the price of foodstuff swelled the grocer's till,
For to fix 'gainst next winter's chill breeze,
Lest our poor families do freeze,
We dug a wee coal hole on God's hill.

But our terrible toil was wasted; we worked in vain,
Two Cossack-mannered coal and iron cops came.
On next winter's cold nights,
We'll have no anthracite,
'Cause the cops caved in our wee coal hole.

Yes, those cops caved in our wee coal hole,
Like coal companies, most coal coppers lack a soul,
Through next winter's chill breeze,
Our poor families must freeze,
'Cause those cops caved in our wee coal hole.

We had dug through forty feet of flinty rock-roll,
We had mucked five hundred tons of mud and clay,
After weeks of slavish toil,
We struck some crop coal,
Which some old-time surface miners had let stay.

Those cops caved in our wee coal hole,
Even before we'd hoisted one needed bucket of coal,
And faith, if they get my prayers,
They'll get hell's hole for theirs,
'Cause they caved in our wee coal hole.

To my poverty they added bitter toll,
They threw my only pick and shovel down the hole,
Then with destructive dynamite,
They put teeth in winter's bite,
When they caved in my wee coal hole.

My mule-driving record proves at Oak Hill mine,
I'm unfairly unemployed for four years' time.
To no soup house I'll be led,
Because I'll dig my family's bread,
Or by cops be killed, in my wee coal hole.

Right demands I keep my family fed and warm,
God put coal 'neath these hills; here I was born.
So call it bootleg or what,
I'll have coal in my cot,
While there's coal in Good God's coal vein.

Starve and freeze us—that's the company's callous aim!
Profit-gluttons, yes, their god is gold and gain.
Eagle Hill's shut down—for what?
Beechwood, Wadesville and Pine Knot—
'Tis not full markets, 'tis foul misers, sons of Cain.

My native land and flag, I bled for you,
Now I'm bulldozed by coal barons' Cossack crew!

Here upon old Mine Hill's side,
My folks were born, here toiled, here died,
So my birthright is: my wee coal hole.

Shove your selfish coal and iron laws on greed's shelf!
Most coal lands were stolen by fraud and pelf.
And may God blast the breed,
Whose religion is greed,
May Satan sear their souls with bootleg coal.

While you're piling greedy profits on your roll,
'Vain you try to flag the flow of bootleg coal.
When all the colliery pulleys turn,
When honest miners bread can earn,
Then you'll be free of bootleg coal.

God's and man's first law is this: protect thyself,
Men can't munch from meatless pots nor doughless delf,
"Honest men earn honest bread
By their brow's sweat," Jesus said.
So don't you dynamite my new coal hole!

To be safe 'gainst next winter's blast,
On God's hill I'll sink another slope or shaft.
Then may God bless the cops,
If they blow out the props
That I put in my new coal hole.

THE BATTLEFIELDS OF FRANCE

I'm proud to say that I'm from P. A. where the mining boys are loyal,
Where they cut that coal in that manly hole, so deep beneath the soil.
They're familiar with the powder smoke, for gas they have no fear,
And among the bravest of the brave are the miners who volunteered.
They love the flag of liberty, the red, the white and blue;
They love the miners' union, and to it will stick true.
Their leaders are all honest men, John Mitchell, Hayes and White,

And in nineteen-two they showed the world how the mining boys could
fight.

FIRST CHORUS

Then hurrah for President Wilson; he is honest, loyal and shrewd
And the miners are all with him for whatever he may do.
Some laid their picks and shovels down and threw away their lamps—
They are fighting for Democracy on the battlefields of France.

And if you want to meet good people, in the coal fields you will find
They are brave and daring heroes that work down in the mines;
They spend their money freely and to strangers they are kind
And that's the class of men you meet in the towns around the mines.
They fought for forty years or more to win the eight-hour day,
At last they have succeeded with a large advance in pay.
And now they will fight for Uncle Sam against the bitter foe;
They will shoulder guns for America and to France they want to go.

SECOND CHORUS

Then hurrah for Mitchell, Hayes and White, to the miners they proved
true,
And the miners are all with them for whatever they can do.
Some laid their picks and shovels down and threw away their lamps;
They are fighting for Old Glory now, on the battlefields of France.

A MINER'S SON

Ah! here I am a miner's son
From the coal fields of P. A.
Ah! here I am a miner's son
From the coal fields far away.

Now don't despise the miner
With the blue marks on his face;

He got them at his hardy toil
  And that ain't no disgrace.

Wherever you may go,
  Wherever you have been,
There's none so fair, no one can compare
  (*Pause for a jig*)
  With the boys of the coal fields green.

I LOVE MY MINER LAD

Six jolly miners of mining you shall hear,
Have traveled through this country for many a long year,
They have traveled East and traveled West, the country all 'round,
To find out the treasure that lies in underground.

Two came from Auckland, two from Newcastle town,
Two from Durham City, a place of great renown.
The miners are such clever men—their equal can't be found—
They turn a stony rock into a sovereign of bright gold.

You should see a miner lad as he walks down the street,
Dressed in his best clothes, he looks genteel and neat.
His teeth are white as ivory and eyes as black as sloe—
You may easy know a miner lad wherever that he goes.

Sometimes he has money, sometimes none at all,
When he has money it is on his comrades' call.
He calls for liquor plenty, pays as the toast goes round—
Here's good health to every miner lad that works in underground!

It's the huntsman's delight in the blowing of his horn,
It's the farmer's delight in the sowing of the corn,
It's the miner's delight to strike the rock in twa,
And find out the treasure that lies down belaw.

I'll build my love a castle, a castle of renown,
Neither lords, dukes nor earls will pull my castle down,
The king loves the queen, the emperor does the same,
And I love my miner lad—who can me blame?

THE MINER LAD

Nay, don't despise the miner lad,
  Who burrows like the mole;
Buried alive, from morn to night,
  To delve for household coal—
Nay, miner lad, ne'er blush for it,
  Though black thy face be as the pit!

As honorable thy calling is
  As that of hero lords;
They owe to the poor miner lad
  The ore that steels their swords—
And perils too, as fierce as theirs
  In limb and life, the miner shares!

Ye gayest of the gaudy world,
  In gold and silver bright,
Who but the humble miner lad,
  Your jewels brought to light?
Where would be your gold and silver,
  But for yonder delver?

Ye brows of pearly diadems,
  Who sit on lofty thrones,
Smile gently on the miner lad
  Who wrought your precious stones,
And rescued from their iron bond
  The ruby and the diamond!

Ye instruments of brass that pierce
The ear with trumpet sound,
Your notes, but for the miner lad,
Had slumbered underground—
Nor imaged bronze, nor brazen gate,
Had graced the trophies of the great!

Then don't refuse the miner lad
The crust of bread—his prayer!
Beneath that blackest face of his
He hides a heart as fair!
The toil of his bare brawny arms
All, all our hearts and houses warm!

SING HO! FOR MINERS

Before the miner pierced the field,
The soldier had no sword to wield;
To sailors Neptune would not yield,
Old ocean like a parchment sealed;
Then ho, for miners! Hey for miners!
They who foremost pierced the field—
They that made old Neptune yield;
Sing ho! for miners, ho!

Then Yankees could not beat the world,
Our thunder on no foes was hurled;
Our stars and stripes, so proudly curled,
Above no waters were unfurled:
Then ho, for miners! Hey for miners!
They that have our thunder hurled—
They that have our flag unfurled;
Sing ho! for miners, ho!

The rail-car had not kept the rail,
Nor steamship sped without a sail;

The lightnings had not told their tale
From northern hill to southern vale:
Then ho, for miners! Hey for miners!
They who laid the shining rail—
They who fiery lightnings hail;
Sing ho! for miners, ho!

Then Mars' trumpet had no tongue,
Nor Vulcan's iron anvils rung,
Apollo's harp was all unstrung;
And science's banners still unhung:
Then ho, for miners! Hey for miners!
For them let Vulcan's anvils ring—
For them let all the muses sing,
Sing ho! for miners, ho!

SING HO! FOR ANTHRACITE

We dig by day and we dig by night,
For the iron ore and the anthracite—
For the ore so gray, and the coal so bright;
Sing ho, for the ore and the anthracite!

The sailor's life has its round of charms,
The storm and chase with their wild alarms;
And he sings as the boatswain pipes to arms,
"Ho! Ho! for the sea with its mystic charms."

The soldier fights for a scanty hire,
Yet pants for the strife and the battle's fire;
As he to the ramparts' heights aspires
Sings—"Ho! for the strife and the battle's fire!"

The farmer treads o'er his furrowed land,
And scatters seed with his careful hand,
And sings as he twists his shining hands,
"Ho! Ho! for hearty harvest hands."

MINSTRELS OF THE MINE PATCH

The miner pants for no gory goal;
In vain to him may the battle roll;
Yet his manly heart and his fearless soul
Sing—"Ho! success to the gleaming coal."

We dig by day and we dig by night
For the iron ore and the anthracite—
For the ore so gray, and the coal so bright;
Sing ho! for the ore and the anthracite.

THE OLD D. & H. GRAVITY

The blowing of the whistles at the breaking of the day
Was the harbinger of labor and the certainty of pay;
There was music in the atmosphere when wheels began to hum;
And a rhythmic sort of cadence in the rolling of the drum.

As long as coal was coming and the engines were in trim,
The boys would keep cars moving till the shades of night were dim;
And then they'd fix up torches, if a break had caused delay,
And work far in the gloaming to assist the trains away.

From Twenty-Eight to Number Nine 'twas up the hill they'd go,
And then descend the Moosic to the level far below;
By gravity to Honesdale, from old Waymart they would run,
And take all kinds of weather till another day was done.

Along the line from Foot of G the "loads" would travel east
Until they reached the old canal where boating now has ceased;
But in the good old summer time, for more than sixty years,
The docks and boats were always manned by scrapping volunteers.

The "lights" came back another track by steam and fans and grade,
And there were men to handle them who never seemed dismayed;
For they could handle slings and sprags or set a brake for fair,
And get a train from plane to plane while things were in repair.

Those good old times, when good old chimes were thrown from engine steam,
Have passed away; but day by day they haunt us like a dream;
For since the year of ninety-eight, when the old road ceased to be,
The romance of a railroad man has less variety.

For the Shepherd's crook and the Horseshoe curve, the spur and pinion wheels,
The old sheave-pit and the balance-box, and the drum with its forty reels,
The cone and sling, the compound brake, and the twist that ground the rope,
Are all in the minds of the old-time men who received a snub to their hope.

Now ponds are lakes with fancy names, and strangers come and go
To see the sights from Fairview Heights, and the fields of Wayne below,
The trains roll by with heavy cars in a modern sort of way,
While the gravity men may show their scars and celebrate the day.

FRAGMENTS

A Pottsville woman recalled the following verse:

May God above,
Send down a dove,
With wings as sharp as razors;
To cut the throats,
Of those old bloats,
Who cut the poor man's wages.

About forty years ago there was an explosion in the Gap colliery at Shenandoah. Wasley, the superintendent, and Reese, the inside boss, went down the mine to investigate the cause, and were suffocated. There was a ballad about them, the following lines of which were recalled by Mrs. Ann Mulhall McAlee of Mahanoy City:

Unconscious of danger with their lamps brightly burning,
And bent on inspection they entered the cave
From which they hoped soon to be returning,
But fate had destined that as their grave.

For death is a cruel, relentless despoiler
Which cuts down alike the rich and the poor.

Obtained from Mrs. Bridget Monahan, eighty-three, of St. Clair, the following lines seem to belong to a love song, which is rare in anthracite balladry:

Down among the coal, down among the coal,
Oh, Jove! it is a lark, all alone in the dark.

Down among the coal, down among the coal,
Waiting to make love to my Jemima.

Dennis P. Coyle of Wilkes-Barre said his father, the late Andrew Coyle used to sing a ballad over a half century ago, the following lines being all he could remember of it.

He's up with a smile on his face in the morning,
And off for a bucket of water he goes,
For men that are lazy with the laziness he's scorning,
Oh God help the workman wherever he goes.
He then puts the tea kettle on for to boil it,
For late was his wife last night mending his clothes,

. . . .

Then wakens his Mary up from her repose.

"Now Mary," says he, "sure the tea kettle's boiling,
And the fire in the grate is as bright as can be.
And soon down the slope, sure, I will have to be toiling
To feed my dear little ones, Mary, and thee.
I know that my miner is honest and pleasant,
And sometimes a prop from its grasp slips away.

* * *

APPENDIX

Biographical Sketches of Traditional Bards and Minstrels

CON CARBON

The best known of all anthracite bards and minstrels was Con Carbon. Born into a mining household in Hazleton in 1871, he went to work in the Audenried breaker at the age of nine. Three years later he was brought to Wilkes-Barre by his parents and there continued his apprenticeship in the mines.

Carbon came into public notice quite early when he revealed the sweetest tenor voice in the Wyoming Valley. He was also richly endowed with Irish wit and a sense of mimicry. But all these gifts were mere handmaidens to his outstanding talent—the ability to articulate in ballad form the thoughts, feelings, experiences, and deepest yearnings of his fellow workers.

When he was still a raw youth and his ballad singing was making him an idol, saloon keepers vied for his presence in their saloons. Of course he did not have to pay for his drinks, but his mere appearance brought increased business. The sordid manner in which his talents were thus exploited disturbed the late Father Curran, his parish priest. One Sunday morning he thundered the warning that the first saloon keeper who dared serve the young minstrel drinks would lose his license. As it was generally accepted that Father Curran was not accustomed to making idle threats, Carbon found every saloon in the parish closed to him. This annoyed him, as he had begun to acquire a taste for the hard stuff. One day soon afterward a friend invited him into a saloon for a drink. Carbon refused, saying, "I can't go in there. I've been silenced by the Church!"

However, his muse did not remain permanently silenced. New ballads came from him in a steady stream, every traditional one increasing his popularity until his name became a household word throughout the region. He was always on demand to sing his own ballads, but his frail health did not permit him to accept even a fraction of all the invitations that rained down on him. As an expedient, he collected some of his songs and ballads which he had printed under the title of *Con Carbon's Own Songster* and sold at ten cents a copy. About twelve years ago his sister, Mrs. James Sheerin, presented a copy to me; its blue paper cover had faded and its pages had become fragile from age, and nearly all the contents were cast in phonetic Irish dialect. Three ballads in the present collection appeared in it—namely, "When the Breaker Starts Up Full Time"; "Mackin's Porch"; and "Gossip in a Street Car." The first two, however, I had already obtained from oral sources. Tradition ascribes the authorship of the following additional ballads to Carbon: "When the Black Diamond Was Burned to the Ground"; "The Hungarian Ball"; "The Hungarian Christening"; "When Jim Gets to Klondike"; "A Greenhorn Makes Good"; and "Me Johnny Mitchell Man."

Con Carbon was idolized not only as a maker and singer of miners' ballads, but as a superb story teller and mimic. His Irish brogue was delicious and his characterizations of the Slavic immigrants were unequaled.

Indeed, nature was profligate with her gifts to this humble mining boy. It is gratifying to record that he used these gifts not to enrich himself, for he died a poor man, but to bring a ray of light and some cheer into miners' lives. No wonder then that the boys who went down the shaft in cages worshipped the ground he walked on.

An instance of such hero-worship was cited by the late Father Phillips, one of Wyoming Valley's most prominent clergymen, with natural gifts of his own to distinguish him. The incident which he describes below occurred at the turn of the century:

I was booked to deliver an address at an A. O. H. meeting one night at Plymouth. A committee escorted me to the stage on which were seated many prominent members of the order, among them being a little old gentleman whose face was handsomely decorated with side-whiskers. While conversing with a member of the committee, the little gentleman in question, who was seated on my right, suddenly said, "Begorra, I wonder what's keeping the talent." I turned and looked at him with surprise, but said nothing. Suddenly he cried, "I wish the talent was here." Again I looked at him with surprise, wondering whether he meant to slight me—me who thought I was the whole thing. Presently, my little friend on the right emitted a roar which would shame the best efforts of a Sioux warrior on the warpath. He threw his hat high in the air, and dancing like a Fiji cannibal over a missionary roast, roared with all the lung power at his command: "Be jabers, the talent has arrived—the talent has arrived!" It seemed in a moment as though bedlam had broken loose. Every man in the audience was on his feet, whooping with bulging eyes and mouth agape: "Hurrah for Con!" I looked towards the entrance, when, lo and behold! I saw Con being carried on the shoulders of two strapping young miners towards the stage. I thought that my little friend on the right would go into convulsions on the wings of enthusiasm. Every lineament of his features seemed to bespeak the esteem in which he held Con. Even his side-whiskers looked as though their every hair waved a welcome to the laughing, rollicking, good-natured Con. It was several minutes before the enthusiasm subsided, only to break forth again in cries of "Let us have 'Me Johnny Mitchell Man,' Con." When Con stepped to the front of the stage, the applause was simply deafening. It seemed to shake the building from top to bottom. He, and not I, was the feature of the evening. Beside him I felt my own littleness. He certainly was a wonderful character.

Carbon died in 1907, and among the tributes paid his memory was a letter to his family from John Mitchell in which the miners' leader told how the minstrel had inspired him during the 1902 strike.

ED FOLEY

Ed Foley was more traditional than Carbon in that he practised his minstrel arts on foot. With his faithful old fiddle under his arm he would stroll from village to village and from one county into another, never riding the railroads or any other vehicle. Once when he had entertained in Wilkes-Barre, his host, warned of his prodigality, bought a railroad ticket for him to Mount Carmel, his home, rather than give him the purse that had been raised by volunteer offerings. As he accepted the ticket he bowed gracefully and thanked his host, but when he reached the depot he redeemed it and squandered the cash in the nearest saloon. How did he reach Mount Carmel about forty miles away? On foot.

Foley was a big-boned, heavy-set man and shabbily dressed. He was simple, prodigal in his eating and drinking habits, and irresponsible, but how the miners loved him! The wonder is how he had the nerve to ask a woman to marry him. Temperamentally unfitted for mining, he was unable to support a family, and his earnings from minstrelsy were too meager. Yet he led two women to the altar, the second a widow with a family of her own. Most of his time was consumed by appearances at christenings, weddings, wakes, balls, and parties and celebrations of all kinds. His niece, Miss Foley, told me that he had a great gift for improvisation. Unconscious of fame and indifferent to the possible interest in him of posterity, he paid little attention to the preservation of his brain children. Some of his ballads appeared on broadsides, a few were scribbled on backs of envelopes and on rough wrapping paper, but most were entrusted to his memory or the memory of his listeners.

Foley was born in Black Heath Patch, Schuylkill County, in 1845, but spent most of his life in the vicinity of Mount Carmel. He died in a Sunbury hospital at the turn of the century.

GIANT O'NEILL

When on October 26, 1936, Patrick J. "Giant" O'Neill died in Atlantic City at the ripe age of seventy-three, the news was received in the hard coal fields with sincere sorrow, as his death ended the career of one of the most colorful characters in anthracite minstrelsy.

In the present collection he is represented by four ballads, namely, "The Hard Working Miner"; "A Stranger at the Scoop"; "A Miner's Son," and "The Battlefields of France." The first two, dating back to the seventies, I obtained from him in the summer of 1925, four years after he had left the region to make his home with a daughter at the seashore resort. We met in the back room of a chop house, where he sang the ballads and danced jigs and hornpipes to the delight of customers.

O'Neill practised the minstrel arts even in Atlantic City. At the height of the season he would stroll in and out of night clubs and hotel barrooms, dancing and singing miners' ballads, first introducing himself with "A Miner's Son."

In stature O'Neill was far from the giant that his nickname suggests, being short, of slender build and soft spoken. But "giant" best describes the position he held among anthracite mine workers during the past century. Of all his gifts, dancing was outstanding; old-timers say the region never had his peer on the dance floor, and probably never will. As explained in the introduction, dancing contests were once the rage in the hard coal region. Local champions would compete at district contests and the winners in turn would dance against the best in the region. Miners would turn out by the hundreds and stake their hard cash on their favorites. In the early seventies O'Neill won the regional championship. His fame won him an engagement with the Welsh & Sands circus. After touring with it several years, he stepped into the rôle of one of the Dublin Dans in Howerth's *Hibernica,* a traveling magic lantern and vaudeville show which toured the country for the entertainment chiefly of Irish audiences. When *Hibernica* broke up in the anthracite region in 1894, O'Neill bowed himself off the professional stage forever, and went back to his former trade as a blacksmith and tool sharpener at various Schuylkill County collieries.

He was still the miners' champion dancer in 1896 when he was challenged to a match by a tall, gangling young mine worker named George "Corks" Kramer of Locust Gap Patch. The challenger's nickname testified to his lightness of foot and skillful interpretations of jigs, reels, clogs, and hornpipes, the most popular dances of the region. O'Neill accepted the challenge and the contest, preceded by much ballyhoo, was held at Locust Gap Patch. A great crowd turned out for the event with Kramer's partisans far outnumbering O'Neill's, for this was Kramer's home.

Giant O'Neill lost his crown in that match, but there were many in the audience who felt he should have won, and they made their expressions known by jeering as the gold medal was pinned on young Kramer's chest. When it was charged that the judges had been prejudiced against the champion, one of them offered to post a bet of $2,500 that Kramer would outdance the Giant again. That was a sizable fortune for those days, and whether or not it was a bluff it had the effect of silencing O'Neill's friends.

The years rolled on, the men grew old and the chance of another match seemed to have passed forever. But in 1935 at the organization of the Pennsylvania Folk Festival, the long-deferred opportunity appeared. When an elimination contest was staged in Pottsville, old-timers, remembering the ancient feud, demanded that Kramer and O'Neill be brought together again. Kramer came to Pottsville from Ashland and the little "Giant" from Atlantic City, and they were selected by the local judges to settle their feud at Allentown, then the seat of the state folk festival. Their appearance formed the climax of that program. Kramer, tall, gray-haired, proudly wearing the gold medal he had won at Locust Gap about forty years ago, towered over Giant O'Neill, a stoop-shouldered, white-haired little old man. There was something pathetic about this contest between two veterans of the anthracite industry. The judges sensed it and, grasping an opportunity to put an amicable finish to the feud, decided that it had been a good contest in which Kramer and O'Neill had danced equally well. The ancient rivals, still breathless from their vigorous stepping, were brought to the center of the stage and, as the spectators cheered and applauded, they shook hands.

POET MULHALL

Martin J. Mulhall—Poet Mulhall they called him—was not a member of the Molly Maguires, yet he is remembered as their chief bard. He was only sixteen when the Mollies were hanged. The spectacle of so many Irishmen, some of them boys like himself, dying on the gallows moved him profoundly.

Secluding himself in his Shenandoah home, he labored feverishly for days afterward and created a ballad for every one of the doomed men. A Shenandoah newspaper, which has since gone out of business, printed broadsides for him. With a different tune for each ballad, he set out on a singing tour of the lower anthracite counties. Most of his traveling was done on foot, but whenever he could he rode the rods. When he came to a patch he sang the ballads and sold broadsides of them. In the Schuylkill Valley, I was told, tears were shed when young Mulhall sang.

Although I could locate none of these broadsides, even with the help of Mulhall's aged sister, I was fortunate enough to find a copy of one of those "hanging" ballads, namely, "Thomas Duffy" as I have told in the chapter on the Molly Maguires.

"Muff Lawler, the Squealer" is another Molly ballad, probably the best known of them, which is ascribed by popular consent to Mulhall. A third ballad in the present collection, though not related to the Mollies, is also a Mulhall composition—"Lost Creek."

Mulhall had had only two years' schooling when he made up his Molly

Maguire ballads. And he was self-taught not only in poesy, but in music and painting. He was also a superb story teller, a folk artist if there ever was one! To one of his artistic temperament, mine work was irksome. He deserted the trade in his early teens, eking out a precarious living by his minstrelsy and performing odd jobs. The early habit of riding the rods, his principal mode of traveling as he grew older, ultimately proved his undoing. It was while hopping a freight that he was killed in the Altoona yards about a quarter of a century ago.

JOHN HORY

Unique was John Hory of Ashland. He did not drink, smoke, dance, play a musical instrument or even sing well. Nevertheless he left behind three fine anthracite ballads: "My Handsome Miner Boy"; "Jake and Jack Are Miners"; and "The Knights of Labor Strike," all of which he permitted me to copy from his notebook. I had been directed to his home by Ashland miners who remembered him as a one-time balladist. I found a seventy-three-year-old miner, melancholic and broken in health. A few years before my visit, he had been working as a door tender in the mines when mules trampled and permanently disabled him. His lean face, stenciled with those characteristic blue-black powder marks, was pallid, and his eyes betrayed the weariness of his spirit. It seemed to me that he was eager for the day

When the angels they will whisper, "Dear old miner you must come,
And we'll row you to the bright celestial shore."

In fact he talked constantly of a joyous reunion in heaven with his wife and a son who had been killed in the mines. Hory has "left this world of woe" and his friends hope that he has had his dearest wish realized.

JACK AND PATRICK JOHNSON

Two brothers, Jack and Patrick Johnson, practised minstrelsy in different localities—the former in Luzerne County and the latter in Schuylkill.

Jack Johnson was born at Summit Hill in 1846, and when he was ten his family moved to Bear Ridge Patch in the Schuylkill Valley. Here he worked in the mines with his brother until 1867, when the little colliery was abandoned and the patch deserted. Jack, then twenty-one, came to Freeland while his brother remained in the Schuylkill Valley. Jack worked in and around the mines of this locality for many years. In 1918, while employed as a hoisting engineer at the Beaver Meadow colliery, he became seriously ill, and died several weeks later in a Philadelphia hospital.

These facts were gleaned from the minstrel's family—John J. Johnson, Jr., superintendent of the Drifton mines, his aged widow and a daughter, Dolly Johnson—during a visit I made some years ago.

Jack Johnson improvised and sang ballads to the end of his days. Unfortunately his son learned to appreciate the value of his father's improvisations too late to write them down, but he did salvage a number of manuscripts, several of which he permitted me to copy. These were: "Bear Ridge Patch," composed in 1896, and "The Miner's Life," which dates back to 1884.

Jack Johnson played the banjo well, and often of a summer evening, as neighbors gathered around his porch, he would play it and sing. He sometimes improvised tunes on the banjo.

Patrick Johnson was an uncommonly good fiddler, as well as a balladist. His best-known ballad was "The Blacklegs." He gave up mine work to become a strolling tea peddler, and his minstrelsy paid him dividends in the form of increased sales. The miners not only purchased his tea but also showered him with hospitality which he earned by singing ballads, playing fiddle tunes, and telling stories on the village green.

DENNIS P. COYLE

Dennis P. Coyle, of Wilkes-Barre, at sixty-seven is the state champion jig dancer, a title won two successive years at the Pennsylvania Folk Festival. He is also a first-rate fiddler and carries in his head a great many old-time fiddle tunes, particularly Irish ones. In some respects he wears the mantle of the late Con Carbon, his boyhood friend and fellow minstrel. They worked in the Audenried breaker and were brought to Wilkes-Barre as boys, and until Carbon's death they lived as neighbors in the East End, Wilkes-Barre's old Irish neighborhood. They often appeared on programs together, and today Coyle is regarded as one of the best interpreters of Con Carbon's mining ballads.

He was my original source of the following Carbon pieces: "When the Black Diamond Breaker Was Burned to the Ground," "Mackin's Porch," and "The Hungarian Ball," and supplied variants of the others. He also gave me his brother Philip's ballad, "Good-bye Number Three," Bob Quigley's "The Start That Casey Got," and the touching "Mickey Pick-Slate." Coyle has a keen wit, a delicious sense of humor, and a marvelously retentive memory. Not the least of his qualities is that he is thoroughly human and friendly.

BARNEY KELLY

A familiar sight in Ashland is old Barney Kelly plodding along the street, his venerable black derby tilted at a rakish angle on his white head, stick in right hand pounding the sidewalks, and his precious violin case under his left arm. You might guess that he was on his way to some local Dinty Moore's for a shindig, but no, he is probably going to Art Stover's home for his regular weekly "practisin'." Stover plays the guitar and the pair have been musical butties for nearly forty years.

At seventy-eight Kelly is too old to be poking around the mines, and as a means of support for himself and his unmarried sister, who keeps house for him, he plays at local shindigs and has "a bit of a job" looking after things at a local hose house. He was never married, and neighbors hint at a blighted romance in his youth. He has more temperament than all the prima donnas of the Metropolitan put together, but miners love him in spite of it, or perhaps on account of it.

Despite his advanced age, Kelly won the anthracite regional old-timers' fiddling contest at Wilkes-Barre in 1937. Like all traditional fiddlers, he plays by ear, and like some, a drop of toddy stimulates his bow. More than sixty years ago his cousin Timothy Kelly gave him the fiddle he plays; taught him the scale and "The Irish Washerwoman." Though he knows hundreds of fiddle tunes, all of them learned by rote, this old tune is still his favorite. Age and many years of rough manual labor at the Potts colliery have not taken too much toll of his nimble fingers.

Whenever I'm in the Mahanoy Valley I call at the ramshackle house that has been his home since his birth. My difficulty is to break away gracefully when he plays for me. At my first move toward the door he would say, "Just one more number, George," and proceed to play a dozen. He has a habit of creasing his left eye when he smiles. He speaks slowly and with a slight tremble in his voice, and sometimes out of the corner of his mouth. His furrowed face is powder-marked only slightly. Having had virtually no schooling, Kelly taught himself to read and write; when he reads he usually wears silver-rimmed glasses which hang halfway down his nose. His memory is amazingly retentive—he scrawled out for me the whole ballad of "The Mines of Locust Dale" which he learned back in 1875—and is equally remarkable for the care with which he keeps written and printed records. On one of my calls at his home he brought out a bundle of old faded newspaper clippings which, judging by one of the clippings, he had been collecting since 1878. From this pile I extracted a copy of the ballad "The Big Hole in the Ground" from the defunct Parker's Mahanoy City *Tri-Weekly Record.*

JOSEPH GALLAGHER *

Panther Creek Valley's best loved citizen is seventy-two-year-old Joseph Gallagher. A native of the patch which he celebrated in his "Dear Old Number Six," he still lives within a stone's throw of it—in a company row house at Lansford. He does not feel as chipper as when I first met him many years ago. His hair has turned white, his gait has slowed down, he breathes with some difficulty, and his sight is poor. Most of his old cronies have crossed the River Styx on their way to "the bright celestial shore." Yet despite his saddened heart and infirmities, he greets me with a cheerful smile and a firm grip, and I never approach his home without a sense of eager anticipation, for I know that he will have something interesting to say. Gallagher has imagination, native intelligence, and Irish wit. He has told me stories and legends of the hard coal fields, and has sung ballads for me, his own and variants of others, and as a bard he has no peer in the valley. He has improvised tunes for his ballads on the fiddle or on a guitar and occasionally has borrowed

* Gallagher died May 6, 1938.

a printed tune. He is represented in this volume by three other works, "John J. Curtis," "Three Jolly Welshmen," and "Dan McCole."

WILLIAM KEATING

At fifty-two, William Keating of Pottsville is old enough to have been part of traditional anthracite minstrelsy, and yet not too old to have discontinued "twanging his harp," as he puts it. He has appeared at both the Pennsylvania and National Folk Festivals, where his distinctive mule driver's outfit has become a familiar sight—patched faded blue overalls tucked inside high-laced boots, his work shirt open at the collar, a dinner pail suspended from one shoulder and a canteen from the other, his teapot shaped open-flame lamp protruding from his miner's cap, and a long braided leather whip slung carelessly around his neck. The favorite ballad of these audiences is his well-known autobiographical "Down, Down, Down."

Short, thin, with few gray hairs, Keating has a boyish appearance, especially in his mule driver's outfit. He was born on March 31, 1886, at Mount Laffee Patch of the third generation of Irish miners.

Keating improvised "October on Mount Laffee's Hills," "Down, Down, Down," and "The Driver Boys of Wadesville Shaft," before he was able to write. Not until he was a thirty-two-year-old soldier at Camp Meade in 1917–18 did he learn to use a pen. He credits the late J. H. Zerbey, Sr., Pottsville newspaper publisher, with the inspiration and encouragement, given during a visit to the camp, which led to his taking writing lessons in camp.

As Keating's lack of early education was typical of so many old-time anthracite mine workers, his reminiscences may be of interest here:

I guess I was born with the "nack" (gift?) of putting (musical) rhyming-Words together; "hold" those Rhymes in my "mind," and recite them Orally, but the want, the Need, the Ability (?) of writing rhymes on paper never became "pressing" nor necessary untill about 32 years After I was born.

My first "need"-to-Write-my-Rhymes-On-Paper, came while I was a slate-picker in Old Glen Dower Breaker, located at Mt. Pleasant. I was

11 years "old" then, and my slatepicker-Buddies often asked me to write my songs and rhymes for them.

But I, (being ashamed of the fact that I could Not write) always "put off" the necessity for writing with one "excuse" or "another"; so (untill I reached the age of 32) "excuses" always "saved" me from the time-Wasting task of writing.

Having been sent To school for Only one year and having "played hooky" Six (All the Summer) months out of That year, allowed me Only 6 actual months in the school-Room. My "grades" in (Mt. Laffee's little Whitish-Gray-painted) school were: Chart Class and First Reader. The only whack I had at (school room) writing was making "crows feet" and "chinese"-scribbling on the Black Board, with Chalk!

From the Schutes I "graduated," instead of from the School. It's (Mt. Laffee)—well-Known: my Parents were, actually, Poor.

All of "the Singing Miners" are Graduates of Toil:

When we were Boys, the Shears-of-Fate
Cut short our share of School:
We're "graduates" from Pickin' Slate,
And Occupations Cruel!
The schute-Boss was our "teacher";
His "example" was a Club!
Ten Hours a day for Pauper's "pay"
We "humped" for Humble Grub!

DANIEL WALSH

Another ballad singer is tall, lanky, gray-haired Daniel Walsh of Centralia, who has won medals in two successive years at the Pennsylvania Folk Festival. He can sing many of the traditional miners' ballads, but the favorite with his audiences and, for that matter, his own favorite, is "The Old Miner's Refrain." A veteran miner himself, gifted with a rich though uncultivated tenor voice, he puts so much heart into his singing that even the most callous cannot resist being moved.

HARRY TEMPEST

Harry Tempest, who wrote "The Twin-Shaft Mine Squeeze" and "Over at Indian Ridge," was born at St. Clair in 1871, and when a child his family moved to Shenandoah. As a young mine worker, he would entertain his fellow workers in the mines with ditties he made up out of his head. He was one of several miners to step from anthracite minstrelsy to the professional stage, and his best-known rôle was as Father John Whalen in the late Daniel L. Hart's play, *The Parish Priest.* The uncertainties of a trouper's life after some years tired him, and he returned to Schuylkill County to engage in business.

When I met him at Atlantic City a dozen years ago he was operating a summer boarding house and reminiscing with his old-time butty, "Giant" O'Neill, who was also living at the seashore resort. Without much urging Tempest sang "The Twin-Shaft Mine Squeeze" and "Over at Indian Ridge" for me. He was a medium-sized, well-built man with broad shoulders and a tinge of iron gray on his massive head of brown hair. His Irish blue eyes reflected the warm human qualities of his character.

The last I heard of him he was living in Corydon, Indiana.

BOB QUIGLEY

Robert J. "Bob" Quigley, a vaudeville headliner with his brother George on Keith's Circuit for many years, was an anthracite balladist and minstrel in his youth. He was born at Carbondale on December 26, 1859, and when he was six years old his family moved to Parsons, now part of Wilkes-Barre. At eight he was working in the Mineral Spring breaker, and from there went into the mines, but he left mine work before obtaining his papers as a contract miner. The gifts he displayed around the mines in his youth—singing, acrobatics, and story-telling—he developed later to become a top-notch vaudeville performer. His first jig and clog dancing was done inside the mines. He also had the knack of improvising ballads about miners. Two of his pieces, "At Paddy Mayock's Ball" and "The Start That Casey Got," which I had previously obtained from other sources, he sang for me in a wavering voice. He said they were based on true incidents. After retiring from the professional stage, Quigley returned to his boyhood home in Parsons, and there, in his seventy-ninth year, he is living a quiet life and enjoying the rich memories of an active theatrical career.

There are a number of other minstrels still living, some of whom have taken part in the Pennsylvania Folk Festival in spite of their advanced age. Among the better known are: Jerry Byrne, fireboss at the Buck Run colliery, and Thomas Rowlands of Edwardsville, singers; James Connors, Centralia, a fiddler; Michael McAndrew of Wilkes-Barre and George "Corks" Kramer of Ashland, jig and clog dancers.

* * *

The following are names of important sources that, with a few exceptions, have not been previously mentioned. They well deserve my heartfelt thanks and the thanks of all who value American folk expressions for the unselfish manner in which they have coöperated in this work.

George Athey, Jerry Byrne, John Byrnes, Dennis Brislin, Harry Brennan, John Curry, Patrick J. Connelly, Justin G. Chadwick, T. J. Clemens, Mrs. Katherine Casserly, Thomas J. Cummings, P. F. Delaney, Mrs. Thomas Donnelly, Michael Derr, Kyran Donahue, William Derby, John Durkin, George English * (aged 90), David Fuge, William Forgay,* Hugh Feeley, Philip Ginder, David P. Ginder, Rev. W. F. Ginder, Con Gallagher, Mr. and Mrs. Thomas Hill, John Heffernan, Baird Halberstadt,* William Irving * (aged 90), James J. Jennings, Mrs. Jack Johnson, Sr., Dolly Johnson, Thomas Jones, William Kinney, James Kenna, Rev. William J. Kelly, Peter Laux, Mrs. Margaret Dalton Libby, John Leinenbach, Jacob Leinenbach, Peter Leinenbach, Charles Leslie, William Leslie, Victor E. Lewis, Mike Maharg, John Maher, Andrew Mattey, Matthew Mahan, Pat McCullough, Edward J. O'Brien, Theodore Ridge, Bernard Sharp, John Schneider, and Rudy Schneider.

WHO WAS THE DISCOVERER OF ANTHRACITE?

This being a collection of folklore, the Ginder incident—the Lehigh field's chief claim to having mothered the industry—has been treated in this volume as a legend, which it really is, rather than as authentic history.

The other anthracite fields have their own "discovery" legends and historic claims which they have advanced, in some cases with much

* Deceased.

warmth, though Indians must have known about anthracite long before the coming of the white man.

The earliest recorded discovery by pioneers occurred in 1762, when advance agents of the Susquehanna Company, surveying a section of Wyoming, reported finding coal outcropping on the right bank of Mill Creek near the Susquehanna river just beyond the northern limits of Wilkes-Barre. The next year, meeting at Windham, Connecticut, the company took official notice of the report and voted to reserve to itself coal found in the towns laid out for settlement.

In the southern, or Schuylkill field, Scull's map of Pennsylvania located coal near Pottsville in 1770. However, the people of Schuylkill County base their claim to priority on the following legend: In 1790 Nicho Allen, a Yankee woodsman living there, camped out one night at the foot of Broad Mountain in what is now Norwegian township. He built his campfire near a ledge of rocks and went to sleep. In the middle of the night he was awakened by a bright light shining in his eyes and an intense heat coming from burning "rocks." He spent the rest of the night trying to solve the source of the mysterious blaze. With dawn came recognition that unwittingly he had set fire to an outcrop of coal. Thrilled by his experience, he quickly spread the report of it along the countryside. The people, however, were skeptical. Their own faith was placed in the Sixth and Seventh Books of Moses. Volumes of awful power, buried deep in these mountains, and guarded day and night by gigantic scorpions—they alone were the source of miracles, in the folk belief. As for rocks, black or any other color, burning, forsooth!

In the same year Isaac Tomlinson found "black stones" lying in the bed of Quaker Run, a stream running across his farm at Shamokin, in the western middle anthracite field. Believing them to be coal he had several pieces tested in a smithy's forge and they burned. A quarter century later, a fourteen-year-old farmer boy named John Thompson took Shamokin's first mined coal to market. Digging it out of the outcrop himself, he loaded it on his two-horse wagon and hauled it to Sunbury where a shoemaker paid him five dollars for the load.

Samuel Preston, a surveyor, first unearthed coal at the Lackawanna river bank near Carbondale in 1804.

A little deer pawed open an outcrop near Hazleton in 1818, and in 1826, while hunting in the same location, which is part of the eastern middle field, John Charles observed a groundhog's hole. Laying down his gun, he reached into the hole, but instead of a groundhog it was coal that his hand had grasped. Prospecting on a commercial basis followed.

The question as to which of the anthracite fields is entitled to the honor of priority in the industry will probably never be settled, in view of the irreconcilable claims. Old newspaper files reflect the bitterness of the age-old controversy, and history books and archives bulge with learned papers on it.

The best case for the Wyoming or Northern field is presented by Ernest Gray Smith in his *History of Wilkes-Barre:* ". . . the Wyoming Valley, in general, led all other districts of the anthracite field in enterprise, initiative and persevering effort in introducing its underground treasures to the world and in particular, it may lay claim to four important circumstances of sufficient importance to perpetuate its name when future mention is made of a great industry which has more than fulfilled, in each succeeding generation, the fondest dreams of its pioneers.

"Amid cross currents of dispute and storms of debate which have beclouded issues for many years, these four claims to lasting fame, in connection with a splendid enterprise stand out without fear of contradiction:

1. That Wyoming, as a district, was the place of actual discovery of anthracite.
2. That the Gore brothers at Wilkes-Barre, first reduced it to commercial use through the instrumentality of the air blast.
3. That Judge Jesse Fell in giving to the world the successful results of his experiments in adapting it to domestic uses rendered a service of immeasurable worth.
4. That the Smith brothers of Plymouth in exploiting the product of their mines . . . were the real pioneers of the industry."

Arguments for the Lehigh field were advanced by the Mauch Chunk *Democrat* in 1890 at the approach of the one hundredth anniversary of Ginder's discovery, as follows:

"Many things have been known to exist from the beginning of time, such as electricity and steam but how to utilize them in the interest of civilization is another matter. The peculiar stone quarries down the Lehigh Valley that have been converted into cement were well known to exist centuries ago. . . . Evidently it is true that coal was known to exist years before 1791 when Ginder discovered it in Summit Hill, but it is also true that the first systematic effort to mine coal and put it in the general market was the formation of the Lehigh Coal Mine Company in 1792—the year following Ginder's discovery, although after shipping several loads popular feeling continued against it and the said company suspended operation. . . . It was not until 1820 that anthracite coal mining and sending it to market had a successful beginning anywhere in Pennsylvania."

This was the year that the present Lehigh Navigation Coal Company, successor to the Lehigh Coal Mine Company, shipped 365 tons of coal to market. From this shipment the U. S. Geological Survey dates the official beginning of the anthracite industry.

While Ginder's title may be challenged in some quarters, there is no doubt whatever that popular tradition recognizes him as the actual discoverer. The Ginder legend has crystallized and its place in American folklore is secure. Its original source was a paper by Dr. T. C. James, a Philadelphia physician, read before the Historical Society of Pennsylvania and reported in *Hazard's Register of Pennsylvania* in 1829. In that narrative Dr. James, after a lapse of twenty-five years, recollected that in the autumn of 1804, he and a friend, Anthony Morris, Esq., became lost in the wilderness of the Mahoning Valley and found a night's lodging in Phillip Ginder's grist-mill. The next day Ginder guided them to the Sharp Mountain spot where he had found coal. As the two gentlemen lingered, "contemplating the wildness of the scene," they were regaled by Ginder with the story of the discovery.

Virtually all subsequent accounts of the incident are based on this James narrative in which Ginder is quoted indirectly. My own departure from it is made on the authority of documentary evidence directed to my attention by Rev. William F. Ginder, Phillip's great-great-grandson and the Ginder family historian. Dr. James, for instance, spells the discoverer's name as "Ginter," and in this form it has come down to our day. But the Ginder family maintains that the correct spelling is with a "d." This is borne out by Phillip's own signature on his oath of allegiance to the Provincial Government, taken on October 25, 1746, when he arrived in Philadelphia from Germany.

The traditional belief that at the time of the discovery Ginder was a desperately poor hunter is also traceable to Dr. James's narrative (". . . he was without supply of food for his family . . ."). This lent drama to the incident but was not in accord with the facts. In 1791, the year of the coal discovery, Ginder had been living in Pennsylvania, and probably in this particular corner of it, for forty-five years. Unless he was far less industrious and frugal than the other German settlers, which seems improbable, he would be expected to have taken up some of the vast tracts of unclaimed land then available. Pennsylvania archives record the fact that in 1786—five years before the discovery—Ginder was in possession of three hundred acres of land in Penn Township, Northampton (now Carbon) County. While this in itself may not be conclusive proof that he was a farmer, the archives show further that in the same year he was taxed with one hundred acres, which must have been under cultivation.

My allusion to Colonel Jacob Weiss's representing himself as the discoverer is based on a copy of the Weiss prospectus for the formation of the Lehigh Coal Mine Company which I found in the Mauch Chunk *Democrat* of April 25, 1891. The copy was made from an original prospectus lent the *Democrat* by Eckley B. Coxe, well-known coal operator.

In 1891, the one hundredth anniversary of the discovery, a bill appropriating one thousand dollars toward the erection of a monument to Ginder was passed by the State Legislature on first reading. This amount was increased to two thousand dollars on second reading. But owing to opposition from other anthracite fields the bill was defeated. The site of the discovery at Summit Hill was for many years marked by a great clay bank thrown up during a quarter of a century of quarrying the Mammoth coal seam. This bank was leveled for a new school building which was named for Ginder. The Ginder family was not wholly satisfied by this tribute to their famous ancestor because the name carved on the school building was spelled with a "t."

The Ginder name is carried on by many of Phillip's descendants in Carbon County. The oldest living descendant is David P. Ginder who, past seventy, lives in Lehighton. A Ginder still cultivates a farm in the Mahoning Valley. The discoverer's son Jacob, born in 1785, farmed in this valley until 1836 when he died and was buried in the Benn Salem cemetery. His grandson, named for him, died in 1912 at the age of ninety-one and is buried near Weatherly.

WAS THE IMPRINTED HAND IN THE MAUCH CHUNK JAIL A HOAX?

The legend surrounding the imprint of a Molly Maguire hand in one of the cells of the Carbon County jail at Mauch Chunk is of a type that is old in folklore. Bob Ripley has a cartoon showing a handprint on a rock at Punjab, India, which is supposed to have been made more than four hundred years ago. "Sikh legend has it," he explains in a note, "that their prophet Nanak was imprisoned by a Mussulman saint, Baba Wali, who attemped to deprive him of water unto death. Whereupon Nanak in great anger smote the rocky mountain side with his hand and summoned forth a clear spring of mountain water. . . ."

A similar handprint may be found on a stone near Welfesholze, Germany. According to its legend, on the eve of the battle fought there in the twelfth century between Emperor Henry V and his Saxon enemies, Hoyer von Mansfeld, the imperial general, swore that he could no more be defeated than stone could take the imprint of his hand. But the imprint was left in the stone, and he lost the battle as well as his life.

In the Mauch Chunk legend, Campbell, the prisoner, was believed to have left an imprint of his hand as proof of his innocence. No one knows how the legend started, but it soon spread to the remotest corners of the region, and even to distant cities. Curious people by the thousands from many parts of the nation have poured into the little mining town to view what was popularly believed to be a supernatural phenomenon. The railroads did a land-office business carrying them from the metropolitan centers on Sunday excursions. This is probably the best-known legend in the anthracite region.

Doubt as to its authenticity has been cast upon it from time to time. Among the skeptics, and perhaps the most outspoken of them, is D. A. L. Davis of Lansford. He has spent his seventy-three years in his native Carbon County and for nearly half a century was editor and publisher of the Lansford *Leader*, a weekly, which has gone out of business. He often saw Campbell on Lansford's streets as a boy, he said. His father, John Davis, master mechanic of the Lehigh & Wilkes-Barre Coal Company was Boss Jones's bed-mate two nights before Jones was murdered by the Molly Maguires.

Davis told me that he had a vivid recollection of the hand on the wall which he first saw with his father in the seventies. Declaring, "I've as good a memory as any man living," he said that his father explained the origin of the imprint as follows:

When the jail was being built, a local plumber was at work fitting pipes in the cell. He was using a primitive type of wrench consisting of chain and lever. Obliged to employ force, he set his foot down on the lever and placed his hand on the wall to balance himself. The plaster still being fresh, the plumber's hand was cast on the wall. When the plaster had dried, the imprint showed up vividly. No one had paid particular attention to it until some time after Campbell and his three fellow Molly Maguires were executed. Then, in that mysterious manner that can be ascribed only to folk lore, a rumor began to be spread through the country that the imprint had been left by Campbell as a mark of his innocence.

Davis said that Sheriff Jacob Raudenbush who had executed the Mollies, declaring that Campbell had never occupied the cell, publicly denied that there was any basis in the legend.

Sheriff Raudenbush whitewashed the wall many times, and so did his successors. Yet the imprint reappeared, each time, however, less distinctly. I asked Davis about this, and his theory was that the oily hand had penetrated the plaster too deeply to be washed away.

Another authority on Molly Maguire lore told me that the prisoners would point up the hand after every whitewash as they had a financial interest in the perpetuation of the legend. Tourists, attracted to the jail by the legend, swelled the prisoners' tobacco fund and frequently gave gratuities to the jail guides.

The myth that the imprint could not be removed was challenged on December 15, 1931 by Sheriff Robert Bowman who scraped the mark off the wall with a putty knife. In a talk which I had with the sheriff several days later, I was told that his act was dictated by a desire to stop the flow of curious visitors who were upsetting his jail routine—and this more than half a century after the origin of the famous legend.

Despite all measures taken to rid the jail of its legendary blemish, there are many folks in the region who say that the imprint will always come back.

SOME HOME REMEDIES

In the summer of 1931, during a week-end ballad hunting in the West End of Schuylkill County, I heard of "Uncle Pete." A descendant of Alsatian pioneers who founded Tremont, and a retired miner, he was one of the best-known practitioners of *hexerei* in that district. But, as I was to ascertain, he powwowed not for personal profit but to help neighbors. Next to the Bible, his most prized possession was a well-thumbed and tobacco-stained copy of Hohman's *Long Lost Friend*.

Calling on him one day with a feigned earache, I had myself powwowed. When I offered to pay him, he refused to accept money, explaining that it was against his principles. But he did accept a small tinful of pipe tobacco. He was a little old man, surprisingly spry for his eighty years. His wrinkled face bore the miner's tell-tale powder marks and was distinguished by a bushy tobacco-stained mustache.

We became good friends and I visited him several times afterward as he was full of local folklore, particularly about herbs, roots, blossoms, and barks. One day I pressed him for formulas of home remedies and specifics used by mining families in that section.

Here they are as he gave them to me:

BLOOD PURIFIER: Mix woodfern, pepper wood, sassafras root and wild cherry bark in equal parts. Cut them up fine and boil in a pot on your kitchen stove. Let the lid off partly like you were cooking whiskey [this was said with a knowing wink]. When it has boiled about half an hour, let it cool off. Then take a teacupful three or four times a day.

NERVOUSNESS: Make a tea of the roots of the moccasin flower which you can pick about the time when the honeysuckle blossoms. Take it twice a day and it'll cure your nervousness.

DIABETES: Make a tea of horsetail leaves which you can find growing along the banks of Middle Creek as it flows from the colliery. It also grows around culm banks. Take two or three cupfuls a day for three days straight. Then for the next three days go to work and pick huckleberry leaves and make a tea out of them and drink that for three days straight. Then you go back to horsetail tea and back again to huckleberry tea, and so on for a month. This will take the sugar out of your blood and cure you of diabetes.

SORE HANDS AND LEGS: Go to work and find the Jimson weed near a colliery engine house ash pile. It's a high bush with an awful smell [here he held his nose]. Fry the leaves in pure, kettle-rendered lard, and lay them on the sore parts. They will stick like a plaster.

FITS AND CONVULSIONS: The root of the water-lily made into a tea is good for them. Drink it before you think you will have 'em comin' on.

Glossary of Anthracite Technical and Colloquial Words and Phrases

AFTER DAMP: Consists principally of carbonic acid gas with some nitrogen, and is produced by a fire or an explosion of fire damp (which see). It cannot be breathed; a single inhalation in its pure state produces immediate insensibility and speedy death.

ARK: A flat-boat in which coal was floated down the rivers to tidewater. It made one trip and was broken up at its destination, the timber sold and hardware returned to the point of origin.

BARN BOSS: The man in charge of the mule barn on the surface or underground.

BASIS: See sliding scale.

BATTERY: In steeply pitching seams, a wooden structure built across the chute to hold back blasted coal.

BILLY CUPS: Whiskey rations served to laborers in Mauch Chunk in the 1820's; named for Billy Speers, the dispenser.

BLACK DAMP: A gas consisting of carbon dioxide mixed with an excess of nitrogen. It is given off by the coal seam and formed during an explosion. Being heavier than air it is always found in a layer along the floor of a mine. It extinguishes light and suffocates its victims. Hence, it is sometimes known as "Choke damp."

BLACKLEG: An opprobrious name for a strikebreaker; turncoat or traitor.

BLACKLIST: A list of the names of workers, especially those active in union organization, against whom all avenues of employment are closed.

BLOWN-OUT SHOT: An ineffective shot in blasting.

BOBTAIL CHECK: A slip of paper which informed the miner that he had no money coming to him at the end of a month's work. See snake statement.

BONY: Coal containing slaty material in its composition.

BOOTLEGGER: One engaged in coal bootlegging. This applies to the worker in bootleg holes as well as the man who cleans the coal in a small, impermanent breaker, and the trucker who conveys the coal to market. Bootleggers call themselves "independent miners."

BOOTLEGGING: Illegal coal mining. The term came into general use in the twenties to describe the method by which free-lance miners excavated company-owned coal from abandoned mines and sold it.

BRANCH: A turnout where miners congregate to wait for empty cars. In mines where the seams lie flat, a spur track into a chamber from the gangway or heading.

BREACH: A large cave-hole caused by undermining.

BREAKDOWN: A fast dance, especially among the Irish. Also a shindig.

BREAKER: A building where anthracite is prepared for market. Because of its peculiar construction, it is the first building in the anthracite region to catch the eye. Many breakers rest against a hillside, built that way to save material in construction.

BREAST: The miner's workshop. Miners in the northern anthracite field call it a chamber and in bituminous mines it is known as a room.

BUCKSHOTS: Early nickname of Molly Maguires.

BURYING: A funeral.

BUTTY: A fellow miner, especially one who works a breast in partnership with another miner. A term used in English mining for two hundred years, and by soldiers in the World War under its other form, "buddy."

CAGE: An apparatus in the shaft on which men and coal are hoisted; same as elevator in a building.

CAR: A small four-wheeled wagon made of wood, iron, or steel in which the coal is hauled underground.

CARRIAGE: Same as cage.

CARTRIDGE: A tube of heavy manila paper filled with black powder once used in blasting.

CAVE-HOLE: A depression on the surface caused by a fall of roof in the mine.

CENTRAL BREAKER: A breaker where the coal from a number of mines in a district is prepared. Central breakers, representing the last word in mining technology, make it economical for operators to abandon many local breakers.

CHAIN GANG: Irish vigilantes who fought the Molly Maguires.

CHAMBER: See breast.

CHECKAI: A Polish word which has entered the vernacular. Freely translated, it means "Hold on!" or "Wait a minute!"

CHOKE DAMP: See black damp.

CHUTE: A narrow passage through which coal descends by gravity from the foot of the breast down to the gangway in mines where the seams pitch sharply. In the breaker an inclined trough down which the coal tumbles by gravity.

COAL DUMP: A hill of stored coal.

COCKO: A piece of slate or bony.

COFFIN NOTICE: A warning containing crude drawings of pistols and coffins sent by Molly Maguires.

COLLIER: Same as miner.

COLLIERY: The mining plant as a whole.

COMPANY HOUSE: A house in which a mine worker lives and pays rent to the coal company he works for.

COSSACKS: Nickname for coal and iron police.

CRACKER: Early term for breaker (which see). Also jocularly for miner.

CRACKER BOSS: An official in charge of the screen room in a breaker.

CREEP: A crush (which see). Any slow movement in which loosened pillars are forced down into the floor of a breast or up into its roof. Also called "squeeze."

CROP-FALL: A caving-in of the surface at the outcrop.

CRUSH: A settling downward of the strata overlying a portion of an excavated seam.

CRUSHER-ROLLS: See rolls.

CULM: All coal refuse finer than rice. Before a market was developed for fine coal, it used to be piled in banks and left for waste; culm banks are now being reclaimed.

CULM BANK: See above.

DOOR BOY: A boy who opened and shut a trap door erected across a passageway in a mine to control the direction of the air currents; automatic doors now perform this task. Also known as trapper.

DRIFT: A water-level entrance into a mine. The opening, about six feet high and eight feet wide, is driven into the coal seam from the outcropping and forms a small tunnel in the coal itself.

DRILL: A tool for boring holes in coal or rock.

DROPPINGS: Drops of water falling from the roof into a gangway or breast.

ELECTRIC MULE: Electric motor.

ENDLESS CHAIN: A device for hauling coal in which a chain passes from the engine along one side of the road around a pulley at the far end and back again on the other side of the road. Empty cars, attached to one side of the chain by various kinds of clips or hooks are hauled into the mine; loaded cars attached to the other side of the chain are hauled out of the mine.

FACE: That part of a breast where the miner performs his daily work.

FAN: A machine propelled by steam or electricity used to force a ventilating current of air through the mine.

FEEDER: A small stream of gas escaping from a coal crevice.

FIRE: An ejaculation shouted by a miner as a warning just before he fires a shot. Also a warning chalked across a barricade at the entrance to abandoned workings where gas accumulates.

FIREBOSS: An executive who inspects an anthracite mine for accumulations of gas before the miners report for work; usually he starts his round at 4 A. M. The loneliest job in the mines.

FIRE DAMP: Light carbureted hydrogen, known as marsh gas, given off by coal seams. Being lighter than air it is found in the roof of a breast or chamber. Highly explosive.

FIVE STARS: Nickname for Knights of Labor in the northern anthracite field.

FLAT: A flat coal seam.

FURNACE: Anthracite mines formerly were ventilated by a furnace erected at the bottom of an air shaft. Being lighter, the heated column of air rose and the outer air taking its place produced the necessary ventilation through the mine.

GANGWAY: A passageway driven in the coal at a slight grade forming the base from which the other workings of the mine are begun.

GOB: Coal refuse left on the mine floor.

GOBBING THE BONE: Cleaning up slate.

GOODS, THE: Molly Maguire slang for passwords.

GRAVITY ROADS: Railroads built in the early days of the industry to overcome mountain barriers in hauling coal from the mines to canals. See switchback.

GUM BOOT BRIGADE: Itinerant miners who bartered gum boots for liquor.

HAULAGE: The system of hauling coal out of a mine.

HAULAGE CHAIN: In the early days chains were used in haulage in and around mines. Wire-rope has displaced them.

HEADING: A passage leading from the gangway. The main entry in a coal mine is laid out with the precision of a main avenue in a city. From it at right angles headings run like cross streets, lined on each side with breasts, or chambers.

HEADMAN: An employee charged with the duty of attending to the signals at the head of the shaft and with assisting in the pushing of loaded coal cars off the cage and empties onto it.

HOEDOWN: Same as breakdown.

HOPPERS: Pockets at the bottom of a breaker through which the processed coal falls as it is loaded into railroad cars; also the cars.

HUNG-FIRE: Delay in a blasting explosion caused by dampness of the powder or by too slow combustion of the fuse.

HUNGARY, HUNK, HUNKY: Nicknames for Hungarians. Generally applied to all Slavic immigrants.

JIG: A machine, working on the principle of specific gravity, used in breakers to separate coal from impurities. It is fast being supplanted by the flotation method operated by means of huge cones.

JIGGER BOSS: A company official who dispensed whiskey rations at Mauch Chunk in the 1820's.

JIMMY: A small railroad car in which anthracite was hauled in early days.

JOHNNY MITCHELL TRAINS: Jocularly applied to freight trains on which striking miners traveled in search of temporary work in the cities outside the region during the famous strike of 1902. Named for John Mitchell, the strike leader.

JUMPER: A bar of steel once used as a rock drill.

KNOCKDOWN: The method by which youthful colliery workers held out a portion of their wages for spending money.

LABORER: A per diem worker for the company. Also one who assists a contract worker in his breast and is paid by him.

LEVEL: Applied to seams which run like floors in an office building. Under and above the seam lie the rock strata.

LOCKOUT: A situation where employers force their employees to quit work.

LOKIE: Diminutive for locomotive. Also applied to electric motors.

MANWAY: A passage in or into a mine used as a footpath for workers.

MINER: A worker who cuts coal in a breast or chamber by contract; the highest skilled worker of a colliery. Used interchangeably in this volume with mine worker and collier.

MISFIRE: A shot that has failed to go off.

MODOCS: Anti-Molly Maguire vigilantes, made up of English, Welsh, and Pennsylvania Germans.

MONKEY HEADING: A narrow and low passage driven in the coal where miners take refuge while coal is being blasted. Chiefly in mines where seams pitch sharply.

MONKEY LADDER: A ladder made of saplings in which the widely separated steps rest in the coal. Used by miners in going to and from their breasts in steeply pitching seams.

MULEWAY: Heavily timbered passage between levels in a mine for the transfer of unattached mules from one level to the other.

NIPPER: An errand boy in the mine.

OUTCROP: A coal seam exposed on the surface.

OUTLET: A mine exit.

PAID CRIER: A professional mourner among Irish mining people, usually a woman; a keener.

PATCH: A mine village, usually built and owned by a coal company.

PATCHER: An inhabitant of a mine patch. Also a mule driver's helper who sprags mine cars and performs other duties along the gangway.

PAY-DAY GAIT: A fast walk.

PICKING ROOM: Same as screen room.

PILLAR: A column of coal left unmined as a support to the roof.

PITCH: The angle at which a coal seam inclines below a horizontal line.

PLANE: Any incline on which a track is laid for the purpose of lowering or hoisting coal in or outside a mine, or on a gravity railroad.

PLATFORM: The place on top of a breaker where the freshly mined coal is weighed by a weigh boss just before it is dumped into the machinery. In the breaker, a flat or slightly inclined floor covered with iron plates on to which coal is run from the main screen-bars and cleaned by platform men.

PLUCK ME: Nickname for a company store; given because of a tendency to overcharge.

POLINKY: A Slavic alcoholic drink of high potency.

POSSESSION HOUSE: A house placed on mining lands in early days to hold a tract against squatters.

POTEEN: Irish for whiskey.

POWDER BOX: A wooden box in a miner's breast or chamber in which were kept black powder, cartridge paper, cartridge stick, squibs, lampwick, chalk, and tools.

POWWOW: A superstitious practice still prevalent among some anthracite miners, more commonly in the middle and southern anthracite fields. Also Slavic superstitions.

PROP: A timber set at right angles to the seam to support the roof.

RIB: A side wall in an anthracite mine.

ROBBING PILLARS: The cutting away of coal left to support the roof after breasts have been worked out, often resulting in cave-ins.

ROCK FIGHT: Nickname for a public dance, evidently referring to the way they sometimes ended in the rough old days.

ROLLS: In a breaker, heavy iron or steel cylinders set with teeth used for breaking coal.

ROOF: The stratum of hardened clay or sandstone that lies over the coal and forms a protection for the miner at his work.

ROUNDHEAD: Nickname for Slavic immigrants.

SAFETY: A safety lamp that can be carried into inflammable gases without igniting them.

SCAVENGER MINING: The taking out of coal so close to the surface as to undermine the top soil, resulting in devastation above ground. Usually engaged in by an independent operator working an old mine on a lease from a major corporation.

SCREEN: A revolving wire-mesh cylinder in a breaker used for separating coal into different sizes.

SCREEN ROOM: That part of a breaker where boys picked slate and bony.

SCRIP: Paper money, redeemable at company stores, issued by early coal companies to miners in payment of wages.

SEAM: Correct technical term for a deposit of coal in the ground. However, vein is in more common usage. Vein is incorrect because the coal lies in a bed or stratum, enclosed by parallel strata of rocks, and does not radiate from a center as do gold and silver veins.

SHAFT: A vertical entrance into a mine.

SHEBEEN: Irish for an unlicensed saloon; a speakeasy.

SHEET-IRON GANG: Anti-Molly Maguire vigilantes.

SHIFTING CLOTHES: Street clothes into which the miner changes on emerging from the mine.

SHINDIG: Same as breakdown and hoedown.

SHOOFLY: Miners' work train.

SHIPPER: An official who inspects the coal in the railroad cars before they are shipped to market.

SIDE-HITCHING: An act in which the mule is hooked by its harness to the side instead of the front of a loaded car to give it enough momentum to slide on to a cage.

SILT: Breaker waste composed of water, coal, slate, pyrite, and clay.

SLATE: Dark shale lying next to the coal beds. It contains impressions of the plant life of distant ages, proving the vegetable origin of coal.

SLATE PICKER: A boy who used to pick slate in the breaker; the work is now done by mechanical pickers.

SLEEPERS: An early nickname of Molly Maguires.

SLIDING SCALE: An arrangement between operators and miners whereby wages were regulated in accordance with the rise and fall of average coal market prices.

SLOPE: An entrance to a mine driven down through an inclined coal seam; also a mine having such an entrance. An inside slope is a passage in the mine driven through the seam by which coal is brought up from a lower level.

SLUSH: Same as silt.

SNAKE STATEMENT: A monthly statement by a coal company on which a crooked line in red ink was drawn to show a miner's indebtedness. The company checked off rent, supplies, and groceries, which often added up to more than a miner's monthly earnings.

SOUNDING THE TOP: Tapping the roof with a pick or bar to test its soundness; the first thing a miner does when he begins his day's work.

SPALL, TO: To fine, as for a breach of mine regulations; to break up coal.

SPOON OUT: To thin out, said of a coal seam.

SPRAG: A round stick of wood, about a foot long, usually having tapered ends, which is inserted between the spokes of a wheel to check a mine car.

SPRAGGER: An employee of a mine who sprags a car.

SPRAGGING: The act of checking a mine car with a sprag.

SQUEEZE: Same as crush and creep.

SQUIB: A long powder cracker once used for lighting a cartridge in blasting.

SQUIRE: An unofficial title given Justices of the Peace in townships, and aldermen in boroughs and cities, who act as magistrates in Pennsylvania's antiquated petty court system.

STABLE BOSS: Same as barn boss.

STONE COAL: Early term for anthracite.

STRIKE: The quitting of work by a body of employees to enforce demands on an employer or resist conditions forced upon them. Also the direction of any horizontal line along or across the seam.

STRIKEBREAKER: Same as blackleg or scab.

STRIPPING: An excavation with steam shovels in which the coal seams are laid bare by the stripping of the surface soil and rock strata. Operators are resorting more and more to this form of mining as it greatly reduces the cost of production, especially the item of labor. It is estimated that for every ton of anthracite that is stripped instead of mined, ten men are deprived of work. Stripping also eliminates the cost of timbering, hauling, pumping, ventilating, and complicated safety provisions.

SUMP: A basin at the bottom of a slope or shaft where water is collected to be pumped out.

SWITCHBACK: An arrangement of zigzag railroad tracks for lessening the grade up a steep hill (Webster). Specifically, the most famous of the anthracite gravity railroads. It was built in 1827 to haul coal from Summit Hill down the Sharp Mountain to the head of the Lehigh canal at Mauch Chunk. The trains carried mules in the rear cars to drag empties up the mountain. In the forties, when the anthracite trade demanded a quicker method of returning the empty cars, a back track was laid across the mountain and two inclined planes built. The use of a Y gave rise to the term "switchback," which was applied to the whole railroad. It was abandoned as a coal carrier in the sixties, and was used as a scenic railway until 1932. In September 1937 it was sold at auction for junk.

TAMPING: The act of packing a drilled hole around a cartridge with fine dirt from the floor of a mine before blasting, to prevent a misdirection of the force of the blast.

TAIL-CHAIN: A chain used in mine haulage. Also tail-rope.

TICK: Credit.

TICK BOOK: An account book.

TOOL BOX: Same as powder box.

TOOL BOX MINER: A lazy miner, specifically one who rests on his tool box while his laborer does his work.

TRAP DOOR: See door boy.

TRAPPER: Same as door boy.

TRAVELING WAY: A passage for men and mules in or into a mine.

TRIP: A small train of mine cars.

TURNOUT: A switch on a mine railroad.

UNION: United Mine Workers of America, the only collective bargaining agency of anthracite mine workers. The union is divided into three districts with headquarters in Scranton, Hazleton, and Shamokin, each headed by a district president.

VEIN: See seam.

WAGON: Underground coal car.

WASHERY: A building resembling a breaker used in reclaiming culm and fine coal from old banks.

WATER LEVEL: A small mine the entrance of which is driven on a grade that permits the drainage of water by gravity.

WHITE DAMP: Carbon monoxide gas, produced by mine fires and explosions. Its presence cannot be detected by the ordinary method of testing with lamps. Odorless, colorless, and tasteless, it is so insidious and poisonous that it causes instant death.

WINDY: A blown-out shot. Also diminutive for window.

WISE WOMAN: A woman, usually one of advanced age, in whose curative powers faith was placed by the sick and injured.

WORKING: Said of a breast or chamber in which appear warnings of an impending crush, such as the dropping of small pieces of slate from the roof, and when fragments of coal break from pillars with a crackling sound like the snapping of dry twigs underfoot.

WORKINGS: Colloquial for an anthracite mining operation.

Bibliography

A. HISTORICAL AND MECHANICAL BACKGROUND OF THE ANTHRACITE INDUSTRY

I. BOOKS

History of the Counties of Lehigh and Carbon. By Alfred Matthews and Austin N. Hungerford, Philadelphia, 1884.

History of Carbon County. By Fred Brenckman, Harrisburg, 1913.

History of Schuylkill County. W. W. Munsell & Co., New York, 1881.

Wyoming and Lackawanna Valleys; Upper Waters of the Susquehanna and Lackawanna Coal Region. Edited by J. A. Clark, Scranton, 1875.

History of Wilkes-Barre. Begun by Oscar Jewell Harvey and completed by Ernest Gray Smith. Four volumes, 1909–1929.

History of Northumberland County. By Herbert C. Bell, Chicago, 1891.

History of the Lackawanna County. By H. Hollister, Scranton, 1875.

Josiah White's History. Given by Himself. One hundred copies printed from original manuscript. Philadelphia, 1909.

The Story of Anthracite. Prepared and Published by the Hudson Coal Company. New York, 1932.

Coal, Iron and Oil, or The Practical American Miner. By Samuel H. Daddow and Benjamin Bannon. Pottsville, 1866.

Coal Catechism. By William Jasper Nicolls. Philadelphia, 1898.

Coal and the Coal Mines. By Homer Greene. Boston, 1889. Revised ed., 1928.

The Great Disaster at Avondale Colliery. By H. W. Chase. Scranton, 1869.

Points on Coal and the Coal Business. By Charles Miesse. Myerstown, 1887.

Black Diamonds. By Sidney Dyer, Philadelphia, 1873.

Geography of Pennsylvania. By Charles B. Trezo. Philadelphia, 1843.

Historical Collections of the State of Pennsylvania. By Sherman Day. Philadelphia, 1843, p. 184.

Adventures in the Mines, or Perils Underground. By T. T. O'Malley, Akron, O., 1892, pp. 143–148.

II. MAGAZINES

Harper's Monthly Magazine. Vol. XV, p. 451. New York, 1857.

III. NEWSPAPERS

Hazard's Register of Pennsylvania. Philadelphia, 1829–30. Vol. III, p. 301; Vol. IV, p. 73; Vol. VI, p. 83.

Mauch Chunk Democrat. August 2, 1890; August 9, 1890; April 25, 1891.

"Historical Gleanings." By Sarah A. McCool. *Shenandoah Weekly Herald,* Shenandoah, Pa. February 7, 1874, to November 27, 1875.

"The Burning Mountain." By "Newob." *Philadelphia Press,* June 25, 1858.

IV. PAPERS

"Development of Mining and Transportation of Anthracite Coal." By Philip Ginder. *Zinc,* house organ of the New Jersey Zinc Company, Palmerton, Pa. August, 1928, p. 242.

Samuel Parker's Report to the Coal Mining Association, 1833, and to the State Senate, 1834.

The Proof That Pennsylvania Anthracite Coal Was First Shipped from the Wyoming Valley. By William Griffith, C. E. Proceedings and Collections of the Wyoming Historical and Geological Society. Wilkes-Barre, 1914. Vol. XIII.

Early Annals of Pottsville. Proceedings of the Historical Society of Schuylkill County. September 2–8, 1906. Vol. II, No. 2.

Early History of Coal Mining and Mining Machinery in Schuylkill County. Proceedings of the Historical Society of Schuylkill County. April 24, 1912. Vol. IV, No. 2.

Coal, its Antiquity, Discovery and Early Development in the Wyoming Valley. Read before the Wyoming Historical and Geological Society, June 27, 1890. Wilkes-Barre, 1890.

V. PAMPHLETS

Anthracite Mining Laws of Pennsylvania, Harrisburg, 1922.

Gases Found in Coal Mines. By George A. Burrell and Frank M. Seibert. U. S. Bureau of Mines. Washington, 1916.

VI. STATE ARCHIVES

Pennsylvania Archives. Third Series, Vol. XXVI, pp. 83–85.

Pennsylvania Archives. Third Series, Vol. XIX, p. 342.

Exhibit "C" of the Immigrants Landing at Philadelphia on file in Division of Public Records, Harrisburg. Shows Ginder's signature when he took the oath of loyalty to the Provincial Government, October 25, 1746.

B. LABOR, ECONOMIC, AND SOCIAL CONDITIONS

I. BOOKS

Anthracite Coal Communities. By Peter Roberts. New York, 1904.

John Mitchell. By Elsie Gluck. New York, 1929.

History of the United Mine Workers of America. By Chris Evans, Indianapolis, 1920.

The United Mine Workers of America as an Economic and Social Force in the Anthracite Territory. By Rev. William J. Walsh. Wilkes-Barre, 1931.

The Anthracite Question. By H. S. Raushenbush, New York, 1924.

Our Times: The Turn of the Century. By Mark Sullivan. New York, 1926.

"The Miners of Scranton," a chapter, page 268, in *Pennsylvania Dutch and Other Essays.* By Phebe Earle Gibbons. Philadelphia, 1882.

A Trooper's Narrative of Service in the Anthracite Coal Strike of 1902. By Stewart Culin. Philadelphia, 1903.

Reflections of an Anthracite Engineer. By George E. Stevenson. New York, 1931.

II. NEWSPAPERS

"One Hundred Years of Anthracite." By Myron D. Edmonds. The Pottsville *Journal,* Pottsville, May 2, 1925 and subsequent issues.

III. PAPERS

Old W. B. A. Days. By Joseph F. Patterson. Proceedings of the Historical Society of Schuylkill County. December 30, 1908. Vol. II, No. 4.

After the W. B. A. By Joseph F. Patterson. Proceedings of the Historical Society of Schuylkill County. Read November 29, 1911. Vol. IV, No. 2.

Bootlegging or Illegal Mining of Anthracite Coal in Pennsylvania: a Census and Survey of the Facts. Report by the State Anthracite Coal Industry Commission. Harrisburg, 1937.

C. THE MOLLY MAGUIRES

I. BOOKS

The Molly Maguires, or Ireland in America. By E. W. Lucy. London.

The Molly Maguires. By F. P. Dewees. Philadelphia, 1877.

The Molly Maguires and the Detectives. By Allan Pinkerton, New York, 1878.

Great Mollie Maguire Trials in Carbon and Schuylkill Counties. Reported by R. A. West. Pottsville, 1876.

History of the Great Riots. By Ed. Winslow Martin. Philadelphia, 1877.

The Pinkertons, a Detective Agency. By Richard Wilmer Rowan. Boston, 1931.

Dynamite. By Louis Adamic. New York, 1931.

The Molly Maguires. By Anthony Bimba. New York, 1932.

The Molly Maguire Riots. By J. Walter Coleman, Richmond, 1936.

II. NEWSPAPERS

Mauch Chunk Democrat, August 1873 to July 1879.

Pottsville Miners' Journal, June 22, 1877.

Pottsville Evening Chronicle, April 1, 1876.

Wilkes-Barre Record of the Times, June 21, 1877.

D. FOLKLORE

I. BOOKS

A Week at Killarney. By Mr. and Mrs. S. C. Hall, London, 1858.

The Song Lore of Ireland. By Redfern Mason, New York, 1910.

The Glories of Ireland. Edited by Joseph Dunn, Ph. D. and P. J. Lennox, Litt. D., Washington, 1914.

The History of Wales. By B. B. Woodward. London, 1850.

The Science of Folk-Lore. By Alexander Haggerty Krappe, New York, 1929.

English and Scottish Popular Ballads. By Helen Child Sargent and George Lyman Kittredge, Boston, 1904.

II. MAGAZINES

"American Folk Music." By Phillips Barry. *Southern Folklore Quarterly,* June 1937, pp. 29–47.

III. NEWSPAPERS

"Where Magic Rules and Men Are Gods." By Margaret Mead. *New York Times,* Sunday Magazine Section, June 25, 1933.

"Hiring a Hall." Column by H. L. Mencken. *New York World,* Sunday Magazine Section, November 15, 1925.

Mahanoy City Press. July 29, 1922 ("The Peddler's Grave").

The Record-American, Mahanoy City, December 1, 1934. (Article on "The Peddler's Grave" reprinted from an earlier issue.)

IV. PAPERS

The German Peddler's Grave. Read before the Historical Society of Berks County, December 14, 1909, by Louis Richards. Vol. II, Transactions of the Society.

Index

INDEX

INDEX

INDEX